D0550506

Politics and Policy Making in Education

Based on interviews with key actors in the policy-making process, Stephen Ball's book attempts to map the changes in education policy, amd policy making in the Thatcherite decade.

The focus of the book is the 1988 Education Reform Act, its origins, purposes and effects, and it looks behind the scenes at the priorities of the politicians, civil servants and government advisers who were influential in making changes. There are direct quotations from senior civil servants and HMIs and three former secretaries of state which provide fascinating insights into the way in which policy is made.

The book focuses on real-life political conflicts, examining the way in which contemporary education policy is related to the ideal of society projected by Thatcherism. It looks in detail at the New Right government advisers and think tanks; the industrial lobby, and the DES, addressing current issues such as the National Curriculum, national testing and City Technical Colleges. Stephen Ball sets these important issues within a clear theoretical framework which illuminates the whole process of policy making.

This book will be of interest not only to educationalists, but also to policy analysts and political scientists.

Politics and Policy Making in Education

Explorations in policy sociology

Stephen J. Ball

Routledge
London and New York

First published 1990
by Routledge
11 New Fetter Lane, London EC4P 4EE

Simultaneously published in the USA and Canada
by Routledge
a division of Routledge, Chapman and Hall, Inc.
29 West 35th Street, New York, NY 10001

Laserprinted from Author's disks by LaserScript Limited, Mitcham, Surrey

Printed and bound in Great Britain by
Mackays of Chatham PLC, Chatham, Kent

British Library Cataloguing in Publication Data
Ball, Stephen, *1950–*
    Politics and policy making in education.
    1. Education. Policies
    I. Title
    379.154

    ISBN 0-415-03507-4
    ISBN 0-415-00931-6 pbk

Library of Congress Cataloging-in-Publication Data
Ball, Stephen J.
    Politics and policy making in education: explorations in policy
    sociology/Stephen J. Ball.
    p.   cm.
    Includes bibliographical references.
    ISBN 0-415-00931-6
    1. Education and state – England. 2. Politics and education –
England. 3. Educational sociology – England. I. Title
LC93.G7B35 1990   90-34343
379.42 – dc20   CIP

Contents

List of figures   vi

Preface   vii

Introduction   1

1 Policy matters!   3

2 Discipline and chaos: the New Right and discourses of derision   22

3 The New Right and education policy   43

4 Industrial training or new vocationalism? Structures and discourses   70

5 Towards the post-Fordist school?   100

6 Curriculum plc: the ERA, policy, partnerships and the school curriculum   133

7 Colouring in the boxes: the struggles over a National Curriculum   173

8 Endnote   211

Appendix 1 List of acronyms and abbreviations   215

Appendix 2 List of interviewees and comment on interviews   217

References   219

Index   230

List of figures

1.1 Educational ideologies   5

1.2 Influences and ideologies in education policy making   7

1.3 Theoretical strategies   10

2.1 Proscriptions: criticism of Keynsian economics   38

2.2 Prescriptions for the market   39

3.1 New Right polarities   45

3.2 The education market place   60

3.3 Pupil-driven funding formula   64

5.1 'What is it to be educated?'   131

7.1 The construction of a National Curriculum subject   186

8.2 Struggles over school knowledge inside the educational   212
    state

vi

Preface

This has not been an easy book to write. In particular it has not been an easy book to finish. I have had to make a number of compromises to get it into publishable and readable form: compromises of scope, length, focus and evidence. The first draft was far too long but still left a great deal that I wanted to say unsaid. It was possible to use only a small fraction of the 1,200 pages of interview transcripts in the text. Many of the people I interviewed are not quoted directly at all. Many small but important incidents and moments have had to be glossed over or left out altogether. Sometimes data was sacrificed for analysis and sometimes analysis for data. Some of the cutting and editing was painful; favourite passages or juicy quotes had to be excised.

Nonetheless, the whole exercise might have been still more difficult if it had not been for the help and support and co-operation of very many people. Trinidad provided encouragement and criticism throughout; she corrected the whole manuscript and put up with me talking about the research at great length; it would not have been finished without her. Liz Cawdron transcribed all the interviews flawlessly (and the Central Research Fund of the University of London provided a grant for this work). Jean Nuttall typed all the letters to interviewees. My colleagues at King's were supportive throughout (it is a great place to work), especially Margaret Brown, Paul Black, Arthur Lucas and Richard Bowe. I also want to thank the following for their pertinent comments and conversation: Meg Maguire, Phil Bassill, Tony Becher, Charles Raab, Jenny Ozga, Naz Rassool, Ann Gold, Geoff Whitty, Charles Batteson, Hiroyuki Fujita, Brian Davies, Tony Mansell, Peter Wilby, Maxine Offredy, Tony Knight, Chris Shilling and Judith Ryder.

Introduction

This book could be described both as an exercise in contemporary history and as a contribution to what Ozga (1987) calls 'policy sociology' which is 'rooted in the social science tradition, historically informed and drawing on qualitative and illuminative techniques' (p.144). I shall be describing and analysing changes in the processes of education policy making in England (not Scotland, Northern Ireland or even Wales) from the 1970s, the period of post-war consensus, to the late 1980s, the era of Thatcherism. I shall also, in particular, be tracing the origins, construction and implementation of aspects of the 1988 Education Reform Act – specifically those aspects which relate to secondary schools and to the school curriculum. The latter – the concentration upon the Act – provides a 'case', a focus, for the former – the investigation of policy making. Together, the process analysis and the case analysis offer the possibility for some theorising of policy and policy making. In this respect I am very aware of Barraclough's view of what can count as serious and worthwhile study. He argues that:

> In the long run contemporary history can only justify its claim to
> be a serious intellectual discipline and more than a desultory and
> superficial review of the contemporary scene, if it sets out to
> clarify the basic structural changes which have shaped the modern
> world. These changes are fundamental because they fix the
> skeleton or framework within which political action takes place.
> (1967 p.16)

The orientation of the study is critical and deconstructive; I adhere to Maurice Kogan's view when he says that 'I assume that it is the task of social scientists to take things apart' (1979 p.5). Where possible this taking apart extends to comments on the likely or actual social consequences of policies. Further, Walker (1981 p.225) argues that: 'The task of social policy analysis is to evaluate the distributional impact of existing policies and proposals and the rationales underlying them'. This will also be attempted.

1

Theoretically and conceptually, the book is probably best described as eclectic or pragmatic. Alternative interpretations and analyses of 'the process' and 'the case' are tried out for their adequacy. In this I am very aware of the complexity of the task I have set myself and of the problem of maintaining coherence. A rationale for the choice and use of different theoretical strategies is outlined in chapter 1. The deployment of these means that the chapters can be read as separate but interrelated essays.

But the careful reader might still want to ask the question 'Where do you stand theoretically and politically?'. The answer to the first part of the question is not easy. I am certainly not a pluralist, at least I do not think I am; I may be a Weberian neo-pluralist, to coin a phrase, but if I am I hold strongly to the tenet of a 'dual polity'. That is to say, the role of representative institutions in social democratic politics is constrained and distorted by the obvious inequalities of power inherent in capitalism. We have a 'deformed polyarchy' (Dunleavy and O'Leary 1987) wherein behind the façade of public politics 'the state also responds, directly, immediately and sensitively to economic pressures from business, both those expressed in overt or latent use of economic muscle, and the considerable presence of business influence inside the various input politics channels'. Some of this is taken up in chapter 5. As to the second part of the question I could not find a better answer than to quote from John Prunty's definition of critical policy analysis:

> The personal values and political commitment of the critical policy analyst would be anchored in the vision of a moral order in which justice, equality and individual freedom are uncompromised by the avarice of a few. The critical analyst would endorse political, social and economic arrangements where persons are never treated as a means to an end, but treated as ends in their own right.
>
> (1985 p.136)

Finally, this book is also a form of ethnography. The interviews with key actors, participants in the policy process, constitute a basis for an ethnography of elite political culture, although no cultural analyses are attempted here (see Ball 1989).

Policy matters!

Policy is clearly a matter of the 'authoritative allocation of values';
policies are the operational statements of values, 'statements of
prescriptive intent' (Kogan 1975 p.55). But values do not float free of
their social context. We need to ask whose values are validated in
policy, and whose are not. Thus, 'The authoritative allocation of values
draws our attention to the centrality of power and control in the concept
of policy' (Prunty 1985 p.136). Policies project images of an ideal
society (education policies project definitions of what counts as
education) and to a great extent I am concerned here to relate
contemporary education policy to the ideal of society projected in
Thatcherism. (In terms of social and economic policy I take Thatcherism
to be a specific and stable ideological system.) Logically, then, policies
cannot be divorced from interests, from conflict, from domination or
from justice. All of these aspects of policy analysis are embedded in
this study. But I do not intend to attempt to portray education policy
simply as a matter of the inevitable and unproblematic extension of
Thatcherism.

Discontinuities, compromises, omissions and exceptions are also
important. Sometimes they are of prime importance. Policy making in a
modern, complex, plural society like Britain is unwieldy and complex.
It is often unscientific and irrational, whatever the claims of policy
makers to the contrary. In particular the 1988 Education Act contains a
number of 'shots in the dark', policies without pedigree. Education
policy is not simply a direct response to dominant interests (see below
the discussion of the educational state) and might best be understood:
'. . . not as reflecting the interests of one social class (commonly the
industrial middle class), but as responding to a complex and
heterogenous configuration of elements (including ideologies that are
residual or emergent, as well as currently dominant)' (Svi Shapiro 1980
p.328).

That leads me to one of the conceptual themes running through the
analysis in this study. At the level of educational ideologies I find

Raymond Williams' (1962) conceptualisation of positions useful and pertinent. Williams identifies three groups and ideologies which emerge most clearly in the nineteenth century as 'influences on the very concept of education' (p.161). One division which separates these groups is 'the idea of education for all and the definition of a liberal education', the former being further separated into a justification based on 'the growth of democracy' on the one side, as against the economic argument for 'industrial prosperity' on the other. In the nineteenth century Williams sees the latter as emerging to dominate the new state system of elementary education which 'led to the definition of education in terms of future adult work, with the parallel cause of teaching the required social character – habits of regularity, self-discipline, obedience and trained effort' (p.162). This view, propagated by those Williams calls the 'industrial trainers', was, however, under attack from both the liberals, whom Williams calls 'old humanists', and the democrats, whom Williams calls 'public educators'. The old humanists, often 'men deeply opposed to democracy', argued that 'man's spiritual health depended on a kind of education that was more than training for some specialised work' (p.162). The public educators put the view 'that man had a natural right to be educated, and that any good society depended on governments accepting this principle as their duty' (p.162). Williams concedes that the public educators 'inevitably drew on the arguments of the defenders of the old liberal education, as a way of preventing universal education being narrowed to a system of pre-industrial instruction' (pp.162-3).

Writing of the inheritance of these nineteenth-century struggles in the twentieth century Williams comments that 'in theory, the principles of the public educators have been accepted . . . In practice the system is still deeply affected by other principles' (p.165). In particular at the centre of education, in the curriculum, the old humanist influence remains strong.

> An educational curriculum, as we have seen again and again in past periods, expresses a compromise between an inherited selection of interests and the emphasis of new interests. At varying points in history, even this compromise may be long delayed, and it will often be muddled. The fact about our present curriculum is that it was essentially created by the nineteenth century, following some eighteenth-century models, and retaining elements of the medieval curriculum near its centre.
>
> (p.172)

I still see Williams' basic typology of definitions as relevant to understanding contemporary struggles over the meaning and purposes of schooling, and especially the curriculum. I shall argue later that in the

	Beliefs	Values	Tastes
Politicians	Market forces	freedom of choice	Independent schools
Bureaucrats (DES)	good administration management system maintenance	efficiency	Central control exams/tests
Professionals (HMI)	Professionalism experience & practice	quality	impressionistic evaluation

Figure 1.1 Educational ideologies
Source: Lawton, 1986, p.35.

1980s the public educators are in disarray and that the field of education policy making is overshadowed by the influence of the old humanists and industrial trainers. The former are vociferously represented both in the ranks of the Conservatives' New Right, and, more modestly, are crucially ensconced in the DES. The latter consist of a shifting and often indistinct alliance of representatives of business and finance, politicians and curriculum developers (e.g. the FEU – Further Education Unit within the DES) with a crucial power base in the DTI (Department of Trade and Industry).

However, the categories and terminology of ideologies and ideological groups employed in the remainder of this study are an elaboration of Williams' threefold division. A finer, more precise identification of ideologies and influences is necessary to capture the complexity of recent education policy making. Salter and Tapper (1981) have already added a new category to this typology – 'educational bureaucrats' – although the ideological position of this 'new, and more powerful interest' (p.83) is not made clear. As we shall see later, in their discussion of the DES, Salter and Tapper see these bureaucrats as primarily concerned with matters of control and the efficiency of the system. While this is undoubtedly appropriate it does not take cognisance of the educational concerns, and influences of and on this group. As the controls over and the discourse about the definition of school knowledge are centralised, the educational bureaucrats of the DES are more likely and more able to have direct influence over that definition. Below I refer to the stance of these bureaucats in relation to matters of curriculum and pedagogy as reformist old humanism. Lawton (1986 p.35) goes further in sub-dividing the powers of the DES into political, bureaucratic and professional. He identifies potentially conflicting groups and ideologies with each of these aspects of power (see figure 1.1).

Even this breakdown remains over simple. It is also necessary to take account of other influences and interests which play upon these key policy makers from the outside. The 'industrial trainers' are one such influence. Another, as already indicated, is the hard-line, old humanists of the New Right, whom I shall refer to as cultural restorationists. The effects of this influence are most evident upon the politicians. (The considerable antipathy between the New Right ideologues and the civil service also comes into play here.) The separation of cultural restorationism from reformist old humanism may seem to rest on a set of fine distinctions. It does. But nonetheless they are important distinctions. One aspect is nicely represented in Johnson's (1989) notion of educational Thatcherism as opposed to Bakerism. Johnson asks the questions: 'Is it a reforming, modernizing movement, a "Great Education Reform" – as *he* says it is. Or is it a return to traditional educational "standards", an educational Restoration – as *she* says it is' (p.95).

Finally, some aspects of the public educator position are represented, weakly perhaps, in the contemporary scene of education policy making by those I shall call the 'new progressives' – that is those advocates, especially as represented in the mathematics and science subject communities, of pedagogical and assessment innovations like the use of investigations and 'practical mathematics', and, crucially, process and graded assessments (see chapters 6 and 7). In mathematics, the Cockcroft Report (1982) articulates and provides authoritative support for this position.

> This well written endorsement of progressive practice was enthusiastically received at all levels by those involved in education, and beyond in the wider community. The report was sufficiently authoritative to deflect criticism which had been levelled at Mathematics teaching and levels of achievement away from a call to a return to basics.
>
> (Ernest 1989 p.2)

As we shall see in chapters 5 and 7, the Cockcroft Report is the object of vociferous criticism from the cultural restorationists of the Conservative, radical right, but receives considerable support from the industrial training lobby. Just as in Williams' account of the nineteenth century, the public educators are caught betwixt and between other influential ideologies. The DES and HMI also inhabit an unclear space

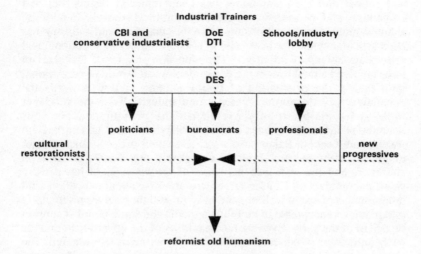

Figure 1.2 Influences and ideologies in education policy making

between these two powerful lobbies. On this and similar matters the DES as a whole represents the sort of 'compromise between an inherited selection of interests and the emphasis of new interests' referred to by Williams (p.172). However, the HMI, in their orientation to practice and to quality, are most clearly affected by, and on occasions articulate and advocate 'new progressivism'. This field of ideologies and influences around the DES is represented schematically in figure 1.2.

The changing processes of policy making in education over the past ten years have, to a great extent, outrun the development of relevant analysis and conceptualisation. In classical policy-analysis terms, education policy making up to the mid 1970s could be described as a 'clientist' system (Ashford 1981), with the teacher unions and LEA lobbies wielding considerable influence. Together with the DES these 'client' groups constituted the so-called 'triangle of tension' (Briault 1976). The policy impetus from the DES was, to say the least, weak: 'the Department has over time developed its own momentum and its own inertia' (Salter and Tapper 1986 p.24), and the office of Secretary of State was very much a political backwater or a way station for new or up-and-coming politicians. Policy was pursued by way of 'disjointed incrementalism' (Fowler *et al.* 1973).

However, from 1976 onwards this cosy, loosely controlled, pluralistic system has gradually disintegrated, the 'triangle of tension' has been broken. The fragile, progressive consensus based on incremental change and school and LEA autonomy has been replaced by conflict and contention, and the assertion of greater centralised controls. In addition a much more direct relationship between education and industry has been articulated and has given rise to a whole variety of vocational and pre-vocational policy initiatives. The education policies of Thatcherism have involved a total reworking of the ideological terrain of educational politics and the orientation of policy making is now towards the consumers of education – parents and industrialists; the producer lobbies are almost totally excluded. The present and previous Secretaries of State have been active in policy initiation, and both Keith Joseph and Kenneth Baker have attached to their office a much greater range of direct powers. Policies are now more clearly political in character, and the influence networks of the New Right have had a significant impact on Conservative Party thinking about education (and other aspects of social welfare) and have proved themselves particularly pragmatic and adaptable in mobilising media and some populist support on behalf of the party. Even so, the unanimity of the government and the party on matters of education policy should not be over-estimated. The Conservative Education Association and other wet groupings have continued to argue against the excesses of the New Right. The Select Committee on Education and Science has, despite its Conservative majority, continued to work within a clientist framework and has maintained an independent and critical, if ineffective, stance towards the government's management of the education service. And the neo-liberal and neo-conservative wings of the New Right itself differ in significant ways on the direction of education policy, particularly the proper role of the state (Belsey 1986). Individual ministers and government departments (e.g. DES and DTI) also differ markedly on aspects of policy.

The basis for description of education policy has changed significantly and the established conceptual tools seem blunt and irrelevant. A set of new desciptors and concepts is needed.

The aim here is not an account of the institutions of policy making. As Bernard Crick is reported to have said, 'too much emphasis on political institutions is rather like sex education with too much emphasis on anatomy'. Rather I shall be attempting to trace a specific set of educational issues and the conflicts, pressures and influences which attend their translation into policy.

One basic task, then, is to plot the changing ideological, economic and political parameters of policy and to relate the ideological, political and economic to the dynamics of policy debate and policy formulation. A major problem will be to establish the links, if any, between these elements, and their links, if any, to policy making.

For the most part I hope to tackle these links and to capture the dynamics of policy in a fairly straightforward way. The most obvious, but not sole, basis of my account of education policy is a set of interviews with primary actors in the policy-making field. (The 'sample' and the methods of this exercise are described in appendix 1.) The field of policy analysis is dominated by commentary and critique rather than by research. Abstract accounts tend towards tidy generalities and often fail to capture the messy realities of influence, pressure, dogma, expediency, conflict, compromise, intransigence, resistance, error, opposition and pragmatism in the policy process. It is easy to be simple, neat and superficial and to gloss over these awkward realities. It is difficult to retain messiness and complexity and still be penetrating. But obviously this choice of research strategy involves a theoretical commitment. I am embracing agency and the ideological category of the individual. In parts of what is to follow I will unashamedly be attempting to explain policy making via what it is that individuals and groups actually do and say in the arenas of influence in which they move. Extracts from interviews have been quoted as extensively as possible. In these interviews people were asked to explain and comment upon the policy-making processes in which they were involved and to articulate their policy concerns; and, analytically, I could be content with that. But I am not content, or not quite. I want to be theoretically more adventurous, I want to subject education policy making to analyses which employ a number of different theoretical strategies. The rationale for the choice of these strategies is as follows.

My analysis here will explore three levels or dimensions of education policy making, each portrayed and reported in terms of an appropriate theoretical perspective. The three dimensions employed are derived from the work of Althusser (1969) and his analysis of the complexity of the total social system as represented by the political, the ideological and the economic. The same analysis can be applied also to any sub-system, in this case education and education policy. The elements of the complexity, the levels, can be considered both in relation to one another and separately.

> Each level, that is, is *relatively autonomous* of each other level (only relatively so, since each level is necessarily affected by the specific effects of each other level; they exist only within a unified system, in which case total autonomy clearly becomes impossible).
>
> (Saunders 1981 p.183)

Such a framework leads to a dynamic consideration of education policy *in relation to* the political and ideological and economic, and the political, ideological and economic *in* education policy (see figure 1.3).

As indicated, each level is to be considered in its own terms, but the contradictions between the levels will also be explored and, in chapter

Education Policy   Level   Theoretical Strategy

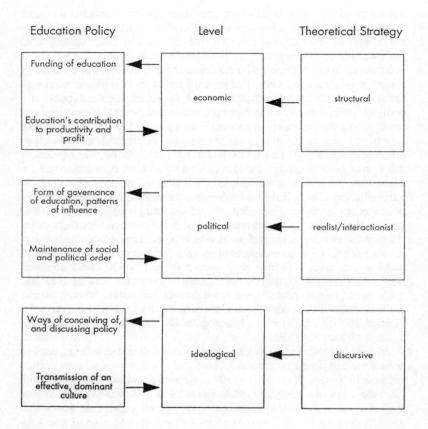

Figure 1.3 Theoretical strategies

4, the question of the dominance or determinacy of the economic level will be examined. Furthermore, the theoretical strategy appropriate for analysis at each level will differ: structural in the case of the economic; realist or interactionist in the case of the political; and discursive in the case of the ideological. The investigation of the economic leads to consideration of both the funding of education and the contribution that education makes to productivity, that is the positioning of education in relation to capital (chapters 4 and 5). The investigation of the political leads to consideration of the forms of governance of education – the politics of education – and the changing role and nature of influential groups and constituencies in the policy process, inside the educational state (chapters 6 and 7). The investigation of the ideological leads to consideration of the ways in which education policy is conceived of and discussed – the limits of the possible – and to examination of education's role in transmitting an effective, dominant culture (Williams 1973) (chapters 2 and 3).

Each level is a source and a resource for education policy making; that is, each level has effects in its own terms on the nature and possibility of policy. Contradictions within and between the levels will initiate change. Each level also provides vocabularies, or discourses (see below) for those engaged in struggle over policy. For example, in the economic, the so-called 'crisis of capitalism' experienced in most western countries in the early 1970s clearly had an impact on education policy making, specifically leading to a re-positioning of education in relation to production (see chapter 4). At the same time, the British establishment clearly faced a legitimation crisis, manifested in an increase in social, industrial and political disorder, which has provoked attempts to rework the school curriculum and pupil–teacher relations to give more emphasis to the social and moral development of pupils and to reinforce key social and national values and, concomitantly, to de-politicise the school curriculum (see chapter 3). Also in relation to these crises, a 'crisis in education', more apparent than real, was constructed in the media out of the critiques launched by the so-called New Right (see chapters 2 and 3). Certain traditional values and meanings in education were regarded as being at stake. Notions like standards, literacy and heritage were mobilised against the 'isms' of education, such as progressivism, comprehensivism, egalitarianism, multi-culturalism, pluralism, relativism.

Looking back to the established descriptors and analyses in the field of education policy analysis there are two odd and difficult absences that need to be accounted for when attempting to conceptualise education policy in the post-war period. The first is the almost total absence of references to education policy in the mainstream literature of social policy. The other 'big spenders' of social policy are well represented. Health is there, social services get plenty of space, employment and housing are fully explored, but education appears not to be an issue for social policy analysts. The second is the almost total absence within what writing there is on education policy of explicit theory, except in some of the more recent work, (such as Dale (1988), Salter and Tapper (1986), Hargreaves and Reynolds (1989) and McPherson and Raab (1988). One way of accounting for both these omissions is to look at the peculiar nature of educational policy making itself, its conceptual oddness.

As noted above, in classical policy-analysis terms education policy making up to the mid 1970s could be described as a 'clientist' system (Ashford 1981). Policy making in the DES was for the most part limited to framing decisions to do with finance, or target setting; direct impact on the curriculum or the organisation of local provision was rare. 'A traditional feature of the English system which gives responsibility for determining the curriculum of schools to LEAs and teachers and not to the central department' (Pile 1979 p.35). Some commentators have suggested that as a result of this the DES through the 1960s and early 1970s seethed with frustrated ambition (Salter and Tapper 1986).

This pluralist scenario, according to Dennison (1984 p.29), worked in a way whereby: 'a neutral government adjudicated, when necessary, between participants who themselves were generating much of the policy'. He goes on 'it was the professional staff (assisted by the LEA) and the examination boards which represented the main interests at institutional level: while nationally the local authority associations, the teacher unions and (to a limited extent) the DES were dominant'. Dennison also makes the point that policy making in the pluralist period was essentially reactive and locked into an assumption of expansion of provision based upon an expectation of continuing economic growth. Policy tended to emerge as a response to the articulation of diverse interests. (See Gerwitz and Ozga 1990 and CCCS 1981 for alternative analyses of this period.)

> Those involved, and the interests they represented (parents, teachers, counsellors and so on) generated a lobby for further spending. Practically, (for example) a special education pressure group was only one among many, ranging from some parents pressing for new school buildings or an additional teacher, through to the national campaigns which usually preceded, and invariably followed, the major educational reports – Plowden on Primary Education, Robbins on Higher Education, etc.
>
> (Dennison 1984 p.32)

But, Dennison concludes, by the early 1980s pluralism was defunct. Around this time, conceptually speaking, we entered a whole new ball game. From the late 1970s theory, and specifically the concept of 'the state', begins to make increasingly frequent appearances in writing by educationalists on educational policy making. This sudden popularity makes the previous absence all the more intriguing. (Perhaps one reason for the late arrival of the state into the educational policy field lies in the relatively crude versions of state theory and narrow [and reified] conceptualisations of the apparatuses of the state which were previously available.)

The tricky question though is whether the shift in conceptual language and theoretical premises – from pluralism to neo-Marxism – simply reflects the changes in the nature of policy making itself or is an independent theoretical break which allows us to see the pluralist conception as inadequate and ideological. If the latter is true, then pluralism is relegated to the status of an analytical fiction and we would need a revisionist history of post-war education policy which provides a more theoretically adequate account (CCCS 1981 have gone some way towards providing this).

However, there are ways of resolving (but not dissolving) the theoretical gap between pluralism and those neo-Marxist theories which give central place to the role of the state. In order to make headway with such a resolution we must divert, at least marginally, into those perennial and difficult debates which inhabit the undergrowth which grows so profusely around theories of the state (attesting perhaps either to their conceptual fecundity or to the ample provision of dead organic matter), that is, the issues of autonomy and determinism, the role of the economy, class forces and class struggle, the state as condensate, the balance of political forces and the question of historical specificity. I will not rehearse these here (see Saunders 1986, Dunleavy and O'Leary 1987) but rather make the bold claim that there is one primary conceptual essence which is discernable across virtually all modern Marxist and neo-Marxist theories of the state: that is, relative autonomy. That is, the relative autonomy of 'the political' and 'the ideological' from 'the economic'. The concept of relative autonomy is a notoriously slippery one, but Hargreaves (1983), drawing upon Wright (1979) and Williams (1978), helpfully links the concept of autonomy to that of delimitation, as opposed to determination. As Wright points out, there is an important difference between recognising that there are boundaries to the possibility of structure and arguing that those possibilities are structurally pre-ordained.

> Structural limitation . . . is especially important for understanding
> the sense in which economic structures 'ultimately' determine
> political and ideological structures: economic structures set limits
> on possible forms of political and ideological structures, and make
> some of these possible forms more likely than others, but they do
> not rigidly determine in a mechanistic manner any given form of
> political and ideological relations.
>
> (Wright 1979 pp.15-16)

And indeed in much of the recent theoretical analysis of education, emphasis has been given to the relative autonomy of education.

> The pattern of English education cannot adequately be explained
> by reference to some master plan drawn up over brandy and cigars
> by the CBI. Nor can it adequately be explained by reference to the
> efforts of crusading politicians, eager to use the education system
> as the key machine tool in their own projects of social engineering.

The education system has continued to expand throughout this
century, with very little direct reflection of the demands made on it
by any of its clients, customers or consumers.

(Dale 1979 p.99)

The point is not that there are no constraints acting upon the form,
process and content of education (there are many), but rather that
education is not immediately and directly produced by these constraints.
However, over the past fifteen years the nature and impact of these
constraints may have changed. This proposition is one of the main
points of consideration in this study.

If such a conceptualisation is to be taken seriously it involves an
attempt to identify empirically the nature of that which is possible in
policy making, that which actually occurs, and the limits of the possible
(and thus, in effect, that which is impossible). (It is somewhat perverse
always to begin with the impossibilities.) A study of policy making in
education in the 1980s makes both of these (accounts of the nature of the
possible and the limits of the possible) eminently feasible. Thus, relative
autonomy is of little help as just a 'mysterious invocation' (Hargreaves
1983 p.27), it must carry some analytical weight and empirical
credibility.

Hargreaves goes on to identify another crucial ingredient for the
analysis of this relationship of the possible to the impossible. Drawing
upon Williams he underlines on the one hand the role of 'agency', the
way that 'we make history', and on the other the definite and objective
'conditions' (the economic) and 'assumptions' (the ideological) which
'qualify', that is again set limits upon, 'agency' (the political). Here then
'the political' is in the foreground and 'the economic' provides the
backdrop as a context, a set of constraints. 'The ideological' is a kind of
stage lighting which keeps the spotlight on the stars and the
behind-the-scenes action in deep shadow, thus maintaining our belief in
the reality of the plot and keeping our concentration on the main action.
For the most part I shall concentrate on the foreground, 'the political',
but a concern with the ideological, with educational discourses, is also
pursued and I shall foray into the economic. Thus, I am not claiming any
kind of licence to avoid or neglect or caricature the role of 'the
economic'. It has a big part to play in the stories I shall try to tell.

Once one takes on board the ideas of autonomy, delimitation and
agency then much of the tidiness offered by cruder versions of state
theory is inevitably lost. We must accept, again as Hargreaves (1983
p.49), points out, 'Multicausal[ity], pluralistic conflict, administrative
complexity and historical inertia' as having equal theoretical and conceptual relevance in understanding actual policy-making processes as
does the logic and development of the capitalist mode of production.

Conflicts and struggles about education may very well be based on or organised around all kinds of non-economic considerations – those of race, gender, religion and professional status, for instance (Hargreaves 1983 p.32).

However, one major problem remains if we adopt a simple model of structural limitation, which is how do we actually explain educational change? How do limits impact themselves on existing practices and bring new practices into being? In some circumstances it might be valid to rely upon internally generated innovations as the source for change but that hardly accounts for the significant shift from social-democratic to Thatcherist forms, values and structures in education, unless we remain content with a purely political account. The idea of structural limitations seems to provide only a weak version of change. It seemingly cannot tell us where educational change comes from, that is how the notion of what is appropriate, rather than possible, is established.

Following on from the framework outlined above I want to consider three possibilities in this study:

(i) The idea that change can be accounted for in terms of the formal political and adminstrative processes of policy making and the struggles and contests between interest groups and parties engaged in the policy process. That is to say, policy changes in education can be traced to ideological shifts and changing patterns of influence within the Conservative Party, to the institutional ambitions of the DES, and to the impact and commitment of Secretaries of State and their ministers.

(ii) Some notion of 'correspondence(s)' between education and the economy, that is a 'relatively stable form of articulation between a distinct form of value production and a distinct form of regulation during a given period of time' (Bonefeld 1987 p.101). This draws upon recent German work on the theory of the state, specifically that of Hirsch. The idea is of a unity encompassing a particular strategy of capital accumulation, a particular ensemble of social forms and class relations, and a particular hegemonic project. This unity is achieved (or attempted) by the increased 'stratification' of society, and social reproduction is increasingly politicised. Education would thus be subject to and, in part, agent of a particular mode of regulation, and a particular hegemonic project. But clearly, although such a conceptualisation reinforces my concern with the political (the state as the functional centre of reproduction (Hirsch and Roth 1986 p.66, quoted in Bonefeld 1987), as far as I am concerned there is a danger that the language and concepts here bring with them a primary assumption of the regulation of social reproduction as 'process without subject' (Jessop 1985). Although the terms project and strategy provide space for agency, subjective decision taking and subjective action, the emphasis is upon structural compatibilities (struggle and strategy would emphasise processes and

15

incompatibilities). Both strategies and struggles are residually accounted for (but at least they are there); and, like most accounts that accept a basically structuralist version of social reproduction, the relationship of education to accumulation is taken to be fairly straightforward. But how far is it possible to talk of *the* relationship between education and accumulation? What does education mean in this general sense? Surely we must try to conceive of, and theorise, a *variety* of relationships, with different education*s*. These relationships will be more or less direct, or indirect or mediated, and more or less significant to different regions of education, accepting that different regions of education are more or less strategically important. The unity of education in terms of any particular mode of regulation will, as a result, be partial. (Of necessity the coverage of education*s* in the substance of this study is limited: the full variety of relationships cannot be explored here.) There is no conceptual problem with the latter if we leave enough scope for hegemonic project*s* and accumulation strategi*es* in relation to the dominant mode of regulation. The articulation of projects and strategies may not be of a piece. This coincides with the point made by Saunders (1981) when he writes of the state as a constellation of sites whose determination by the economy is both general (the dominant mode of regulation) and varied, rather than specific and identical. In some respects this again allows for a resolution of traditional pluralist, procedural versions of educational politics and reformed structuralism. Kogan (1982 p.6), for example, describes educational change as:

> negotiated through conflicts between and within bureaucratic,
> economic and social demands. In an increasingly complex society
> group interests and the ideologies supporting them are experienced
> chiefly through highly bureaucraticised institutions which establish
> their own logic of development. But nothing is automatic. Changes
> occur, sometimes accidently, when the right configuration of
> feelings, ideologies and power coincide.

The hegemonic project of Thatcherism perhaps represents one such configuration. But the consequences for change are not foregone. Thus I am struggling here with not wanting to 'give away' materialism but neither wanting to accept an unproblematic, law-governed, normative version of social and educational change. We desperately need to account for the inconsistencies of social reproduction, and the 'cracks, fissures and contradictions' (Holloway 1987) which appear within Thatcherism, to avoid the temptation of making history from theory, and analyse the 'heresies' of reality (Bonefeld 1987). The reality of fiscal crises, changed strategies of accumulation and mode of production, and concomitant changes in the mode of regulation and the role of the state are not in question; but their effects in the field of education cannot just be read off (as many writers want to do).

(iii) The role of discourses. Power is invested in discourse, equally, discursive practices produce, maintain or play out power relations. 'Implicit in the question of the restructuring of education, then, is the question of how the state exercises and imposes its power in part through the *production* of "truth" and "knowledge" about education' (Donald 1979 p.100). What Donald suggests is the need to separate debates about education, from policies, from changes in schools. 'The debate about education is often constructed at some distance from the processes it purports to describe. It has however, through policies, a real effect upon the educational system itself' (Finn, Grant and Johnson 1977 p.148).

The notion of discourse deployed here derives from the work of Michel Foucault. Discourse is the key concept in Foucault's theory of the relationship and inter-relationship between power and knowledge. It designates the conjunction of power and knowledge. Foucault puts forward the view that knowledge and power are inseparable, that forms of power are imbued within knowledge, and that forms of knowledge are permeated by power relations.

> No body of knowledge can be formed without a system of
> communications, records, accumulation and displacement which is
> in itself a form of power and which is linked, in its existence and
> functioning, to the other forms of power. Conversely no power can
> be exercised without the extraction, appropriation, distribution or
> retention of knowledge. On this level, there is not knowledge on
> the one side and society on the other, or science and the state, but
> only the fundamental forms of knowledge/power . . .
>
> (Foucault 1971 p.66)

Power and knowledge are two sides of a single process. Knowledge does not reflect power relations but is immanent in them. Discourses are, therefore, about what can be said, and thought, but also about who can speak, when, where and with what authority. Discourses embody meaning and social relationships, they constitute both subjectivity and power relations. Discourses are 'practices that systematically form the objects of which they speak. . . . Discourses are not about objects; they do not identify objects, they constitute them and in the practice of doing so conceal their own invention' (Foucault 1977 p.49). Thus, the possibilities for meaning, for definition, are pre-empted through the social and institutional position from which a discourse comes. Words and propositions will change their meaning according to their use and the positions held by those who use them. Knowledge is that of which one

17

can speak in a discursive practice. Meanings thus arise not from language but from institutional practices, from power relations, from social position. Words and concepts change their meaning and their effects as they are deployed within different discourses. This is important, as we shall see later, in the use of terms like 'freedom' and 'choice' by the New Right. Conflicting discourses may arise then even within a common language.

Thus, discourses construct certain possibilities for thought. They order and combine words in particular ways and exclude or displace other combinations. We do not speak the discourse. The discourse speaks us. However, in so far as discourses are constituted by exclusions as well as inclusions, by what cannot as well as what can be said, they stand in antagonistic relationship to other discourses, other possibilities of meaning, other claims, rights and position; this is Foucault's 'principle of discontinuity'. 'We must make allowance for the complex and unstable process whereby discourse can be both an instrument and an effect of power, but also a hindrance, a stumbling block, a point of resistance and a starting point for an opposing strategy' (Foucault 1981 p.101). According to Pecheux (1982) discourses are constructed through struggle, 'meanings are gained or lost through struggles in which what is at stake is ultimately quite a lot more than either words or discourses' (Macdonell 1986 p.51). Again this is important when we come to look at the emergence of the educational discourses of the New Right during the 1970s and the construction by them of a powerful 'discourse of derision'. It is through such 'discursive processes', as Pecheux calls them, that particular words take on particular meanings. Furthermore, this discourse of derision acted to debunk and displace not only specific words and meanings – progressivism and comprehensivism, for example – but also the speakers of these words, those 'experts', 'specialists' and 'professionals' referred to as the 'educational establishment'. These privileged speakers have been displaced, their control over meaning lost, their professional preferences replaced by abstract mechanisms and technologies of 'truth' and 'rationality' – parental choice, the market, efficiency and management. A new discursive regime has been established and with it new forms of authority. Foucault says 'Discourse may seem of little account, but the prohibitions to which it is subject reveal soon enough its links with desire and power' (1971 pp.11–12).

The field of analysis becomes more complex, but we may now have a set of tools with which to begin to try to explain things (pluralists, it would seem, could only describe things); explanations are not going to come easy, they are not going to be simple or straightforward, and our answers may indeed beg other questions.

To return to the point where I began, it may be that the new ball game begun in the late 1970s or early 1980s, let us say 1976 for sake of convenience, does us the service of making the role of the educational state more apparent, and the relations between the state, the education system and the economy more real (but no less complex). The social reforms which characterised the era of social democracy (CCCS 1981) have clearly and decisively been ended. Education is now discoursed in very different terms. It is to be made more disciplined (greater state intervention and monitoring and more centralised control) and more efficient (reallocation of funds and cuts in expenditure). As a result the endemic tensions between the demands made on education by capital, its technical contribution towards ensuring the continued accumulation of capital, and the role that education plays in the maintenance of the conditions of capital accumulation, its ideological contribution, are also made more visible (This is explored more fully in chapter 4.) Capital, or, more accurately perhaps, representatives of business and industry, can now take its place of direct influence in the arena(s) of educational policy making, but that influence is not simply foregone or unopposed. The policy communities (Richardson and Jordan 1987) may have shifted profoundly but the field is by no means open. In a sense social-democractic pluralism has been replaced by elite-pluralism. Old, conservative (and old-Conservative) interests are at odds with new, manufacturing capital with finance capital, the Treasury with the DTI, the neo-liberals with the neo-conservatives, wets with drys, Elizabeth House with Number 10, the DES with itself, Conservative Central Office with the Shires.

The ball game may be new and the teams may be different from before but there are just as many teams, maybe more. While I sit in the beleagured bleachers, ducking the fly-balls and malicious hits into the crowd, this is the scene on which I aim to offer my ball-by-ball commentary. I will look at the past performances of the teams, review the form of the players, profile the coaches and analyse the moves and plays.

The educational state

I take the state to be a practical and institutional entity, a thing as well as a set of functions. It is identifiable in terms of particular agencies, and in some respects individuals. I see issues like system regulation as explicable only by reference to the purposeful deliberation of and action by individuals. The state cannot have intentions unless these are expressed in terms of social mechanisms. It is an apparatus; it is concerned, in part at least, with its own ends; it is managerialist (Saunders 1979) and bureaucratic, and greatly preoccupied with short-term 'crisis management' (Offe 1984). But this is not meant to imply a neutral state.

While it may be set apart from class relations, sectional interests are clearly reflected in its policies, as a result of either direct representation or the exercise of influence on or over the state. Again, though the state is not autonomous or independent, its independence is constrained by a variety of factors, particularly its reliance upon and relationships with private production and capital accumulation. It is, as explained previously, relatively autonomous.

The educational state, therefore, is that conglomeration of sites and agencies concerned with the regulation of the education system. But:

> if the state in education is understood not as a single and unified entity but as a set of 'agencies, departments, tiers and levels, each with its own rules and resources and often with varying purposes' (McLennan *et al*. 1984), then it becomes possible not only to avoid conspiratorial explanations but also to trace the dynamics of state action in different historical periods. The state is the locus of power and control but the mode in which these are expressed and the agencies through which these are mediated change in relation to wider socio-political developments.
>
> (Grace 1987 p.196)

These sites and agencies of the educational state contain and represent contesting interests in policy formation and policy debate. As Grace goes on to point out, the mandates of governments and the will of ministers are for ever confronted by the energies, skills and vested interests of civil servants involved in the administration and bureaucracy of the state apparatus. The central state often finds itself in conflict with elements of the local state. Policy inputs into government and the state apparatus from teacher unions, employers, local authorities and others are rarely consensual. The policies and priorities for education of the DTI (Department of Trade and Industry), DOE (Department of Employment), MSC (Manpower Services Commission), and Home Office may be very different from the DES. Within the DES ministers and officials do not always concur with the HMI (Her Majesty's Inspectorate), and the FEU. has had several moments of out and out conflict with the Secretary of State. And, as we shall see, relations between the DES, the Schools Council and the SCDC (School Curriculum Development Committee) have often been strained. Some system regulation and system management in education are actually carried out by quangos, appointed bodies, intermediary agencies and even, in the case of examinations, by quasi-commercial organisations. Thus we need to be aware of centre–periphery relations within the educational state itself. As McLennan, Held and Hall(1984, p.3) note:

abstract statements about the state are always a shorthand for this
conglomeration and must be consistent with an exploration of its
dynamics . . . In order to understand the relations and processes of
the state and their place in civil society, we must grasp the way the
state is embedded in a particular socio-economic system . . .
together with its nature as a site of political negotiation and conflict.

Thus, throughout the study my emphasis is upon conflict and
incoherence within the state and within and across the various sites
which make up the state. These conflicts take the form of general and
particular disputes over and struggles for control of the meaning and
definition of education. Specifically I shall highlight the disputes over
pedagogy, curriculum and assessment (the three message systems of the
curriculum), and thus what it means to be educated, which have arisen
between elements of the New Right, certain 'reformist' representatives
of big business and industry, and the DES and HMI.

2

Discipline and chaos: the New Right and discourses of derision

> in any society the production of discourse is at once controlled,
> selected, organized and redistributed according to a number of
> procedures whose role is to avert its powers and its dangers, to
> master the unpredictable event.
>
> (Foucault 1981 p.53)

In this chapter and the following I intend to examine the impact of the
so-called New Right on education policy in two different but related
ways. First, I will introduce and discuss the substantive views of the
New Right and, via the concept of *discourse* (see chapter 1), I shall
argue that these views have come to constrain the possibilities of policy
and policy debate. Then, in chapter 3, I shall consider the impact of the
New Right in education policy in more specific terms.

Discourse provides a particular and pertinent way of understanding
policy formation, for policies are, pre-eminently, statements about
practice – the way things could or should be – which rest upon, derive
from, statements about the world – about the way things are. They are
intended to bring about idealised solutions to diagnosed problems.
Policies embody claims to speak with authority, they legitimate and
initiate practices in the world, and they privilege certain visions and
interests. They are power/knowledge configurations *par excellence*.
Indeed, Foucault suggests that there are two arenas within which
'procedures of exclusion', the control over discourses, is most strict in
our society; they are sexuality and politics. 'We know very well that we
are not free to say anything, that we cannot speak of anything when and
where we like, and that just anyone, in short, cannot speak of just
anything' (Foucault 1981 p.62).

What is presented here, then, is a discursive account of education
policy through the 1970s and 1980s. It is not an account of events as
such and it is by no means exhaustive, although I will suggest that
certain events are of special discursive significance. Rather I am con-

cerned with a number of emergent theories and key issues in policy debate and the manner and effects of their articulation (see Laclau and Mouffe 1985). In particular, I shall draw attention to the way in which these emergent discourses were constructed to define the field, articulate the positions and thus subtly set limits to the possibilities of education policy.

The New Right and education: the beginnings

Foucault distinguishes between beginnings and origins. The latter provide a basis from which causality and narrative can be deployed. Origins, once found, are often taken to constitute an explanation of things; they are also commonly the starting point for the evolution or development of things. In contrast, an interest in the former (beginnings) involves not a reconstitution of the past but rather an attempt to make the past intelligible.

I take as my beginnings, then, not one point in time but, in fact, two. The first, the year 1969, is the date of publication of the first of the *Black Papers* (Cox and Dyson 1969), a series of right-wing, populist pamphlets which mounted a trenchant critique of all aspects of progressive and comprehensive education. The second, the year 1976, is the date of Labour Prime Minister James Callaghan's much-publicised speech at Ruskin College, Oxford, in which he appeared to take up basic aspects of the *Black Paper* criticisms, and in which he initiated The Great Debate on education. Something of the differences between origins and beginnings is highlighted in the following comment made in interview by Stuart Sexton.

> The turning point, not just in education, was in turning away from Heath-minded conservatism, to the re-emphasis of individual freedom and the market, that things worked better if you let people run their own show, rather than bureaucrats, etc. That was really brought in and encouraged by Mrs Thatcher when she assumed leadership of the party.
>
> It irritates me when people claim that the 1976 Callaghan Ruskin speech was the turning point when it jolly well wasn't. It was an attempt by the then Labour government to recapture some of the initiative we had captured. Norman St John Stevas' Parent Charter speech in Stockport was more important a year previously. It got less publicity because it wasn't James Callaghan. Callaghan said nothing new but it was the Labour government saying it, climbing on the band wagon. They then carried on the bad old ways under Shirley Williams anyway and if you look at that 1976 Education Act . . .

Nonetheless, Sexton, like a large number of the rest of my respondants, identified the Ruskin speech as being of major discursive significance. The speaker, the setting and the nature of the text (see chapter 6) all came together to provide legitimation for a conception of the problems and possibilities of education and to empower certain groups and constituencies to speak authoritatively about education and to marginalise other groups.

1969

The first of the *Black Papers* (Cox and Dyson 1969) on education was primarily concerned with Higher Education and the political involvement of students in the events of 1968. For many of the writers in the collection the causes of such student unrest were seen to lie in the lack of respect for and challenge to traditional authority (both the authority of texts and of institutions); and indeed much of this critique arises from inside the academic establishment. Typically, C.L. Mowat argues: 'We forget at our peril the mediaeval origin of universities as guilds analogous to the craftmen's guilds, in which the masters, journeymen and apprentices were all bretheren but not all equal' (Cox and Dyson 1969 p.13). The basis of the critique is within the tradition of what Williams (1962) calls 'old humanism'. It contains both a defence of the elitist, liberal curriculum and an attack on the destabilising effects of progressivism. The discourse being generated here links education with traditional social and political values and with social order. In the rest of the series the criticisms tend to focus more particularly on schools and especially upon comprehensive schools, the products of DES Circular 10/65, and progressive primary schools, the progeny of the Plowden Report. But the underlying concerns are essentially the same no matter what the specific object of critique. A new ideology of education was being synthesised under the 'mobilizing myth' (Levitas 1986 p.8) of education in 'crisis'. State education was portrayed as having disintegrated into chaos; and, having established an imagery of crisis and chaos, the *Black Papers* writers were not slow to offer their solution. The call was both for a return to pre-comprehensive, pre-progressive forms and methods (the reinvention of tradition or cultural restoration) and for new ways of exerting discipline in and over education.

> In the name of 'equality of opportunity' the egalitarian seeks to destroy or transmogrify those schools which make special efforts to bring out the best in talented children . . . in his impatience the egalitarian takes the alternative course of levelling down the higher standards towards a uniform mediocrity . . . This leads him to decry

the importance of academic standards and discipline – and indeed
learning itself.

(Maude 1969 p.6)

Through the *Black Paper* opus as a whole three major substantive
themes are reiterated, each of which involves direct criticism of
comprehensive and progressive education. The first is that academic
standards are in decline, particularly standards of literacy and numeracy.
For many commentators the nation had to look no further to explain
Britain's economic decline. The oil price rises (of 1973 and 1974) and
the world trade crisis aside, Britain's recession could be blamed on
comprehensive schools, progressive primary education and bad teachers
... and all this despite the absence of clear evidence of decline in
standards and the existence of counter evidence of no decline (Bullock
1975), and more pupils than ever before leaving school with
examination passes (Wright 1977). Crucially, as part of a complex,
interrelated discourse of critique, this refrain remained largely
impervious to disconfirmation. It entered into the generally accepted
'what we all know about school', precisely because of its composite
interdependence with other thematic choices in the discourse. In this
way, the discourse is self-generating, self-reinforcing, it constitutes an
'imposition of the real' (Baudrillard 1988) – where the opposition
between things as presented and what's really going on begins to
dissolve. Signs take on a life of their own, their own circulation. Schools
in public debate are 'imaged', judgement and rational critique become
impossible. The second and third themes have the same dubious
empirical status but, taken together, they do powerful political and
ideological work, effectively deconstructing the fragile possibilities of
comprehensive schooling.

The second theme is that of dangerous, politically motivated teachers
preaching revolution, socialism, egalitarianism, feminism and sexual
deviation. Here the link is between comprehensive schools and social
disorder. Teachers of English, guardians of national literacy, were in
particular indicted on this count. Attempts by a painfully small number
of teachers to bring aspects of working-class culture into the school
curriculum and to develop forms of critical literacy were regarded as
massively subversive. Thornbury (1978 pp.136–7) captures the mood of
ideological subversion in his description of English teachers in London.

Young English teachers in the 1960s revived the romantic
nineteenth-century notion of 'enthusiasm', encouraging the
working class child to remain a literary primitive ... Many of the
new English teachers indoctrinated themselves and their classes in
attitudes critical to the police, local government bureaucracy,
industry and employers. They did not hesitate to encourage this

ideology in the children's writing, or classroom discussion . . . The new wave of English teachers was committed to the comprehensive school, to unstreaming, subject integration and team teaching.

Brian Cox took up this theme again in the 1980s in a more generalised attack, claiming that education policy since the 1960s had been dominated by left-wing educationalists, 'whose aim is revolution, not by armed over-throw of the government, but by transformation of institutions from within' (1981 p.5).

Significantly education did not stand alone in the 1970s as an object of political suspicion; this kind of analysis can clearly be situated within the context of the general Conservative Party attack on socialism, trade unionism and egalitarianism which was being formulated in the early 1970s. The shadow cabinet conclave at Selsdon Park in 1970 produced an election strategy which centred on the issue of law and order and which was aimed to fuel a national disquiet based on the idea of 'a nation under threat'.

The reaction, into which the *Black Papers* fitted, was to a loss of legitimacy in traditional authority, including the authority of the state, which was increasingly evident in the later 1960s. (What Habermas [1976] calls the 'legitimation crisis'.) Established values of all kinds were subjected to challenge. This leads on directly to the third educational theme of the *Black Papers*, that of indiscipline. Again the comprehensive schools and progressive primaries were identified with a decline in standards, this time standards of behaviour. The comprehensive and open-plan primary classrooms were portrayed as unruly and ill-disciplined, with the teachers unable or unwilling to assert their control. The schools were subject, it was argued, to vandalism and disfiguring graffiti. Lack of classroom control spilled over into the rest of the school and thence onto the streets. The rising level of juvenile crime, particularly street crimes, were in part laid at the door of the comprehensive school (the other 'popular' explanation treated such crimes, newly dubbed as 'mugging', as essentially crimes of black youth, see Hall *et al.* 1978). Teachers and black youth provided relatively unpopular and susceptible groups (in very different ways) which could be constructed as specific scapegoats for general social problems. The streets and the classrooms were no longer safe places to be. A 'moral panic' was being constructed, and taken up with enthusiasm in the media, with teachers 'named' and cast in the role of 'folk devils' (Cohen 1980).

This formed the basis for a powerful and effective 'symbolic crusade', a 'moral enterprise' where 'someone takes the initiative on the basis of interest and uses publicity techniques to gain the support of the organizations that count' (Cohen 1980 p.112). In this respect the *Black*

Paper writers possessed the sort of legitimating values, enterprise and power which Cohen (1980) suggests are the necessary basis for successful moral entrepreneurship. The crusade was to save the future, by turning to the past, to save the school system. It was made clear that teachers could no longer be trusted with the education of the nation's children. All aspects of the progressivism of the comprehensive school – curriculum, teaching methods and social relationships – were being thoroughly debunked in the critical discourse of the *Black Papers*. However, the degree of impact achieved would have been inconceivable without the ideological support of the greater part of the media for the educational project of these cultural restorationists. The *Daily Mail* and, more recently, the *Sun* and the *Daily Star* have played a particularly important role in a sustained campaign of 'teacher-bashing' (CCCS 1981). Furthermore, a number of key events provided particular focus for the elaboration of the discourse of critique.

In particular, the events at William Tyndale primary school brought the possibility of linking all three of the *Black Paper* themes. Here were politically motivated teachers, making no attempt to teach traditional basic skills, who were deliberately abdicating from their responsibility to discipline and control their pupils. It revealed teachers to be unaccountable to their community and their employers. It

> showed that teachers could run the schools in ways that clearly contradicted many of the shared assumptions on which the education system rested. Teachers could be in effective day to day control of the schools, and they could use that control in ways not welcome to the school managers or its funding authority.
>
> (Dale 1979 p.96)

Within the framework of the emerging rightist education discourse the lessons of Tyndale were obvious – teachers needed to be made more accountable, they needed to be more closely monitored and controlled. A similar message could be constructed out of Neville Bennett's much-publicised report, *Teaching Styles and Pupils' Progress* (1976). The analysis of data from a variety of primary classrooms purported to show that children did notably better on a whole range of measures in formal rather than informal classroom regimes. Significantly the BBC *Horizon* programme based on the book was entitled *Lesson for the Teacher*. Teachers were being told again that they had got it wrong.

There are many other examples to choose from, headlines, articles and television programmes mobilised and reiterated a set of simple myths, slogans, silences, stereotypes and emphases. They all pointed to crisis, to schooling out of control. There is little or no space in this discursive terrain for alternative interpretations. The blame was clear.

And many parents, fearful for the future of their children, were ready to accept an analysis which would apparently lead towards a shift of control over education away from teachers to them. The discourse is not one of despair, for the construction of blame also constructs solutions (a point to which I shall return below). As with the other expressions of cultural progressivism the cultural restorationists with their emphasis on the heritage, the known and the valued, could tap the evident popular distrust of the new and the difficult. In this way elitist conceptions of art, literature, music and education could actually be passed off as popular. Traditional patterns of the distribution of cultural capital were thus reinforced.

In more general terms the *Black Papers* anticipated and contributed to two key aspects of contemporary Conservative politics or what has come to be called Thatcherism. First, in the sphere of cultural politics they provided an intellectual basis for and legitimation of anti-progressivism (not only in education but also in art, music, and the theatre). Progressivism is identified unequivocally (but mistakenly) with egalitarianism. (The more recent incorporation of progressive methods into vocational education schemes has illustrated the absence of an inevitable relationship between progressivism and liberation [Bernstein 1975].) And this is one more indication of the possibility for words and concepts to be wrenched out of one discursive ensemble and reassembled in an entirely different metonymical relation in another discourse.) Progressivism is also linked to the decline of traditional values and the purportedly concomitant potential for social unrest. It also relates to the Thatcherite critique of permissiveness generally.

The second key aspect pointed to a relationship between the decline in traditional values and moral decay, which is also linked to the devaluation of the family, and the family writ large – the nation. Here a set of sacred objects, statements and concepts are thematically welded into a powerful regularity. Racial politics (and immigration laws) are bound with a rediscovery of Nation (massively underpinned by the jingoistic effects of and exploitation of the Falklands war). These in turn are articulated with attacks on trade unionism ('the enemy within') and student radicalism. The whole package is tied in turn to the virtues of the traditional family which are set over and against the 'rise' in sexual permissiveness, pornography, abortion and homosexuality. These affinities within the discourse capture and evoke a whole range of commonsense fears and concerns. A great deal of the popularism of Thatcherism has its basis in this corpus. The discourse is realised in the style and practice of Thatcherism which Hall and Jacques (1983) describe as a form of 'authoritarian populism'. Keith Joseph provides an apt illustration of the populism and the discursive packaging.

We were taught that crime, violence, wife-beating, child-beating
were the result of poverty; abolish poverty, and they would
disappear . . . By now, we are in a position to test all these fine
theories in the light of experience . . . Real incomes per head have
risen beyond what anyone dreamed of a generation back; so have
education budgets and welfare budgets; so also have delinquency,
truancy, vandalism, hooliganism, illiteracy, decline in educational
standards. Some secondary schools in our cities are dominated by
gangs operating extortion rackets against small children. Teenage
pregnancies are rising; so are drunkenness, sexual offences and
crimes of sadism . . . the decline is spreading. We know that some
universities have been constrained to lower their standards for
entrants from comprehensives, discriminating against the more
talented because they come from grammar or independent schools
. . . If equality in education is sought at the expense of quality,
how can the poisons created help but filter down?

(*The Times*, 21 October 1974)

Returning to education specifically, Macdonell suggests 'any discourse
concerns itself with certain objects and puts forward certain concepts at
the expense of others' (1986 p.3). Thus, in this area of concern it is
sensible to consider that which is excluded or displaced in the new
emergent dominant discourse. In other words what previous
possibilities, for example, for comprehensive schooling are rendered
impossible by the intervention and take up of the *Black Papers*? What is
the world that we have lost?

It is all too easy in a field of ideological struggle, like education, to
respond to retrenchment and restructuring by romanticising the past.
However, it is difficult to point with any confidence to a period in the
recent educational history of England that could be described as the
golden age of the comprehensive school. The CCCS (1981) review of
educational policy in the 1960s makes it clear that the 'noise' of educational reform in the emergence of comprehensive schooling was often
not matched by real changes in educational practices. The reviewers
also argue that while 'There was a distinctive social democratic
"moment" in the formulation of policy' in the 1960s, 'it was always
caught within sharp limits' (p.111). And they highlight the incoherent
nature of the policies and reforms being advanced in this period, which
were 'uneasily adjacent, often incompatible and held loosely together
by ambiguous key terms' (p.106). Their conclusion on the 1960s is that
while the implementation of circular 10/65 (via which the Labour
government of 1964–70 made its only *request* to Local Authorities for
comprehensive reorganisation, there being no legal framework for such

reorganisation until 1976) 'encouraged a national movement towards comprehensives . . . the meaning of the movement was never in any way radical' (p.129). Throughout the short period of so-called progressive consensus (say 1965–69) the meaning and practice of comprehensive schooling remained a focus of conflict and indecision. The discourse of reform was fractured, incoherent and often contradictory. Several ideological models, in effect a set of contesting discourses, were invested in aspects of practice in schools (see Ball 1981) and in the arenas of policy formation.

Neither the teacher unions, nor the DES, nor the LEAs (Local Education Authorities), nor the Labour Party were clear in their support for or vision of comprehensive schooling. There was no politically significant institutional site from which the discourse of comprehensive education could be mounted without equivocation. The failure of the discourse was therefore a failure of both theory and practice.

In some sense the lack of coherent definition and positive guidance allowed for a convenient policy hiatus. While this hiatus gave some grassroots innovators room for manoeuvre, it also gave the much larger number of conservatives or doubtfuls the room to carry on more or less as they had before. The tendency to regard 1965 and the introduction of comprehensives as a point of break in English educational history also tends to obscure the extent of continuity from previous practice. More than anything else the policy hiatus allowed a version of the grammar school curriculum to become firmly and unproblematically established in most comprehensives (Ball 1981, Riseborough 1981, Reynolds and Sullivan 1987). To a great extent when critics of current government policy look back to the previous period with regret and a sense of loss, that which is considered lost is the small minority of attempts at innovation in a small minority of schools, and, perhaps more importantly, the possibilities for change, unrealised for the most part, which the situation in the late 1960s seemed to offer.

In general terms the inchoate, fragmented and contested discourse of comprehensive education failed to win the hearts and minds of parents and employers. There was certainly no attempt by the Labour Party to fashion a broad-based national political discourse into which comprehensive education would naturally fit. Indeed many of the major Labour politicians of the Wilsonian period were only too willing to parade their personal belief in the efficacy of grammar schooling as the best route of social mobility for bright working-class pupils. This further undermined any possibility of consolidated class support for comprehensives. The hegemony of the grammar school and the O-level curriculum was never successfully challenged (except within a handful of varietist schools such as Countesthorpe College, Sutton Centre, Vauxhall Manor, Stantonbury), and such support as was forthcoming from the Labour Party was articulated in traditional Fabian terms, as a project of improving class access. There was little or no attempt to examine and reconstruct the ideological form and content of the education on offer – what is to count as being educated. Thus the discourse of comprehensive education was a discourse of vagary, of uncertainty and of polarity, embracing as it did extremes from the most radical to the most pragmatic (many Conservative LEAs sanctioned the building or reorganisation of comprehensives straightforwardly on the basis of cost-effectiveness). In effect, the comprehensive movement failed to bring off a meaningful discursive formation. The dispersion of statements (Foucault 1972 p.38) addressed to comprehensive education remained arbitrary and chaotic, and lacked the rules of formation (the conditions of existence) for a discursive formation. The voices of the public educators, always muted and somewhat discordant, were thus rendered silent within policy debate.

Against this discursive background, as political and economic conditions began to change in the early 1970s it is hardly surprising that comprehensive education provided a soft target for Conservative critics. But the irony embedded in this argument is that the motifs of crisis, or chaos, and of rampant unremitting change appear ever more circumstantial and illusory. They are built upon a small number of exceptions. The thrust of comprehensivism was poorly rooted and represented in practice and easily dismantled by critique.

The offensive of the Right against comprehensive education contains throughout a number of distinct but discursively related aspects and bases. In contrast to the comprehensive movement the Conservatives have sucessfully managed to integrate and maintain and manage a high degree of contradiction and incoherence within their critical educational discourse. Indeed, the disparate aspects of the discourse have served all the more effectively to outflank putative resistance.

1976

There are a number of symbolic, practical and pragmatic reasons why the bulk of my analysis of education policy begins from the year 1976. The main symbolic reason is the presentation in that year of James Callaghan's Ruskin speech and the ensuing Great Debate. As noted already a number of my respondents had comments to make about the significance – political and educational – of the speech and its aftermath. Whatever Callaghan's intention the speech gave powerful encouragement and added legitimacy to the 'discourse of derision' mounted by the *Black Papers*. In discursive terms it marked the end to any possibility of serious public opposition to the critique of comprehensivism and progressivism. It cleared the ground for a shift of

31

emphasis on the Right from critical deconstruction to radical reconstruction. The shaky edifice of comprehensive theory and practice in areas of the curriculum, assessment and pedagogy could now be dismantled with impunity. Hold-outs against change, defenders of comprehensivism, could now be picked off as both subversive, damaging to the interests of children and the nation, and reactionary, irrationally persisting with old, disreputable ways. In terms of policy the sayable and unsayable were thenceforward carefully demarcated. A classic division between madness and reason is erected: the madness of egalitarianism, social engineering and democracy in education over and against the reason of tradition, discipline and authority. To engage in the discourse of madness would be to court exclusion from the arenas of policy. From 1976 only certain policies were possible, only certain policies were sane or rational. Thus, in those places where policy was being made only certain concepts, conceptions, proposals and pleas were utterable or at least hearable. And indeed only certain interests had the right to speak, to plea, to be heard. Some old interests and lobbies were now being firmly excluded, the folk-demon teachers and their unions were one such group, teacher educators and academics another, the LEAs would soon be another. In contrast, new voices were being listened to in the corridors of power, in particular, the voices of industry, given special credence by Callaghan's Great Debate, and the various voices of the now increasingly well-organised and articulate New Right. Digby Anderson, Director of the New Right, Social Affairs Unit, explained:

We are interested in taking things which have not been looked at very critically and doing something on them . . . in the late 70s it was fairly clear there was an orthodoxy about education, it wasn't difficult to know where to go to find the sorts of things that might be interesting and provoke better debate. And I don't think anyone would deny that the breadth of the education debate has improved . . . we have pushed back the boundaries of what is sayable, and now there are a number of things which are sayable which weren't sayable ten years ago.

The deconstructive/reconstructive thrust of the *Black Papers*/New Right discourse works at a variety of levels producing a series of 'binary oppositions with positive and negative poles' (Kenway 1987 p.42). Two of these oppositions are fundamental to the whole edifice of critique and response in the assault on education policy making. One is the setting of expertise and against commonsense. The role of expert knowledge and research is regarded as less dependable than political intuition and commonsense accounts of what people want. The other rests on what Kenway calls the 'people-powerbloc distinction': 'Powerless individuals were juxtaposed against a self-serving, unresponsive bureaucracy' (p.42). (I shall examine more of these juxtapositions and polarities in more detail later.)

Interestingly and crucially these fundamentals represent opposing conceptions of power/knowledge relations in education policy. As Kenway also points out, the effectiveness of such polarities is related both to the divisions they generate – parents against teachers, scholarly research against the popular media – and the *unities* they conjure up – parents as a group, of a kind, teachers as a group, of a kind. The interests of all parents are cast together as the same; the culpability of all teachers is cast together as the same. 'Disparate and contradictory interests [are] activated and welded into a common position' (Kenway 1987 p.43). In effect the discourse of the *Black Papers* constructed a new social-subject in the field of education policy, a subject which would be crucial in the development of the New Right's policy initiatives in the 1980s – the concerned parent; the parent as consumer of education. And through and around this new subject another key polarity was established, a polarity of control – professional control versus accountability. Out of the ashes of William Tyndale, of *Teaching Styles and Pupil Progress* and The Bullock Report rose the phoenix of *parental choice*.

In all this, then, the power/knowledge ensemble of the education policy establishment, the triangle of tension (teacher unions, DES and LEAs) was profoundly dismembered. Again the concerned parent is cast as a figure of reason and sanity naturally opposed to and set over against the wild experimentation and unorthodoxies of the uncaring teachers (like those of William Tyndale) and 'loony left' authorities like ILEA, Brent and Haringey. As Hall explains ' . . . the work of ideological struggle is therefore equivalent to the work of articulating/disarticulating discourses from their previously secured position in an ideological field' (1980 p.174). But clearly the discourse of the concerned parent does not stand alone in the New Right's ideological work. It is at the centre of a series of interpenetrating discourses and both affects and is affected by them. For example, the discursive themes of standards and excellence articulate straightforwardly with the role and concerns of the archetypal concerned parent in terms of basic elements of the general political discourse of Thatcherism, that is possessive individualism and personal initiative. Thus, the concerned parent aims to do the best for his or her child, given the harsh realities of the competitive world. The child needs a decent education and good qualifications which will enable him or her to get on. The emphasis is upon individual betterment and competition. The parent's duty is to ensure that they choose the best education for their child, even if that means that the children of others will have less than the best education. In this condensation excellence is a competitive acquisition, it is a form of differentiation, of comparison.

Education is thus displaced from its political and collective context, and notions of mass or common schooling no longer have a valid or logical role to play in this scenario. The concerned parent is thus recruited as a discursive subject of Thatcherism. If the parent makes a poor choice, it is said, then that is his or her problem.

In classic Foucauldian terms the 'dividing practices' provided for by this discursive complex both *totalise* and *individualise* the social-subject, the concerned parent. All parents are taken to have shared interests in opposing liberalising reforms in education but they compete individually, via their children, for the scarce rewards of educational success.

We should note a further significant element of these educational and political discourses. Many of the key elements in these discursive ensembles – individualism, choice, competition, etc. – are ramified from recently re-emergent Conservative philosophies, particularly that of Neo-liberalism. Neo-liberalism, which we will shortly examine more closely, rests firmly upon notions of freedom of choice, market forces and quality by competition (strongly counterposed to the worth or possibility of equality). Excellence and standards, and the advocacy of practices like streaming, corporal punishment and the use of formal exams, all pursued dedicatedly in the *Black Papers*, also resonate with some of the root concepts of neo-conservativism – tradition and authority, order and place.

Political philosophy and social policy

The last of the *Black Papers* was published in 1977. From that point on the discursive cudgels of the conservative educational offensive were taken up by a variety of related and overlapping New Right agencies and groups, ranging from the Centre for Policy Studies, The National Council for Educational Standards and the Social Affairs Unit to the Institute of Economic Affairs and The Adam Smith Institute. What makes them markedly different from the rather informally produced *Black Papers* is the degree and sophistication of their organisation and strategies for dissemination (see Labour Research 1987, Vol.76, No.10 and Bosanquet 1983), and the extent to which their critiques and proposals are theoretically informed by philosophies of neo-liberalism and neo-conservatism. CCCS make the point that:

> Little could be said by way of characterizing the Conservative
> Party's educational 'thought' from the inter-war years into the
> early 1960s. The whole idea would be paradoxical. There was no
> right wing figure comparable to Tawney (Eliot's writing was
> remote from prescription, Bantock's never found much resonance),

while little importance was attached to the whole area of social
policy except as reluctantly found necessary.

(CCCS 1981 p.191)

By the 1980s the intervention of the crusading, radical, New Right had
changed all that. Neo-liberal texts, particularly the work of Hayek, and
monetarist theories like those of Friedman, are paraded as a basis for
social and economic policy making. And neo-liberal and neo-
conservative philosophers like Adam Smith and Edmund Burke are
being re-examined and reworked by contemporary Conservative intellectuals like Roger Scruton and Peter Quinton (see Salisbury Review).

Before looking specifically at the engagement of these theoretical
discourses with education policy I want to sketch very briefly and
schematically the main theoretical tenets of neo-liberalism and
neo-conservatism.

Neither of these assemblages of economics, philosophy and social
theory are of a piece. They each encompass a range of positions and
perspectives. Neo-liberalism, for example, is used as a generic term to
cover Friedman's economic liberalism, Nozick's libertarianism (the
advocacy of the minimal state), and Hayek's Austrian economics. For
our purposes Hayek is most pertinent and most influential, Nozick
(1974), even in these circles is regarded as somewhat of an extremist. He
argues for no state intervention beyond the protection of life and
property and thus the absolute freedom of the market.

Hayek's work rests on a critique of socialism, statism and
Keynsianism. He is opposed to trade unionism, to government interventions into the economy and to state welfare. They each, he argues,
distort and inhibit the free and efficient workings of *the market*. Trade
unions artificially push wages above the level which would be set by the
free market. They also advantage some workers, those in strong unions,
and thus disadvantage others, ununionised or in weak unions.
Democracy itself is a major problem in all this; according to Hayek
'political feeling aroused in a democracy would have certain practical
results in terms of rising public expenditure and growing centralisation'
(Bosanquet 1983 p.14). State welfare is wasteful, depresses competition
(that is, without state benefits unemployed workers would be motivated
to accept jobs at lower wages and thus drive down wages generally) and
reduces incentives. Indeed Hayek suggests that collectivism has an
effect of moral distortion, the national character can be damaged (1986
p.159). Also welfare involves the substitution of state judgements about
output for those of the market. State judgements are inevitably biased,
the market is not. Furthermore, according to Hayek, welfare payments
are based upon coerced transfers of income between individuals.
Government intervention in the economy is also unfair and inefficient

and once started is difficult to stop. It leads to socialism and what Hayek graphically calls 'the road to serfdom'. Mrs Thatcher is a very orthodox Hayekian in this regard. 'I have' she said 'always regarded part of my job as – and please do not think of it in any arrogant way – killing Socialism in Britain' (*Financial Times*, 14 November 1985). According to Hayek, government failure is more common and more likely than economic failure. The market embodies a superior rationality. Governments once embarked upon social or economic expenditure programmes are confronted by and susceptible to interest and client group pressures for more or new expenditures. And elections are imperfect public-choice mechanisms, they encourage governments to attempt to buy support.

Much of Hayek's analysis of the ills of collectivism are focused on a rebuttal of Keynsian economics. Keynsianism is identified with a politicised economy, an economy where decisions are made by public agencies, and with economic strategies which rely heavily on government expenditure and thus on high taxes and high levels of public sector borrowing. The result, it is argued, is inflation and government overload, or what is called 'ungovernability' (King 1975). Overload is used in two senses; the first is the vast and increasing responsibilities of modern democratic governments, and the concomitant increases in intervention in and control over people's lives; the second is the extent to which the increases in state expenditures outrun the growth in the national product to the point where the state has insufficient resources to meet its accumulated responsibilities. This also relates to Friedman's 'theory of bureaucratic displacement'; the theory suggests that 'increases in expenditure will act rather like "black holes" in the economic universe, simultaneously sucking in resources and shrinking in terms of "emitted" production' (Friedman and Friedman 1980 p.155). (The National Council for Educational Standards has devoted considerable time and energy to attempting to prove this maxim.) All this can lead to a decline in public confidence and a loss of legitimacy by the state. Thus: 'By attacking Keynsianism as a discredited and failed theory New Right economists were trying to knock out the lynchpin on which so much of post-war intervention in the economy rested' (Gamble 1986 p.40).

As an alternative to all this Hayek argues for two things: for free markets and for individual freedom. Markets, according to Hayek, are better than central planning authorities at coping with rapid social and technological change and with uncertainty, by continuous adaptation to unpredictable change. Decentralised markets also maximise creative entrepreneurship, that is the search for new ways to make profits. 'Through the pursuit of selfish aims the individual will usually lead himself to save the general interest, the collective actions of organised groups are almost invariably contrary to the general interest' (Hayek 1976 p.138). Furthermore, the market is unprincipled, it allows no moral priorities in its patterns of distribution. It may not produce equality, indeed equality would be unhelpful in market terms, but it is not unfair. 'Since inequality arises from the generation of innumerable individual preferences it cannot be evil unless these preferences are themselves evil' (Joseph and Sumption 1979 p.78). It produces a natural economic order and the poorest, the losers in the market, will benefit from the progress of the society as a whole. There are no intentional effects in the market, no possibility of things like institutional racism – that would be arbitrary and inefficient. The market is spontaneous. There is no one to blame for failure but the failures themselves. Fault must lie in the culture, the family, or the individual. For Hayek, as for Mrs Thatcher, society is a meaningless aggregation. There can be no commonly agreed social definitions of either need or worth, so attempts at social justice are always biased and unfair because only some are selected to benefit. These are political judgements, they require a concentration of power and thus smack of totalitarianism. These are the enemies of freedom.

Hayek's definition of freedom is very precise and very narrow. It is a freedom 'from', rather than a freedom 'to', that is an absence of coercion. Thus, it differs fundamentally from post-war conceptions of freedom that rest upon notions of citizenship rights. It is solely a freedom to have control of one's own behaviour, the removal of interpersonal constraints. It is a freedom to choose. Even if the choice is between starvation and exploitative labour, for Hayek this is a real choice. It is real freedom. You can starve if you want to. There are always alternatives in the market.

> The fact that the opportunities open to the poor in a competitive society are much more restricted than those open to the rich does not make it less true that in such a society the poor are much more free than a person commanding much greater material comfort in a different type of society.
>
> (Hayek 1986 pp.76–7)

Thus, freedom is market freedom, very much the basis of 'on yer bike' Tebbitism. State activity can only serve to reduce freedom, thus the role of the state in Hayek's view must be limited to the maintenance of those property rights and legal procedures which provide the conditions necessary for the market to operate. All else – health care, pensions, education, etc. – can be left to the market. Clearly both the rhetorical commitment in the early phases of Thatcherism to the 'rolling back of the state', and the privatisation programme of the latter period rest on se twin premises of individual liberty and market freedom. Property rights rather than person rights are celebrated. However, while it is arguable that the impact of the New Right on economic policy has been more rhetorical than ideological, it certainly has provided an impetus for a whole variety of social policy initiatives in social security, health and education, aimed at destroying the basis of the post-war political consensus. My general point here is that the role of the New Right, as well as its direct impact on policy in some areas, has been discursive, that is it has facilitated a discursive reworking of the parameters of political possibility and acceptability. Some aspects of the once unproblematic consensus are now beyond the pale, and policies which might have seemed like economic barbarism twenty years ago now seem right and proper.

1 State and public intervention in the economy, especially attempts to control levels of unemployment by government spending produces a *politicized economy*, which restricts competition and generates inflation.
2 Socialism is atavistic, based on the politics of envy. All government decisions are less likely to work than the trial and error of the market.
3 State intervention and public spending encourages pressure group policies, interest groups press for increased and expanded shares of government expenditure.
4 Politics based on public spending solutions to economic problems encourage *promisory democracy*, the use of expenditure promises to influence voters.
5 Notions of *social justice* or *redistribution* are politically biased, relying as they do on partisan definitions of *need* and worth.
6 Welfare and citizenship rights rely on the *coerced* transfer of income between individuals and are *unfair*, i.e. high taxes.
7 High taxes and transfer of income reduces initiative, incentive and creativity *and* personal responsibility, create dependence and distort the national character.
8 State provision of services eradicates *choice* and *competition*, reduces *efficiency*, stifles innovation and removes personal *liberty*.
9 State professionals are an inefficient, self-serving clique determined to maintain restricted access, restrictive practices and resist innovations.
10 Trade Unions distort the market and competition by artificially raising wages above the real market level and are unfair because they damage the interests of some workers and advantage others.
11 To implement the politicised economy and policies of social redistributive justice requires massive state concentrations of power and gives rise to practical and financial *ungovernability*.

Figure 2.1 Proscriptions: criticism of Keynsian economics

1 Decentralized markets maximise creative entrepreneurship and are better at coping with uncertainty and rapid social and technological change - ensuring progress and civilization.
2 Markets render no moral priorities or claims to justice, it is neutral - a natural order.
3 Inequalities are *fair* because the market is unprincipled, its effects are unintentional, there is no deliberate bias - hence no racism or sexism.
4 Inequalities are inevitable and acceptable - indeed necessary. Inequality produces incentives.
5 This provides for maximum *LIBERTY*. Liberty is the absence of coercion, maximum control over one's own behaviour, an absence of interpersonal constraint (freedom *from*). This leaves us with the *real* choice, even if between exploitation wages and starvation.
6 The key is *market competition* based on *economic individualism*. The privatised provision of *all* services produces *efficiency* and *choice* for the individual *consumer* (which produce greater expenditure).
7 The state should have minimal responsibility for maintaining property rights, and the legal framework of the market, and national defence.
8 Liberty ensures the creation and dispersal of knowledge. Choice in the market encourages the pursuit of new ideas and methods.
9 Extensions of market relations and privatisation are extensions of freedom. Hence attacks on the welfare state and union rights as a moral crusade.

Figure 2.2 Prescriptions for the market

Those who stress the political orthodoxy of Thatcherism are in one sense right but only to the extent that they fail to take note of the deeper shifts in which yesterday's outrage becomes tomorrow's norm, in which what was only a short while ago unthinkable becomes today's green paper and the policy of the future.

(Schwarz 1987 p.125)

But clearly, that which is the New Right, and indeed that which is Thatcherism, does not begin and end with economic orthodoxies and a minimal state. In fact, aspects of the New Right present a very different view of the role of the state and give emphasis to social rather than economic orthodoxies; that is neo-conservatism.

In the renewed theoretical project of neo-conservatism freedom is again a central concept, but again it is a concept which is narrowly defined in a careful metonymical relation to a set of other concepts, like nation, authority and human nature. Specifically, freedom is taken to lie in a willing subordination to the nation. Thus, according to Roger

Scruton, 'the value of individual liberty is not absolute, but stands subject to another and higher value, the authority of established government' (1980 p.19) or Peregrine Worsthorne, 'social discipline is a much more fruitful theme for contemporary conservatism than individual freedom' (1978 p.150). While the neo-liberals see the community as founded upon economic relations, the neo-conservatives see it as founded upon social bonds arising out of a common culture and sense of national identity, held together, and, if necessary, enforced by strong government. Thus, the essence of social order here is neither individualism nor the mutuality or collectivity of society, but nation. Here there is no such thing as society, there are individuals and there is the nation. The citizen is interpellated not by choice but by duty. The social-subject of neo-conservatism is the loyal, law-abiding family man (or housewife/mother), holder of and believer in traditional values and sober virtues. Over and against this ideal citizen/parent is set an alternative subject: the carrier of alien values or alien culture, the agitator/trade unionist, sexual deviant, or working, single-parent mother, permissive/liberal, and progressive teacher – in other words 'the enemy within', the traitor.

In all this family and nation, morality and law are bound together in a discursive unity. The 'naturalness' of the traditional family, of fixed gender roles and 'normal' sexuality, of family loyalty and allegiance, fit neatly to the 'naturalness' of national loyalty, of order and place, of historic continuity. And out of this comes a 'natural' fear and suspicion of 'outsiders' and the rejection of alien values which undermine social cohesion.

> There is a natural instinct in the unthinking man . . . to accept and endorse through his actions the institutions and practices into which he is born. The instinct is rooted in human nature.
>
> (Scruton 1980 p.119)

Thus, cultural variation becomes a social 'problem', a threat to the preservation of national identity. Racism is simply a defence, a natural reaction; but it is a racism based on assumptions not of innate superiority but rather of cultural difference, and implicit cultural superiority. As a result, not surprisingly, the neo-conservatives are vehemently opposed to internationalism (like the idea of a European State) and multiculturalism.

> The enemy, the 'multiculturalist', is presented in purely negative terms as activists and agitators. They 'damage', prompt a 'backlash', 'purge', 'sanitise' and commit 'multiracialist assault'. They also argue (passionately), 'impede', 'assert', 'insist' and 'issue

guidelines'. They are emotional rather than reasonable, and deviant by association and by assumed political attitudes.

(Seidel 1986 p.118)

This ensemble of strength and allegiance, nation and culture, nature and normality is often portrayed by commentators as the basis in Thatcherism of 'authoritarian popularism' (Hall 1983). These aspects of Thatcherism are taken to articulate with certain popular prejudices and baser forms of jingoism which are fostered in the tabloid press, and with the resonant traditional themes of order, standards and duty. As noted already, Thatcherism operates via these themes in terms of common-sense, oppositions which set normal against abnormal, order against chaos, the hardworking against the scrounger, discipline against decay, nature against ideology.

> ... the successes of Thatcherism in shifting the ideological
> conjuncture – in imposing and normalising the springs of
> authoritarianism – go very deep, especially on the issues of race,
> law and order (such that principled, rather sensible liberals can be
> branded treacherous) and family and sexual life. And indeed one
> mark of the power of this cultural transformation is precisely the
> fact that it has been so speedily normalised ...

(Schwarz 1987 p.145)

Clearly, as we may see, when taken together, the neo-liberal and neo-conservative elements of the New Right display a number of vital contradictions. The existence of these contradictions must sound for any analyst of contemporary politics a series of important warning bells. First, there is the obvious danger of holding too firmly to the loose aggregation which is commonly referred to as the New Right. Second, there is the danger of attempting to translate directly between philosophical discourses and political action. Thatcherism represents an amalgam of and a selection from these philosophical discourses and clearly the emphases within Conservative policies have shifted several times since 1979. Thus, Jessop *et al.* (1984) suggest that 'Thatcherism must be seen ... more as an alliance of disparate forces around a self-contradictory programme' (p.38). Furthermore, pragmatism, expedience and so-called intuition all play their part in forging a distinctive set of policy discourses inside government. Opposition from dissenting ministers and civil servants, contradictory advice from advisers, and, on occasion 'popular' dissent (for example, over NHS cuts) all mediate and disrupt the relationships between philosophies and policies. And Thatcherism is not necessarily homologous with Conservatism. Dimitri Coryton, Chairman of the Conservative Education Association:

> she [Mrs Thatcher] is very much the outsider, she hasn't gone
> through that 30 year period of building up colleagues in the House
> of Commons . . . so when she did come to power, she actually drew
> to her some fairly bizarre and peculiar individuals. People who
> were not part of the mainstream, and who were, in the case of
> education, often not really all that well informed. The basis was
> ideology not practical experience and they have the massianic
> fervour of the ideologue. The expert is dismissed as a vested
> interest so the inexpert ideologue has the field.

Alan Hazelhurst MP, Mark Carlisle's PPS (Parliamentary Private
Secretary):

> There was a fairly important sea change, with the election of Mrs
> Thatcher and a feeling of dissatisfaction with the 'failure' of the
> Heath years, and those of us who came into parliament in 1970
> originally, as the supporters of the party and the then party leader,
> were put into eclipse. People were looking for new brooms and
> questions were asked: 'Are you really part of the new system . . . ?'
> When you're in government, especially now perhaps, things get led
> from the top and I think you get one or two things appearing in the
> manifesto and are genuinely surprised by what you find.

The work of the New Right intellectuals in and around the party is not
just one of advocacy, it is also one of opposition – that is opposition to
policies which are regarded as ideologically unsound, in their terms
(like, as we shall see, the National Curriculum). Policies within the
Conservative Party are a matter of continuing dispute, although
disputation is neither always welcome nor easy, 'it's especially difficult
at the present time to be dissenting voices within the Conservative Party.
You are set upon more savagely if you are dissenting, it doesn't matter
who you are.' (Alan Hazelhurst); ideological purity, expedience and
career advancement, among others, are factors which come into play in
particular policy struggles.

There are also ways in which the different philosophical emphases
work effectively together either by impacting on different fields of
government policy or by mutual reinforcement, for example in relation
to civil liberties or the role of the strong state acting to preserve the
freedom of the market (see Levitas 1986 p.103). Having shaded in some
of the general features of the deconstructive and reconstructive
discourse of the New Right in relation to education and social policy, in
the next chapter I will look more specifically at the elements of New
Right education policy.

3

The New Right and education policy

Thatcherism in education, as elsewhere in policy formation, is an amalgam, a blending of tensions, a managing of nascent contradictions. But the important point is that, analytically, education is no longer separated off from other areas of social and economic policy. It is no longer a backwater of policy. It is now in the mainstream of the political ideology and policies of Thatcherism.

However, when seeking to identify the impact of the New Right on education policy the differences and tensions identified must be carefully borne in mind. There is no way that education policy can simply be read off from the philosophical discourses of the New Right of whatever variety. Nonetheless, the Education Reform Act (ERA) does display a remarkable number of New Right imprints in its various provisions. (The actuality or degree of direct New Right influence on the 1988 Education Act and other aspects of Conservative education policy is taken up later.)

I want to begin by examining two particular texts, which in the field of education may be said to represent (very loosely) neo-liberal and neo-conservative thinking. For the former I will take Stuart Sexton's 1987 pamphlet from the Institute of Economic Affairs, Education Unit *Our Schools – A Radical Policy* (Sexton was a political adviser to Norman St John Stevas, Mark Carlisle and Keith Joseph), and for the latter, the Hillgate Group's (1987) pamphlet *The Reform of British Education*. The Sexton pamphlet was written in advance of the publication of proposals for the Education Reform Act, and is based upon a private paper prepared for Sir Keith Joseph. The Hillgate document is a form of response to those proposals but picks up themes from an earlier paper entitled *Whose Schools?*. The similarity of the title of this earlier paper to the title of Sexton's is some indication of a degree of commonality in the primary concerns of the two groups. Both deal fundamentally with the 'ownership' of schooling. Who shall define and control the meaning of the school, of education? The answer in each case is apparently the same, in straightforward neo-liberal terms it is the consumer/parent.

The aim, we believe, is to offer an independent education to all, by granting to all parents the power, at present enjoyed by only the wealthy, to choose the best available education for their children.

(Hillgate p.1)

To produce the quality and choice that we expect in education, to improve our schools, we need to change the way that we fund and manage them. Making the education service fully responsive to parental choice and student needs, with a direct financial relationship between provider and consumer, is the way to better standards, and a far better way than administrative tinkering and political exhortation.

(Sexton p.2)

(I shall return to the differences in emphasis in these statements in a moment.)

In each case there is a complex ensemble of interdependent key concepts deployed. The policies and reforms associated with or conjured up by one concept logically, in terms of the political theories upon which they draw, relate to other concepts and their attendant policies. Baroness Cox (of the Hillgate Group, CPS, NCES etc.) expressed this quite pertinently in interview:

Freedom, freedom of choice, accountability, readily available information because you have to have informed choice, and accountability implies information. Diversity of provision which again implies you've got choice, you've got to have choice between genuine alternatives, choice implies diversity. So they are the kind of things that we tried to think how do you implement those in policy terms, taking those fundamental Conservative values. And those are the kind of values that are, I think, being developed in policy proposals, and in Gerbil (Great Education Reform Bill). It would be surprising if there wasn't a congruence [with New Right thinking]. Those ideas are part of a changing climate of opinion and a changing political climate. Obviously many tributaries go into that river.

On this basis both documents proceed discursively, employing a number of simple divisions and polarities to mount a series of arguments for the root and branch reform of schooling. As noted above, such polarising work as this is typically done by setting reason against madness and commonsense against dogma. Thus, the primacy of the parent and parental choice is set against the domination of 'powerful bureaucratic interest groups' which are 'strongly influenced by socialist ways of thinking' (Hillgate p.1). The interest groups stand for 'mediocrity in the name of "social justice"' and against 'merit, standards and

achievement'. Similarly, Sexton (p.4) predicts that his proposals for
'parent power' will be 'bound to offend an enormous vested interest,
namely that great army of civil servants, both local and central, now
concerned with running education'. The exposition of polarities of
falsity and truth, and the identification of sacred and profane, or
demonic objects, con- tinue throughout the two documents and are
summarised in figure 3.1.

Sacred	Profane
Parental Choice	Producer Control
Accountability	The Educational Establishment
Cultural Heritage	New subjects
Tradition	Multiculturalism/relevance/minority languages
Political Unity	Politicised curriculum
The Family	Personal, Social and Health Education (PSHE)
Latin and Greek	Social science/Peace studies
O and A levels	GCSE
Sit down, terminal timed exams	Continuous, coursework assessment
Privatised examining	Teacher education/ professionalism
Grammar Schools	Comprehensive schools
Selection	Mixed-ability
Pupil entitlement	Totalising central powers
Market forces/opting out	Teacher unions/LEA services/in-service education
Opted out/independent schools	LEAs (and the ILEA in particular)

Figure 3.1 New Right polarities

Now, from what has been discussed in the previous chapter, drawing
on the *Black Papers* and the philosophical discourses of the New Right,
a number of these oppositions and identifications should be predictable:
the support for grammar schools as against comprehensives; the
emphasis on tradition and cultural heritage as against new forms of
knowledge; a call for public accountablity rather than control by the
educational establishment; the opposition to multicultural and anti-
racist education, and the argument for pupil entitlement in the form of
vouchers. Sexton goes into considerable detail in his document in outlining a scheme for the introduction of education vouchers.

But there are several new elements which extend and elaborate on
Black Paper themes or take up explicitly the work of the New Right
theorists. Also, in comparing the texts there is a distinct difference in
emphasis over issues related to the curriculum and matters of internal
school organisation. Sexton is content to limit himself to a fairly ortho-

dox Hayekian, free market argument – choice, vouchers, comparative
testing, publication of results, abolition of teacher unions and fixed rates
of pay, and the privatisation of LEA services. I shall pick this up again
later. The Hillgate Group concur with virtually all of this neo-liberal
theology but also go beyond it. They are not content just to prescribe a
form of market control based on parental choice; they also wish to shape
and constrain choice by the proscription of certain aspects of the school
curriculum and the prescription of others. In particular, they clearly
intend to incorporate the school into the neo-conservative agenda of
nation-building, the maintenance of traditional divisions and elitism,
and the exclusion of minority or 'alien' cultural forms.

I will look in more detail at three of the areas of discursive work
which cut across the various polarities listed: the curriculum, teachers,
and forms of evaluation and assessment.

The curriculum

This is one of the areas of thematic consistency which began with the
Black Papers. At the centre of the New Right assertions is a dispute
about the valid and true contents of, or criteria for, the school
curriculum: relevance and multiculturalism versus tradition and cultural
heritage, 'politicised' versus neutral subjects, or, in simple terms, true
versus false knowledge.

Thus, relevance in the school curriculum, the adaptation of lessons to
the 'emotional repertoire' of the student, means 'that the harder and
more durable parts of the curriculum have often been set aside' (Hillgate
p.3). Certain competences are thus threatened which 'the state has a duty
to perpetuate'. For otherwise 'the knowledge, skill and culture upon
which our society has been founded' may be 'irretrievably lost' (p.3).
Knowledge, skill and culture will be sacrificed to 'opinionated vague-
ness'. Subjects like lifeskills, peace studies and attempts at multicultural
education are seen as most damaging in their effects. As regards the
latter, it challenges 'the traditional values of Western societies ... the
very universalism and open-ness of European culture is our best
justification for imparting it' (p.3). The universalism and openness of
European culture is set against 'the desire to lock ethnic minorities
within their own languages and customs' (p.3). The task is to set aside
'misguided relativism' and to 'reconcile our minorities, to integrate
them into the national culture, and to ensure a common political loyalty'
(p.4). Multicultural education is treated with scorn, 'in an atmosphere of
"multiculturalism" the opportunity will be taken to teach, as first
modern languages, the languages of ethnic minorities, to the detriment
of French, German, Italian, Spanish, Russian and Arabic which connect
more directly with our national culture and national interests' (p.17).

The discursive work done by these kinds of argument is enormous. Not only are non-European cultures emptied of all worth, but attempts at cultural maintenance are taken to be damaging to the minorities themselves and tantamount to political subversion.

The politics of and in the school curriculum has been one of the major concerns of the New Right educationalists in the 1980s, and has been taken up by the Hillgate Group and others in publications produced by a variety of New Right organisations or 'fronts: the Social Affairs Unit (O'Keeffe 1986), the Education Research Centre (Scruton *et al.* 1985), the Sherwood Press (Palmer 1986), the Institute for European Defence and Strategic Studies (Scruton 1986). Most of this writing concentrates on the issue of the alleged political bias in areas of recent curriculum development like peace studies, urban studies, world studies and also health education, variations on the *Black Paper* theme of the subversive teacher. So, in *World Studies: Education or Indoctrination* (1986) Scruton argues that world studies 'masquerades as a "discipline" whose aim is to produce an open mind towards the differing cultures and varying conditions of humanity' but that 'In reality its purpose is quite opposite . . . It is designed to close the child's mind to everything but the narrow passions of the radical'. In *Education and Indoctrination* (Scruton *et al.* 1985) a similar argument is aimed at the growing 'politicisation of subjects'.

> First, difficult and disciplined parts of the subject are removed or downgraded, so that educational achievement can no longer be represented as the mastery of a body of knowledge. Second, texts and subjects are chosen, not for their intellectual or literary merit, or for their ability to further pupils' intellectual grasp, but for the political attitudes which are conveyed in them, and pupils are taught to consider the acquisition of such attitudes as the true mark of educational success.
>
> (pp.8–9)

Scruton *et al.* argue for a distinction between a politicised position and a political one. The former is seen as goal-oriented – all action and institutional life being aimed at the achievement of over-riding political concerns. This leads to intolerance and 'unending struggle' and 'violent change' in pursuit of unexplained 'social justice'. This is cited as a pedagogy of indoctrination. The latter treats politics as a process, multifarious and conflicting 'whereby differences are recognized and, where possible, accommodated or resolved'. Not only in this view are the 'new' subjects irredeemably 'politicised' but some established subjects may also be perverted by 'deteriorated-liberal, Marxist and progressive perspectives' (Barcan 1986). Anti-racism receives a similar critique (Palmer 1986).

> The anti-racist curriculum, like all 'antisms', is said to be a denigration of the cultural heritage and therefore a deprecation of the very framework of tolerance which permits radical critique of existing British institutions. It is anti-educational and illiberal.
>
> (Quicke 1988 p.10)

As elsewhere in the corpus of the discourse the new studies and subject matter are taken to be political and biased, while traditional disciplines and content are taken to be unquestionably neutral and objective; the new are taken to embody attitudes, while the old convey only knowledge free from behavioural or attitudinal imperatives. The politicisation is seen as part of a process, if not a left-wing plot, which has the effect in society of threatening core values and the moral fibre and security of the nation.

> The implications of politicisation of education reach far beyond schools and colleges out into the wider society and into the future. We have touched on the effect of peace studies in undermining the political will for defence. Other effects include a 'drip' effect, a general erosion of appreciation of, and loyalty to, what is good for our country, in our cultural heritage, in our traditional values and in our moral standards. And in adult education, there is in some places a "feeder effect" a deliberate turning out of committed Marxists into key posts, such as teaching, social work, trade unions, the media and local government.
>
> (Speech by Baroness Cox in the House of Lords Debate on Education-Avoidance of Politicisation, 5 February 1986, Policy Research Associates, p.15.)

In all this the reference points, the models for good practice are the grammar, direct-grant and independent schools 'because they provide a visible demarcation of quality and are the repository of traditional moral and cultural values and educational standards. In an ordered world it is essential to have high status models to which others can aspire' (Salter and Tapper 1985 p.176). The cultural restorationist mission is clear.

As elsewhere, the effect and possibility of the discourse is achieved by virtue of the fact that the remarks are made, figures (of whatever status) quoted, the arguments put. Whereas there is no real need of recourse to proof, evidence, logical adequacy or statistical rigour, there is frequent recourse to 'social givens lodged in the "British personality" and in the meaning of national culture' (Quicke 1988 p.18). The organisations and the people are there to be quoted; the publications are produced for the effect that they will have. The significance of the organisation behind the discourse is the production of a body of unified statements, a nexus of regularities. The 'form of stating' (Cousins and

Hussain 1984 p.88) is what is significant here. The organisations created by the New Right produce an institutional site that makes it possible for the statements to be made in an authoritative fashion. Margaret Thatcher has taken up the restorationist agenda with enthusiasm. In her speech to the 1987 Conservative Party Conference, she argued:

> Too often our children don't get the education they need – the education they deserve. And in the inner cities – where youngsters must have a decent education if they are to have a better future – that opportunity is all too often snatched from them by hard-left educational authorities and extremist teachers. Children who need to be able to count and multiply are learning anti-racist mathematics – whatever that may be. Children who need to be able to express themselves in clear English are being taught political slogans. Children who need to be taught to respect traditional moral values are being taught that they have an inalienable right to be gay.
>
> (CPC Brighton, 9 October 1987)

The teachers

I have already given some account of the deconstructive, teacher-bashing work done on established notions of teacher professionalism and teacher autonomy, by the conservative educational offensive. In some respects both the Hillgate Group and Sexton continue this bashing in our examplar texts. For both, many of the problems outlined above are related to and serve teachers' interests, although how and why is never made clear (see Demaine 1988). The Hillgate Group are straight-forward: 'we have no confidence in the educational establishment, which has acted as an ideological interest group, and which is unlikely to further the Government's aim of providing real education for all' (p.10). Both are broadly dismissive of teacher-training and in-service education: 'why assume that Local Authority advisers and in-service training are necessarily blessings?' (Hillgate p.30). (One is tempted to ask 'why not?'.) Sexton suggests that 'Some education departments, at both universities and non-universities are said to be so unacceptable as to be worthy of closure' (p.20). By whom and why he does not trouble the reader with, but it is said! And he urges 'new measures on the training courses for more practical training on how to teach' (p.20) and the 'need for a shift away from educational theory' (p.21). The antipathy towards teacher-training reaches incredible and scornful proportions in the Social Affairs Unit document *Detecting Bad Schools: A Guide for Normal Parents* (note again the deployment of 'normal') (Anderson 1982):

Teachers with Cert Ed after their names have studied nonsense for three years. Those with BEd for three or four years. Those with PGCE have had a rest for one year studying nonsense after doing a proper subject and those with MEd or AdvDipEd have returned for super nonsense.

(p.11)

In one respect the campaign against teacher-training is an attack on a key site for the speakers of progressivism and comprehensivism. To devalue the speakers and their rights to speech is to debunk the discourse they represent. The sense of virtuous outrage, of real culpability and deserved comeuppance, aimed at teachers, which runs through much of the *Black Paper*/New Right analysis, was expressed in interview by Baroness Cox when she talked about the 1985–86 Industrial Dispute:

There were a critical mass of teachers, and it's up to them to look at their own consciences, but in terms of the profession I think it was tragic, who did take it out on children and children did suffer for a long time and the fact that a sizeable number of teachers did this up and down the country. It was't just in ILTA (the Inner London Teacher's Association) and Manchester. I'm afraid that teachers have got to live with the consequences of that. I happen to know conscientious teachers who did try to go on teaching, in very hostile circumstances who got a tremendous amount of intimidation. If you allow that to happen in a profession you've got to pay the price.

But there is also indication of a reconstructive thrust, the formation of a new 'petty professional' teacher. For example, both Hillgate and Sexton suggest that 'Staff without formal teaching qualifications (who have not had their brains stuffed with the dubious material now taught in so many teacher training courses) could be appointed' (Hillgate p.27). This clearly lays the groundwork for the Licensed Teacher Scheme, announced by Kenneth Baker in 1989, although the pressing problem of teacher shortages provided an added spur. In good Hayekian terms Sexton urges the introduction of 'a 'free market' instead of a statutorily controlled national rate of pay' (Sexton p.18). This would mean 'an improvement in the right kind of teachers being in the right kind of jobs and with the appropriate rates of pay' (p.18) with differential pay rates regionally and for different subjects and for performance. (The Adam Smith Institute *Omega Report* [1984] and the 'No Turning Back Group' of right-wing Conservative MPs [1986], have made similar proposals.) Again this is now being brought about – the Advisory Committee on Teachers' Pay and Conditions of Work, set up by Kenneth Baker to replace the pay-bargaining system of the Burnham Committee, has recommended experiments with regional variations in pay, and LMS provisions of the 1988 Education Act will undoubtedly encourage the institutionalisation of pay differentials. Furthermore, Sexton argues that teacher employment should be based on a contract specifying 'expected duties and responsibilities' (Sexton p.19) and 'it would be open to the individual teacher to accept such a contract (which includes a presumption of professional status and therefore no strike)' (p.19). He goes on to argue that

> it would be appreciated by the truly professional teacher if, having agreed to such a contract, the teacher took on a new, recognised professional status, perhaps Fellow of the College of Teachers. Employers would inevitably give preference, and pay, to such contractual professional teachers, and very quickly those teachers unwilling to accept such professional responsibilities, would, by their own self selection, be weeded out.

> (p.19)

These new professionals would no longer be college trained but apprenticed or articled. After all 'to teach is an aptitude, and ... formal qualifications do little in themselves to develop it' (Hillgate p.36). Naturalism again.

The nature of this new teaching and the new professionalism remains unclear, but certainly whole areas of decision making about the curriculum, about pedagogy and about assessment which may previously have been the concern of teachers are now to be pre-empted by decisions lodged elsewhere. The anti-union thrust of Hayekian orthodoxy is clearly evident here. The model for the new professional is taken from commerce rather than from public service – with pay to be negotiated individually. The emphasis is upon performance measured by 'objective' indicators or 'outputs' via appraisal or testing. Indeed National Testing is seen in these terms as teacher testing. Sir Rhodes Boyson MP (*Black Paper* writer and editor and political conduit for many of the New Right proposals) described this in interview as one of his prime concerns while a Junior Minister at the DES, to get teachers made more accountable, more disciplined. He supports the National Testing introduced by the ERA for these reasons:

> I do believe there should be accountability, the parent should see where his child is compared with the school and the country at any point of time. And everybody else is tested – I don't see why teachers aren't tested. They can then argue how they are tested but the testing has to come. That I've advocated over the years and I won on that one. Really it's a test of teachers. We know how much is being produced in Ford compared with Japan, 40 per cent less

51

cars, 10 per cent less or whatever. Anybody who has been in schools knows that somebody is twice as productive as another as a teacher. And if a boy goes into class A instead of class B he will do far better. But the poor teacher also knows that or suspects that and doesn't want that test being available, but the parent wants it. It is too complicated to try and test teachers, they have tried in various parts of America, but what I'd like to see is the teachers tested. If you test the teachers you can leave the pupils alone. They'll knock the children into shape properly.

This leads quite neatly to the general issue of testing and assessment.

Evaluation and assessment

The interesting point about the role of assessment, or, more accurately, testing, in the New Right discourse is that it bridges between a neo-liberal, free-market concern, for the making of comparisons between schools and teachers, in order to facilitate informed parental choice, and the neo-conservative distrust both of teachers and of new teacher-based forms of assessment. Sexton emphasises the former but would prefer that examinations be seen to 'be independent of government' (p.26). The Hillgate Group emphasise the latter. They see testing and the publication of results as an effective form of accountability for and control over schools (pp. 14-15), 'Information about attainment plays a central part in assessing the effectiveness of teaching' (p.15). Again, this is a well-established position in New Right writing. This goes alongside a belief in the superiority of traditional forms of O and A level examining, and a commitment to the privatisation of examinations 'with employers, universities, and other interested bodies, getting together to set examinations that *they* would wish students to pass, rather than those which have been devised by people detached from the worlds of scholarship, employment and industry' (p.20).

But testing, despite its role as a basis for market comparisons and consumer choice, does not sit easily with the strict neo-liberals. As National testing it can be seen as a way of imposing uniformity on schools, when the neo-liberals value diversity. Sexton recognised this as a problem in interview:

Testing, funnily enough, and you may say that there is a contradiction here, but Rhodes Boyson and I wrote a paper way back in 1978 about the need for assessment, testing if you wish, of children at certain points in their career as a tool for both teachers and parents to see how well their children are doing. As a tool for taking remedial action if they were not doing as well as they should be. And we thought that some kind of nationally understood standards would be desirable so that one could say little Johnny has got to stage six in reading and he really ought to be at scale eight at that age and we were thinking only of reading, writing and numeracy. And what you now see is that idea blown up into seemingly far more competences, skills and knowledge. [He is referring to the TGAT (Task Group on Assessment and Testing) proposals.] It's like having a public examination several times during your school career. Now that's not what Rhodes and I expected or wanted and I am highly sceptical that in practice we can achieve what they are looking for. If they would limit it to a generally agreed understood level of literacy at the age of seven that would be a big step forward. If they cared to then say the level of literacy and numeracy at age eleven, super. If they start getting more detailed than that they will get themselves in real trouble. Testing and the curriculum go together, even by what I have just said I would be dictating the curriculum to the extent of saying children should know how to read, but that is the minimum that most parents would say yes to, and children should be reasonably numerate, of course they should. In one sense the market dictated that there should be an acceptable level of competence in the basic skills, I am now trying to define what is acceptable competence.

What these comments also indicate is the extent to which other influences play upon and intervene in the policy-making process, and the role of the New Right intellectuals as critics as well as makers of policy.

These kinds of preferences are also set against a marked hostility towards the new GCSE (General Certificate of Secondary Education) examination introduced under Sir Keith Joseph. ' . . . little trust can be placed on the GCSE examination – devised as it was by the very educational establishment against which the Government has now been compelled to take legislative measures' (Hillgate p.19) (see also North [1987] and Worthen [1987] for New Right critiques of GCSE). And the substantive problem with GCSE for these writers is that it allows too much control over examining to the teacher by the use of continuous assessment, and many of the syllabus guides are 'infected by the same politicised attitudes, the same hostility to merit and discrimination, and the same egalitarian tendencies as have brought the country's educational system to its present sorry condition' (Hillgate p.20). Further, the principle and practice of a single examination for all pupils is regarded with suspicion. The New Right preference is for differentiation by ability in all aspects of schooling.

In interview Sexton saw a single examining system determined by the state as an infringement of parental liberties and free-market choice:

And I would couple with that Clauses 5 and 12 of the Bill which will give the Secretary of State the power to say that you may take these public examinations and no others. So that if I wanted to do the International Baccaleureat at a maintained school I will not be allowed to. And there are a lot of doubts as to whether the GCSE is acceptable and I would say it's not. But under this new Bill, Baker will be able to insist that our children do the GCSE whether we rather they do Scottish O level or not.

What is being advocated here is a free market in examinations rather than state control and delimitation of examinations as provided in the 1988 Education Reform Act.

Update

In the summer of 1989 the government announced its decision to abolish GCSEs assessed wholly on coursework. From 1994 all GCSEs will involve an end-of-course 'timed and unseen' test under 'controlled conditions'. The government also rejected SEAC proposals and decided to limit GCSEs to cover only attainment at levels 4 to 10 in the National Curriculum. The *TES* (22.9.89, p.2) reporting Mrs Angela Rumbold's speech to the Joint Council for the GCSE, commented that Mrs Rumbold (Junior Education Minister) failed to allay fears that the latter would 'lead to the re-establishment of a dual assessment system'. The criticisms of modern assessment techniques made by the cultural restorationists rest on a profound distrust of teachers' assessment and of the GCSE. These criticisms would seem to have found their mark.

Let me pick up two further issues raised in the Hillgate document which are helpful in understanding the educational project of the New Right and its theoretical bases. First, there is strong support in the document for the provision in the original Great Education Reform Bill that London Boroughs be allowed to opt out of the Inner London Education Authority (ILEA). (An amendment was later accepted by the government which actually abolished ILEA.) The interesting thing about the Hillgate response is again its mixture of dogma from both neo-liberal and neo-conservative sources – that is the ILEA is seen as profligate, inefficient and politically subversive.

The ILEA incurs excessive costs; it displays overall poor standards of attainment; it has tolerated or even encouraged a politicised curriculum and the introduction of politicised appointments and teachers; finally, the entrenched commmunist and neo-communist domination of the Inner London Teachers Association, with consequent continuing high levels of militant activity, obliges a democratic government to do whatever it can to destroy that Association's power-base.

(p.26)

The first part of this condemnation follows on from a number of studies produced by Hillgate contributors, under the banner of the National Council for Educational Standards (Marks *et al.* 1983) which have attempted to correlate levels of educational expenditure with outcomes (usually measured in terms of public examination passes). The argument that is pursued is that higher-spending education authorities do not have higher rates of passes, and that good teaching rather than expenditure is the basis of examination success. In some versions this argument seems to suggest a negative correlation, that if less is spent more will be learned. In this and other respects the Labour-controlled ILEA, the highest-spending authority, is a prime target for criticism. No quarter is given for special educational needs or problems. And the assault on the ILEA introduces once again the potent imagery of politically subversive teachers. Anderson (1982) notes at least that 'Teachers are not particularly political people' but goes on, 'but those that are include Trotskyites and proselytising lesbians' (p.21). He advises parents to 'Look for these tendencies on the teachers' own noticeboard' (p.21) when choosing a school for their child.

The second importance of the long-standing attacks on the ILEA is discursive. The ILEA provides a focus for critical incidents – poor results, inappropriate teaching apppointments, politicised subjects, egalitarian projects. It stands as a symbol of irrationality, of extremism, of madness, of the profane. The media have done a great deal to make ILEA highly visible. It has become a rallying point of opposition to progressivism and comprehensivism; and it serves as a condensate of all that has gone wrong with British education. It is the epitome of what is wrong with all schools, all teachers. To oppose ILEA is to stand for sanity in education. This kind of argument, stressing the inevitableness of things – ILEA must go – is taken up in a Conservative Political Centre pamphlet written by John Bowis MP (1988), *The ILEA – The Closing Chapter*. He says:

> I have never been one to damn ILEA out of hand. But however fair one tries to be, however good some areas of ILEA work may be, and however effective past ILEA publicity may have been, the more unmistakable becomes the conclusion . . . The system has failed the children and failed the parents and the community.

(p.7)

The ILEA is taken to be 'a left-wing lobby' (p.6). Its status as an elected body – left-wing or not – seems to have no role in this kind of evaluation, left-wingness being more significant than democratic elections. Bowis quotes the anti-ILEA *London Evening Standard* with approval:

> It is now generally accepted that an education authority which shows the worst results for the largest expenditure per pupil, which soaks up 8 per cent of all education spending to educate just 4 per cent of the country's children, and whose administrative costs have risen by 20 per cent in real terms in the last eight years, despite an actual fall in London's school population, is irreparably inefficient and wasteful.
>
> (p.37)

In educational matters the ILEA seems to have played a similar symbolic role to that of the GLC and the Metropolitan Authorities in the case of economic policy. That is, the problem with the ILEA for the Conservative Party intellectuals is that it stands for an alternative (Duncan and Goodwin 1985). In discursive terms it is a counter-text, it stands for that which is unthought in the discourse of the New Right. It served as a form of disidentification, a set of 'political and ideological practices which work on and against what prevails' (Macdonell 1986 p.40).

Finally, I want to comment briefly on Sexton's and the Hillgate response to the National Curriculum. As far as Hillgate are concerned it is a highly ambivalent and contradictory response. The cracks which can emerge between neo-liberal and neo-conservative orthodoxies are visible. In neo-liberal vein the Hillgaters are dubious; a national curriculum is 'alien to the British educational tradition' (p.10) and it 'concentrates too much power in the hands of central government' (p.11), but 'The remedy, however, is not to reduce the power of the Government, but to make it accountable' (p.11). They are clearly caught somewhere between a minimalist and strong state position; between parental choice and 'the duty of the state' (p.3); between free market diversity and rigid adherence to the absolute verities of 'true' knowledge; between trust and distrust of autonomous teachers and trust and distrust of parent/consumers. In the apparent clarity of oppositions the Hillgate document is deeply unclear and muddled. However, the discursive effectiveness of the document and the campaign it represents, and their impact of policy formation, seem to indicate the greater importance of the relay than the message (see Bernstein 1985 and Wexler and Grabiner 1986).

Sexton is opposed to the idea of a detailed National Curriculum on straightforward free-market grounds. He outlined the Hayekian position in relation to the national curriculum very clearly in interview:

The National Curriculum is a great mistake. If you have a genuine free market in education and schools, by that I mean the choice of the customer, the parents and children to choose from a variety of schools and of course the corollary of that has to be the ability of the schools to respond to that diverse market so devolve management and all that is part of that package. If you have got such a free market as you have in the independent sector then one product of that free system is that the curriculum will evolve to what the customers are looking for. And in fact if you look at the independent schools there is a remarkable similarity between the curriculum of the various independent schools because that is what the customers want. Dictated by exams, dictated by companies, by whatever you like. But they provide what the customers are looking for. So if the government had the strength and conviction of pressing forward for devolved management then they should be happy to allow the curriculum to evolve in response to parental demand and student demand, that's one argument. By doing the very reverse of that and centralising that and when we say centralising it what you really mean is that a committee of fifteen bods, the great and the good as they are called, are going to decide in great detail what the market is better able to decide. So my second argument against the National Curriculum is that they would do a less effective and efficient job in deciding whether it is French or German we ought to be learning or whether children ought to do French and German or whether Russian is appropriate or whether now they should start learning Chinese. That's the kind of detailed decision which the NCC [National Curriculum Council] is going to be asked to make. So you are substituting fallible people, or fifteen of them, or ultimately the Secretary of State advised by them, instead of the diversity that you would get by freedom of choice.

The third argument is that they will inevitably fossilise that curriculum, whatever they decide in 1988; governments being governments and civil servants being civil servants, it would take them another five years before they wake up and say we ought to be doing something after computers or whatever. And who introduced computers? Not the maintained schools – Arundel introduced it, that was the first school to say it is about time we had a computer in here. So there are several arguments which show that the National Curriculum will not produce a good curriculum, will actually fossilise whatever they decide rather than allow in flexibility. It will attempt to put a curriculum for all children and of course children are very different and that is why people prefer different schools because they suit them or don't suit them. And of

course it is obsessive centralisation to set what children shall learn
by law and thereby by implication nothing else will be taught. It's
incredible.

This is a classical Hayekian statement, the spontaneous order, continuous adaptation and efficiency and freedom of choice of the market
is set over and against the unfair, inefficient and fallible processes of the
centralised state. The curriculum should be determined by what parents
want and by enterprising schools reading the changing circumstances in
which they work. The issue of devolved management, which is part of
this package, is picked up in the following section.

Clearly, the New Right project, and in particular the *Black Paper/*
Hillgate thrust, does address itself to the centre of controversies about
educational practice and to a number of real ambivalences experienced
by many parents in their dealings with schools. The coherence of the
message lies in the steadfast reassertion of certain preferred discourses
organised around the bourgeois, liberal–humanist approach to
education. In treating the comprehensive/progressive discourses as an
aberration, as irrational, the New Right are attempting to 're-naturalise'
the previously dominant, previously unproblematic conception of
education. They are what Wexler and Grabiner (1986) term 'cultural
restorationists', seeking to revalorise traditional forms of education. The
three message systems of schooling – curriculum, pedagogy and evaluation – are tightly inscribed, one within the other, in the deconstructive/
reconstructive strategy. But as well as reassertive the project is also
radical. For the New Right have given a whole new set of accents to the
issue of control, the governance of education. As we have seen, control
is reconstituted on the twin bases of central state control – of the
curriculum, of testing and of teachers – and free-market, parental
choice. These modes of regulation are intended both to provide social
and political stability and to isolate and neutralise, as far as possible, the
influence of reformist public educators – the egalitarians.

The New Right discourse is in some respects exemplary. The
transformations achieved by it, the spaces it opens up and closes down,
from within which subjects may take up a position, and the objects of
which they may speak, with which they may deal, are articulated in
terms of specific displacements and exclusions. That is to say, part of the
significance of the discourse is the impossibility of reply. The culpable
teacher, the implicated educational establishment, are excluded from
valid participation in the debates which affect them directly and within
which they are spoken of. The discourse rests upon their failings and
their culpability, thus their responses, their anguish, their outrage can all
be set aside, for 'they would say that wouldn't they'. As we have seen,
in their construction of possible policies they represent perfectly the

Thatcherist *cri-de-coeur* that 'there is no alternative', for alternatives are thoroughly excluded and discredited. The discourse replaces groups (the articulation of interests) with mechanisms: the neutral exercise of the effects, the forces of the market, freedom of choice, the decisions made by individual parents/consumers, on the one hand, and the application of technologies of measurement, testing, management, appraisal, on the other. The teacher is thus recreated in the tight vice of performance indicators and public reputation. Interestingly, both these aspects – technical–rational organisation and individual choice – are redolent with the utilitarianism which so preoccupied Foucault in his analyses of the emergence of modern social institutions – prisons, hospitals, factories, schools. Here again policy as politics, as ideology, is apparently replaced by policy as rationality – efficiency replacing social justice. The discourse of the New Right thus effectively depoliticises education.

Furthermore, the other key emphasis on nature, the natural, again stressing the inevitability of things, obscures the role of theory as a basis for policy making. The point here about theory, the theoretical bases of the New Right, is that the theories provide a source for the construction of a political discourse. They can be set over and against other 'discredited' theories. The discourse exploits them, deploys them, justifies itself by reference to them, but in no sense is it solely constituted or captured by them. Thus, to continue to ask questions about logical contradictions is, in a way irrelevant, or at least is relevant only at the level of practice, policy itself that is, rather than at the level of theory. The test of the discourse is its effectiveness, not its coherence: what it does, not what it says. The extent to which the possibilities of policy making have been captured by and through this discourse is finally an empirical question. Clearly, though, as we have seen, the ERA (Education Reform Act) displays a considerable extent of such impact. However, the New Right do not constitute the only discourse in contest in the education policy process, as we shall see.

The education market place

Finally in this chapter I want to look at one aspect of the ERA which bears most clearly the imprint of the New Right discourse – the LMS (Local Management of Schools). While this aspect of the ERA is seen by many commentators as a technical measure, with the National Curriculum getting most attention and attracting most controversy, I would argue that the LMS proposals are the most significant aspect of the ERA, certainly the most clearly ideological aspect, and the aspect likely to have the most radical, long-term impact on the form and content of schooling.

The Education Reform Act is clearly not an easy document to read –
it is complex, multifaceted, and the product of several different sets of
interests and influences. For most teachers and parents the significance
of the Act lies in its direct and immediate effects on their classroom
work or on the prospects of their child. The Act, even those sections
related specifically to schools, tends to be interpreted and responded to
as bits and pieces. But it is not in its conception or its purposes a bits and
pieces Act. At the heart of the Act is an attempt to establish the basis of
a education market. The key provisions of the Act replace the principle

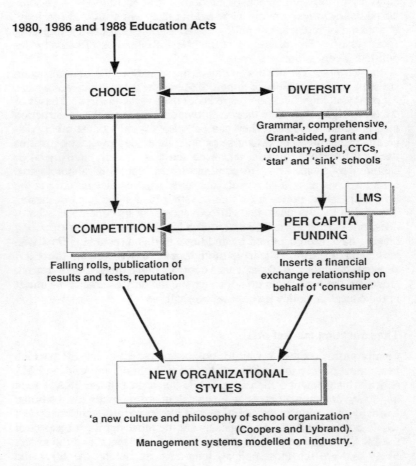

Figure 3.2 The education market place

of equal access to education for all with the principle of differentiation in the market place. In order to appreciate the ways in which an education market is being established by the ERA several pieces of the Act have to be put together and linked to previous Conservative education policy. The elements of this market are *choice, competition, diversity, funding* and *organisation* – (see figure 3.2).

Parental *choice* has been one of the fundamentals of Conservative education policy since 1979 (see Norman St John Stevas' Parents' Charter). Where feasible, Conservative ministers have argued that parents should be able to send their children to the school they wish, the school they think best. Local authority controls over school numbers and parental choice have been reduced in several pieces of legislation since 1980, and the ERA allows all schools to increase their intakes up to the level of their standard number, based on 1979 figures. Thus, there will no longer be fixed limits in intakes other than this 1979 standard number. Local authorities will no longer be able to plan to balance intakes between schools or to protect schools against the effects of falling rolls.

This relates then to the second principle of *competition*. Again the ERA builds upon and extends previous legislation; the 1980 Education Act required schools to publish their examination results and to hold compulsory Open Evenings. Many schools have begun to attend to the development and protection of their public image and reputation as a result. Glossy brochures have been produced; some schools have called in public relations consultants; care is taken to ensure that the local press are invited to cover school activities. The open enrolments provided by the ERA will heighten this competition, especially in areas where there continues to be spare capacity. In areas of reduced or falling rolls all schools, except those already over-subscribed, will now be competing to raise their numbers to the 1979 level. In other words, they will be attempting to attract pupils away from other schools in their locality. In Hayekian terms competition between schools would best serve not only the consumers, parents, but also the nation, by ensuring an orientation to 'continuous adaptation'. Behind this is also the effect of competition in weakening the power of the producers, teachers. 'The interests of organised producers are therefore always contrary to the one permanent interest of all the individual members of society . . . ' (Hayek 1979 p.151). But the principle of a Hayekian market rests upon *diversity*. Choice in his sense is only real if there are diverse products to choose from. The argument would be that if all schools are comprehensive, all giving the same service, then there is no choice. Any attempt to make the provision of schooling equal for all, the same for all, would confound the market. The control and determination of school provision must thus be taken out of the hands of government and left to the market:

the predominant model of liberal democratic institutions, in which
the same representative body lays down the rules of just conduct
and directs government, necessarily leads to a gradual
transformation of the spontaneous order of a free society into a
totalitarian system conducted in the service of some coalition of
organised interests.

(Hayek 1973 p.2)

For Keith Joseph, the fundamental problem with the education system,
the source of all other difficulties, lies in the very fact that it is a state
system and a compulsory system.

we have a bloody state system, I wish we hadn't got. I wish we'd
taken a different route in 1870. We got the ruddy state involved. I
don't want it. I don't think we know how to do it. I certainly don't
think Secretaries of State know anything about it. But we're landed
with it. If we could move back to 1870 I would take a different
route. We've got compulsory education, which is a responsibility
of hideous importance, and we tyrannise children to do that which
they don't want, and we don't produce results.

The ERA introduces a greater variety of schools into the education
system and breaks the LEA monopoly of state schooling. There are now
Grant Maintained Schools, those which have opted-out of local
authority control and are funded directly by the DES. There are CTCs,
(City Technology Colleges) in theory funded by industry, in practice
massively underwritten by direct DES funding. And the processes of
competition and choice already at work have also tended to increase
differences between LEA schools, between comprehensives. Some have
good reputations and some bad. In some cases such reputations are
based on the previous histories of the schools, or on bad local press
coverage, or unfounded gossip and rumour, or deliberate smear. But all
these things have an effect. Even prior to the 1988 Act, of course, there
was no common system of schooling. There are still approximately 200
grammar schools; 6 per cent of school-age children attend private
schools, some of them funded by the DES under the Assisted Places
Scheme; in some authorities, like Bromley, there are comprehensive
schools and super comprehensives; some authorities still pay for some
of their bright pupils to attend private schools, and in many areas the
grant-aided and voluntary-aided Church schools are regarded by some
parents as more equal than their LEA counterpart schools. The point is
that Conservative policy has supported and encouraged these
differences between schools and the ERA introduces even more variety
into the market.

It's Margaret Thatcher's way of saying that 'I brought consumerism into education'. I don't suggest that she sees schools quite like supermarkets, nevertheless, what she is saying in effect is, that just as parents have every right to shop where they think fit, when it comes to buying goods, so they have every right to shop where they think fit when it comes to their child's education. And this is the way they can bring it about.

(David Hart: General Secretary of
The National Association of Head Teachers)

But despite this basis for a proto-market in education there is one fundamental factor missing from this situation which means that it is not, as yet, a real market. That is, the choices made by the consumers do not impact directly upon the income or well-being of the producers; in other words there is no financial exchange. A real market is driven by rewards and by failure. According to Schumpeter (1979) the market system is of necessity severe and violent, based upon 'competition which strikes not at the margins of the profits and the outputs of the existing firms but at their foundations and their very lives' (p.84). In other words, if it is to work, the market must impact directly on the producers. Keith Joseph indicated, as an avowed follower of Hayek, that his own thinking ran along these lines.

I think that national agencies tend to be producer lobbies, like nationalised industries. One of the main virtues of privatisation is to introduce the idea of bankruptcy, the potential of bankruptcy. That's why I like opting out . . . of course I wanted vouchers. Simply because you transfer in one go from the producers to the consumers . . . I don't claim that all consumers are wise, of course not, but some will be able to exercise choice which they can't exercise now.

As Keith Joseph indicates, the New Right advisers in and around the government have sought to remedy the absence of the idea of bankruptcy through their advocacy of *vouchers*. The idea here is that all parents are given vouchers for each of their children with a certain fixed value according to age and that these can be exchanged anywhere in the education system for educational services – including the private sector if the parents are able to top up their vouchers to meet the private fees.

'The voucher would restore the [market] link by giving the parent purchasing power . . . The education voucher would be a halfway house to the eventual policy of leaving income with tax payers to use for education' (Seldon 1977 pp.68–9). The government would redeem the vouchers in terms of cash payments to the schools. Such a scheme was experimented with in parts of Kent, and DES civil servants convinced

Sir Keith Joseph that a national scheme would be unworkable and too expensive, and perhaps too radical for many in the Conservative Party.

> I was a frustrated enthusiast for vouchers, who was forced to accept that, largely for political reasons, it wouldn't be practicable . . . You would have a very controversial piece of legislation, which would take two or three years to carry through, with my party split, and the other parties unanimously hostile . . . It's not like imposing comprehensivisation. It's imposing freedom.
>
> (Keith Joseph)

There is therefore no provision for vouchers in the ERA, but there is a next-best alternative. There is, in effect, a cash exchange for services being introduced by the mechanism of *per-capita funding*. From April 1990 onwards almost all schools (except small primaries) will begin to move to a situation where the majority of their funding will be based on the number and type of pupils they can attract (75 per cent of the LEA block grant will be distributed on this basis). Each pupil who comes through the school gate will carry with him or her a cash bounty, and the staffing, materials, facilities and equipment the school wants or requires will have to be paid for out of the monies accumulated in this way.

> I think, persuaded by the New Right, the government has devised a formula which is pupil-driven, which, with certain exceptions, is so based upon the concept that if a pupil arrives at a school they bring money with them. It is very close to a voucher system.
>
> (David Hart)

The actual figures for pupils in each age group from one LEA are shown in figure 3.3.

Description	Value
Nursery	997
Reception	965
Infant Yrs 2+3	648
Junior	671
Lower Secondary	886
Upper Secondary	1243
Lower Sixth	1576
Upper Sixth	1576

Figure 3.3 Pupil-driven funding formula, London Borough of Hounslow
Source: The London Borough of Hounslow, Education Committee, *Local Management of Schools*, Draft Scheme for Consultation, April 1989.

This means that competition between schools is now very real. The ability to attract pupils will affect staffing levels and the overall level of service which any school can deliver. A civil servant (D) with responsibilities in this area explained:

> ... certainly this government is quite clear that it wanted to produce diversity from amongst which parents could chose, and it makes no apologies for that. And of course, even LMS, there is a logical link that money will flow to or from a school as pupil numbers flow to and from a school. Therefore, you give schools a financial incentive to attract pupils and retain them ... This will give them an incentive to be responsive to the wishes of parents.

This is also seen as going some way towards the break-up of public-sector schooling.

> It breaks down this distinction between the way that public-sector things operate and private-sector things operate. To that extent it reduces the differences between the sectors.

Those schools which already have relatively fewer numbers than their neighbouring schools, for whatever reason, and were protected by LEA funding arrangements, will immediately begin to lose cash, as budgets are adjusted. Schools which have relatively more pupils will gain a cash bonus, and subsequent changes in numbers, as schools are more or less successful in keeping or increasing their numbers, up to their 1979 standard number, will gain or lose cash accordingly. In some areas schooling will become a cut-throat business as schools with spare capacity attempt to market their services in direct competition with one another. Clearly the DES are expecting that some schools will not survive in the market place, they are expecting 'bankruptcies'. In effect 'the weak will go to the wall', some schools will lose numbers to the extent that they will no longer be viable, some schools will close. The exact same principle which operated in the first term of the Conservative government with regard to British manufacturing industry will be applied to schools. A part of the process is linked to an ideology of freedom of choice, but the market is also being sold in terms of raising standards alongside the National Curriculum.

> ... they represent two prongs in a series of policies designed to secure higher standards ... On the one hand, trying to establish common standards across the country, on the other, seeing the varied mechanisms of increased local control and competition, within the present government's philosophy as key methods, and perhaps the most efficient for actually achieving increases in standards ... There's probably a sense in which two different philosophical strands are involved in the two approaches, but I

don't think that means that they're necessarily inconsistent or incoherent

(DES civil servant F)

The market thus is being used as a disciplinary mechanism. By seeking out inefficiency, by responding to large-scale movements of fashion and taste, and by rewarding successful schools, the market will eliminate the poor schools.

> And of course this was the point that was very forcibly put to Ministers during the passing of the Bill, and to the Department in the consultation on the open enrolment proposals. And the other aspect of this is that local authorities said that it would make their task of managing the education service locally very much harder, because they would find themselves very hard put to compensate for a poor school, with not very many pupils. On the other hand, I suppose Ministers would say that it remains the case that there is quite a large surplus of school accommodation, still throughout the country . . . and the authorities have not yet fully realised the potential for taking places out of use, and Ministers would say that if parental views, as expressed through choice of school, help authorities to take hard decisions about school closures that may be necessary, then painful though it may be, that may actually be beneficial.

(DES civil servant F)

This is what Hayek describes as the short-term 'creative destruction' of the market. Thus, to a great extent, planning judgements are to be set aside. If at some point the 1979 standard number limit is abandoned, and this is not out of the question as rolls begin to rise again in the 1990s, those schools which are successful in the education market may even be able to undertake their own building programmes or bid to take-over their ailing competitors. Conversely, however, in areas which are experiencing population inflow the market does not operate at present because places are scarce. But some areas may find themselves denuded of schools altogether, and most vulnerable are those poorer inner-city areas with older schools with poorer facilities. Those parents with the money and time and ability to move their children to schools in the leafy suburbs will do so. Those parents who work long hours, who do not own cars, who don't want their children undertaking long journeys on costly, dwindling, unsafe public transport will be left with the choice of declining schools until they have no choice at all. In research done on the open parental choice schemes which have been operating in Dundee and Edinburgh this is exactly what was found to be happening. The Scottish researchers report:

Most of the schools which lost numbers were situated in the least prosperous housing schemes while most of the schools which gained substantial numbers were located in mixed inner-city areas. Thus, unlike moves between primary schools, which mainly take place within relatively homogenous areas, moves between secondary schools frequently involve transfers between catchment areas with different social characteristics. Moreover, in both cities, the schools which gained most pupils were all previously selective schools.

(Alder and Raab 1988 p.176)

The researchers also suggest that:

To the extent that parent choice enables some pupils to attend more 'effective' schools, they may be expected to benefit. However, a large influx of pupils into an 'effective' school may reduce its 'effectiveness' just as a large outflow from an 'ineffective' school may reduce its 'effectiveness' further.

(p.176)

This last point is important because it underlines the point that, at least in the short term, the motivation for almost all schools is to attract as many pupils as possible, in order to maximise their income. Other consequences of increasing numbers will seem less important.

The last aspect of the education market displayed above is that of *organisation*, for alongside the introduction of pupil number-related budgets is the introduction of devolved budgets. That is to say, again from April 1990, more and more schools will be given control of their own budgets directly. They will get and they will spend the money; they will employ, hire and fire teachers and other school workers; they will buy equipment, pay for maintenance, for heating and lighting etc., they will have to balance their own budgets. The budget will be the ultimate responsibility of the school governors, with the headteacher managing 'the school in accordance with the Articles of Government, reflecting the governing body's management policy. He or she will have a key role in assisting the governors in formulating the management plan and ensuring the involvement of staff . . . '(Local Management of Schools, Hounslow). The model of organisation which the ERA implies is clear: it is that of governors as Board of Directors and headteacher as Chief Executive. Headteachers emerge as key figures in the ERA reforms.

The Secretary of State certainly needs heads. They are the lynchpins of the system, and he can't deliver the reforms without the Heads. And he has to recognise that in pay terms soon, and in terms of our negotiating rights and conditions of service . . . On the other hand the Education Reform Act lays down a major challenge to our members. Because I am not sure that the state system can be seen to fail. I don't subscribe to the wildest of scare stories about the government wanting to wind up local education authorities and create twenty-seven and a half thousand self-governing institutions. But, nevertheless, there are people in the New Right who certainly would like to move to a voucher system. And the Local Management of Schools system is as close as you will get to a voucher system. There are people on the New Right who would like to see the abolition of Local Education Authorities . . . If we are going to stop these persistent attacks on the state system, one way of doing it as actually to make ERA work . . . I don't mean grant-maintained schools or CTCs, I mean the engine room of the act, the National Curriculum.

(David Hart)

Schools are to become businesses, run and managed like businesses with a primary focus on the profit and loss account. In the DES commissioned report on LMS, Coopers and Lybrand (1988), accountants, make the point that the new budgetary controls will require 'a new culture and philosophy of school organization' (p.2). The parent is now the customer, the pupils in effect the product. Those schools which produce shoddy goods, it is believed, will lose custom. And it would appear that in the government's view shoddy goods mean poor results in national tests. The introduction of national tests alongside the provisions of the education market provides parents with a simple and crude but direct point of comparison between schools. Given that schools are also required to provide a fixed National Curriculum it is tempting to refine the business model slightly and see the education market as a system of franchises, what one writer has called 'Kentucky Fried Schooling' (Hargreaves 1989 p.10).

While the curriculum may be national, accountability is now firmly local. The onus is on individual schools to achieve successful implementation.

Politicians are always adept at shifting the blame, and this is an Act where not only national but local politicians can shift the blame down to school level . . . The local politicians could turn around in the future and say, 'Well don't blame us, they were given the budgets, they were told they could do what they like'.

(David Hart)

In these terms then the setting up of an education market is tied to, rather than in tension with, the National Curriculum and National Testing provisions. The dualism in the ERA, the centralism and the introduction of market forces, also has another effect which articulates with the general thrust of government social and economic policy – it reduces further the planning and budgetary powers of Local Authorities. A former senior civil servant (B) at the DES commented:

> I don't think the Bill is all that much about more parental choice, more parental power. The Bill is undoubtedly about the curriculum, there is no question about that. It is actually central to the Bill, and in addition, the Bill, it seems to me, is about reducing the power of local authorities, that's what the Bill is about. Some of the power goes to the Secretary of State and some of the power goes to the governors and the heads. And a little bit of it goes to the parents. That's what the Bill is about. And, suppose you were to take as a hypothesis that that is actually the thrust of the Bill, then you can see that any measure that goes in that direction is welcome. Even if, in fact, it may do little more than give a bit more push to some of the other things.

The taken for granted assumption in all this is that business methods and market forces are the best ways, the most appropriate ways, to plan and deliver education. There is little discussion of whether education can be considered as a product, a good, like cars and chocolate bars or hairdressing. What the ERA does is to treat political ideology as though it were commonsense. The LMS scheme is a massive social experiment. (Some of these issues are taken up again in the following chapter.)

4

Industrial training or new vocationalism? Structures and discourses

Writing in his autobiography about his speech at Ruskin College in 1976, James Callaghan summarises his concerns and arguments as follows:

> Teachers, I said, must carry parents with them. Industry complained that some school-leavers did not have the basic tools to do the job and many of our best-trained students from university and polytechnics had no desire to join industry. Why was this? Why did so many girls abandon science before leaving school, and why were thirty thousand vacancies in science and engineering at universities and polytechnics not taken up, while the humanities courses were full? Were we sacrificing thoroughness and depth of courses in favour of range and diversity? I favoured a basic curriculum with universal standards. 'The essential tools are basic literacy and numeracy; the understanding of how to live and work together; respect for others; and respect for the individual. This means acquiring basic knowledge, skills and reasoning ability; developing lively inquiring minds and an appetite for further knowledge that will last a lifetime.' The goal of education was to 'equip children to the best of their ability for a lively constructive place in society and also to fit them to do a job of work' and, I emphasised, 'not one or the other, but both'. In today's world there would be fewer jobs for those without skill, and I concluded by asking for a positive response and not a defensive posture in the debate which I hoped would begin.
>
> (Callaghan 1987 p.411)

I have already indicated in the previous chapter how the Ruskin speech both drew upon and gave impetus to the New Right's advocacy of parental choice. In chapter 6 I shall follow the take-up of curriculum matters from the speech within the official discourses of the DES and HMI. Here I want to examine in particular the various vocational discourses mobilised by and around the speech, and their claims about the relationships between education and the economy. The speech did not initiate these discourses but it gave them legitimacy in the education 'policy community'.

According to James Donald (1979), the Ruskin speech, the Great Debate which followed it, and the Government Green Paper, *Education in Schools* (Cmnd 6869) which was published in July 1977, all played their part, discursively, in 'the creation and imposition of a 'new settlement' to replace the old consensus in education' (p.107). In part this kind of deconstructive/reconstructive process (as outlined in chapter 2) is achieved through the logics displayed in the texts: the speech, the debate and the paper. These texts conjured up a commonsense and real account of schools, the purpose of which 'was the validation of existing knowledges through a sort of populist empiricism' (p.106). The discursive strategies of the speech have similarities with those employed in the *Black Papers*, but the overt tone of the speech is somewhat more system-friendly, if no less critical. The Green Paper, while also taking up a neutral, even-handed, even disinterested stance, based on assertion, reported fact, and friendly critique, is nonetheless 'an elegant political and epistemological manouvre to create a rationale for fundamental changes in social democratic discourse' (Donald p.106). The success of the texts lay in their credibility. Describing the response of the NUT to the Green Paper, Donald says: 'Unable to challenge the status of the Paper's truth, reading it as it asks to be read, the Union's discourse is politically ineffective because it has become residual'(p.107). Donald goes on to point out that an understanding of these texts, their work and their effects also involves looking at their 'correlation with a range of political and economic practices', that is at their context, 'the institutional conditions which made this discourse and not another "happen"' (p.108). This is taken up in the second section of this chapter.

For now I want to pursue chronologically and analytically the 'new vocationalist' impetus provided by the three texts. It is important to begin with the point that these texts, and the many others which quickly followed, do not articulate a single, straightforward vocational message. A number of interrelated criticisms of the vocational inadequacy of schools and school leavers are mounted (see Dale 1985).

1. That schools, particularly those identified with the ideology of progressivism, fail to instill in their students the habits, attitudes and self-discipline which employers require from their workers. They do not encourage and produce good workers (or, perhaps more accurately, good employees). (However, there continues to be considerable disagreement within the vocationalist *oeuvre* as to what the right habits and attitudes are.)

2. That schools, particularly those identified with the ideology of pro-gressivism, are neglecting basic skills and teaching other inappropriate things, which means that school leavers are unprepared for the technical demands of the workplace.

3. That schools generally maintain and perpetuate a bias towards the academic and against the practical, vocational or industrial, thus en-couraging students away from courses like engineering or careers in industry. This position is often identified with the writing of Corelli Barnett (1972) and Martin Wiener (1981) and continues to be put. For example, in 1986, Industry Year:

> We all need industry but we fail to recognize the valuable
> contribution it makes to society. We are an industrial country with
> an anti-industrial culture, as recent surveys of attitudes show. This
> is the *root cause* [my emphasis] of our relative decline, and it is
> this which Industry Year is attacking.
>
> *(Industry Year* 1986)

The other point to be noted from this illustration is the identification of attitudes located within education and culture as the primary factors in the explanation of industrial and economic decline. Political and economic factors are taken to be of less importance.

4. Related to the above, schools in general are criticised for failing to teach students about the world of work or about the economic im-portance of industry within society, that is they do not make pupils aware of the source of wealth creation within capitalist societies.

A later addition to these criticisms more directly associated with neo-liberalism and the ideology of Thatcherism was:

5. That schools fail to develop the skills of, or positive orientations towards, entrepreneurship and enterprise.

Clearly there are contradictions embedded in the schools/industry discourse, for example between the encouragement of assertive, in-dependent entrepreneurs, who would found their own businesses, as against fostering attitudes of deference within a body of potential em-ployees. Jamieson (1986 p.26) notes that:

> It is difficult to describe the schools/industry movement. There are
> two major difficulties. First, it doesn't stand still. The number of
> groups, organizations and government agencies constantly grows.
> Secondly, it has no one focus of attention, save it wants to change
> the education system in one way or another.

However, the polyvalency of the discourse is one of its great strengths. It has developed as a practical political reponse to a multifaceted industrial crisis (basically a crisis in the profitability of capitalist industry) and is directed to different levels and aspects of the crisis. It is in part a reponse to the failures and weaknesses of British industrial management and the need to develop a new cadre of skilled and enthusiastic managers. It also relates to Thatcherism's faith in small business to provide the basis of industrial recovery and thus produce a real and lasting reduction in unemployment. But it is also a response to the high levels of industrial unrest during the 1970s, from the 'three-day-week' to the 'winter of discontent'. Further, it is addressed to the low levels of productivity which played their part during the 1970s in rendering British exports uncompetitive. And it is fairly straightforwardly a response to employers' complaints about ill-disciplined and ill-prepared young workers. Finally, the schools/industry movement is part of a large-scale effort directed towards the social management of high levels of youth unemployment.

Many of the specific criticisms carried by these arguments are addressed directly at teachers. In many cases the fault is seen to lie with teachers' attitudes, lack of understanding, political orientations or incompetence. This was most forcefully put, a few months before the launch of the Great Debate, in an influential article written by Arnold Weinstock, Chairman of GEC, with the title 'I Blame the Teachers'.

> Teachers fulfil an essential function in the community but, having themselves chosen not to go into industry they often deliberately, or more usually unconsciously, instil in their pupils a similar bias … And this is quite apart from the strong though unquantifiable impression an outsider recieves that the teaching profession has more than its fair share of people actively politically committed to the overthrow of liberal institutions, democratic will or no democratic will.
>
> (Weinstock 1976)

In a straightforward way this kind of assault articulates perfectly with the contemporary discursive thrust of the *Black Papers* criticisms of comprehensive and progressive education; it is also a discourse of derision. A very similar kind of commonsensical analysis is employed with a similar kind of plea for sanity set against the extremism to be found among teachers. Not surprisingly one of the threads running through the various schools/industry schemes is the attempt to influence and change teachers, primarily by getting them to spend time in industry, to expose them to the paramount reality of work. Errant schools and lax or left-wing teachers provided potent, and popular, explanations for Britain's dire economic condition in the late 1970s. And the national humiliation involved in making representations to the IMF for financial support could neatly be displaced.

There are some relationships between new vocationalism and neo-liberal theories, particularly in their common emphasis on the importance of individual endeavour. At the heart of the analytical complex of new vocationalism stands the deficient individual – the school leaver. The explanation of Britain's economic regression and lack of competitiveness is taken to be the lack of individual motivation and skills. Thus, according to the DoE/DES (1986) White Paper *Working Together – Education and Training*, 'motivation is all important so that attitudes change and people acquire the desire to learn, the habit of learning, and the skills learning brings' (1.4). The diagnosis and the solutions appear to be simple, far too simple for many commentators – instil motivation, develop the right attitudes and habits, and economic recovery will be achieved. As Stronach (1988) puts it 'In vocationalism, the individual stands naked before history' (p.57). As in Hayek and Adam Smith it is the endeavours of individuals that provide the order and benefits of capitalism, not the plans and interventions of governments. 'In all the middling and inferior professions real and solid professional abilities joined to prudent, just form and temperate conduct will seldom fail success' (Smith 1976 p.119). However, despite some discursive similarities in their critiques of schools the New Right and the industrial trainers are by no means identical in their analysis of the faults and possibilities of schooling.

Again, though, the new vocationalist discourse is organised around a set of polarities, of problems and solutions. Lack of motivation is set against motivation, lack of skills against skills acquired, wrong attitudes against right ones, bad habits against good, lack of preparation for work against being prepared. As Stronach (1988 p.60) puts it 'the personalising of economic competitiveness (be motivated, get skilled) offers both an economics of recovery and a metonymics of blame (if *you* were trained and motivated *we* wouldn't be where we are today)'. Indeed, Stronach offers an original and pertinent analysis of new vocationalism. Like many others he rejects the simplicities and audacity of the basic claim, that individual attributes are directly related to national economic well-being, and argues instead that new vocationalism can be best understood as ritual. 'It is not cynical to argue that these initiatives are essentially responses rather than solutions to "the problem" ' (p.66). They 'address' the problem. 'Our vocational initiatives are also contemporary dramas that ritually involve young people in enacting solutions to economic decline' (p.66). As a ritual, vocationalism serves 'to reassure the powerful as much as it seeks to mystify the powerless' (p.67). It is, Stronach argues, a form of 'archaic recovery', regeneration, a return to a 'mythicised tradition', a time when workers knew their place, knew their job and capitalism boomed.

Each of the areas of critique listed above once planted in the political imagination of the major parties, and well fertilised by the discursive outpourings of the Great Debate, was eventually to bear policy fruits. Schools/industry and the new vocationalism quickly became an industry in its own right as innumerable schemes, programmes, initiatives and courses were launched and continue to be launched. Some of these are listed for illustration in Figure 3.1. Each one of these initiatives offers a response, a solution, to one or more of the areas of concern and deficit.

However, as already indicated, beneath, or beyond, an apparent simplicity and commonality in the vocational impetus there is a degree of dissonance and dislocation. Industry itself is not, of course, of a piece. The needs or concerns of big and small, manufacturing and finance, local, national and multinational, and traditional, service and high-tech businesses are not the same. Industrialists, or those who speak for them, do not necessarily speak with one voice. Those who speak on behalf of industry do not always get things right.

> The movement is a diverse collection of employer and trade union
> groupings; especially constructed educational or quasi-educational
> 'projects'; government statements and exhortations – all designed
> to put pressure on the education system to change both the content
> of what is taught, how it is taught and how it is assessed and
> examined.
>
> (Jamieson 1986 p.1)

And yet, to an extent at least, as far as policy making is concerned, the momentum of the discourse rolls over the possibility of making fine distinctions – the point being that while the discourse of new vocationalism does not serve or embody the voice of industry in any pure sense, it does embody the voice of industry in a real sense. That is to say, over a short period business people have become strongly represented in decision making and advisory capacities in all spheres of education policy. Their presence allows the voice of industry a range of sites from which to be heard again, symbolising that something is being done. The appointment of industrialists to various boards and advisory positions transforms experience and interest into expertise (Miliband 1973). Vocationalism has given voice and authority to one set of interests – business – while stifling others. This is about control as well as content.

From its beginnings at Ruskin it has been a political discourse. Strategically the various vocational initiatives have played a key role in reworking the governance of education and changing the possibilities of policy making. TVEI has provided a potent examplar. 'TVEI has emerged as a prototype for implementing educational policy and change' (Gleeson 1987 p.1). As Dale (1985) argues, TVEI has played a major part in changing the content and orientation of schooling, but in the process the ways and means of changing schooling itself have been changed.

> TVEI does not follow any of the three main routes of bringing about major educational change in Britain either in the nature of its aims or its methods. It is neither a programme drawn up by and in consultation with praticising educators, aimed at improving the content and/or delivery of (parts of) the school curriculum (the Schools Council model); nor does it follow the Plowden, Advisory Committee, model, where representatives of a wide range of interests join with the 'great and the good' to scrutinize, and recommend a series of more or less major changes; nor does it follow the model of legislative change, which encouraged comprehensive schooling, for instance, or raised the school leaving age. Rather, it might be argued, it follows a business or commercial model, moving resources into a new 'line' when the existing one is proving ineffective. At the centre of its aims is improving the service to a particular group of customers, clients and consumers – it does not seek to improve the service to those already seen as (too) well catered for. Its mode of operation is executive rather than legislative or advisory.
>
> (Dale 1985 p.43)

In retrospect the TVEI scheme can be seen as the precursor to an increasing variety of forms of categorical funding: directed payments from the centre, from the DES as well as MSC, which are specifically earmarked and which just by-pass Local Authority decision making on educational expenditure. As Dale is suggesting the MSC has sponsored a new style of policy making and new forms of policy evaluation. The speed of implementation of TVEI and the relative ease with which the compliance of LEAs was achieved served to demonstrate the potential for quick, radical, top-down reform in a system on the defensive, with low morale and reduced funding. The intrusion of the MSC (and the DoE and DTI) in the spheres of influence previously dominated by the DES, the LEAs and teacher unions further reduced and weakened the institutional basis of the old consensus in education. New voices now had a legitimate say in education policy making. The locus of this new discourse in business and commerce articulates the cause of the industrial trainers, and it has a long history stretching back into the nineteenth century (see Reeder 1979 and McCullough 1986).

Beck (1983), looking back at the outcomes of the Great Debate, argues that 'Perhaps the most damaging educational legacy of the Callaghan Government's policy of linking educational practice to industrial regeneration was the legitimacy it gave to forms of educational practice which substitute political socialization for evidential education' (p.229).

As indicated already, we can identify a key element of style within the social practices of this discourse. Teachers and schools were to find themselves signing contracts with the MSC for the delivery of TVEI courses, and departments or schools, and authorities are in competition for scarce funds, having to make bids and develop effective presentations. The logic of capitalism begins to bite deep into the processes of schooling.

The structuralist scenario

We have looked briefly at some aspects of the new vocationalist discourse; I now want to put that discourse into a non-discursive, economic context. This will enable us to look a little more closely at the economic policies of Thatcherism, and to see how these policies affected education. I will try to link education to capital by looking at changes in the economy and social policy. Thus, we can pursue the aim of setting education within a broader policy perspective. The substantive issue is this: How does education policy over the past ten years look if we attempt to understand it in structural terms, in relation, that is, to the national and international crisis of capitalism of the mid 1970s and the concomitant fiscal crisis of the state? That is the 'increasing budgetary gap created in public finance in advanced capitalist countries because of the historical process of socialization of costs and privatization of profits' (Castells 1977 p.415).

The notion here is that particular policy ideas and policies-in-practice have certain economic conditions of existence, and when the latter shift, or are percieved to have shifted, then the existing policy repertoire breaks up and a potential is created for a new repertoire.

The structuralist argument proceeds generally as follows. In times of economic growth, high employment and full use of productive capacity, taxation from the profits of capital enables the state to develop welfare services and satisfy demand for increases in the standard of living of workers. Several things are achieved:

1. Policy concessions maintain stability and stifle potential conflicts. Dissatisfaction can, in effect, be bought off. And the development of the social wage – the provision of public health, education, housing, transport services and social welfare – reduces pressure on wage demands aimed at employers.

2. The state takes on responsibility for the disorganising effects of capital (e.g. unemployment, poor health and environmental damage).

3. The state can take over the burden of reproducing the relations of production for capital, thus reducing costs by the provision of public housing, public health and education and training.

4. The state stands in place of industry when social needs do not produce solvent demand (i.e. when they are unprofitable for private enterprise), e.g. recreation, housing and education.

Under these conditions the spheres of production (industry/business) and reproduction (social welfare/education) are strongly separated. Social welfare and public services are firmly within the sphere of reproduction.

In the mid-1970s, in Britain and many other western industrial societies, the economic basis of these social democratic policies began to change dramatically, hastened by the oil price rises of 1973-75. There was:

1. Serious decline in the rate of economic growth.
2. Massive increases in inflation.
3. Rapidly rising rates of unemployment.
4. Currency instability.

These changes in economic conditions had severe knock-on effects for the state and for economic policy. Falling profit meant falling revenue from taxes. In order to increase net profitability, capital pressured the state to reduce taxation (e.g. corporation tax, employers' national insurance contributions). The state lost fiscal input in both respects. There were further demands from capital for the state to take over reproduction costs (e.g. apprenticeships and training, pension and health schemes): demand for public funds as a direct assistance to capital in the form of subsidies, regional aid, export credits, the setting up of enterprise zones, etc.; and demand for the relaxation of development controls – enterprise zones, development corporations, suspension of planning controls – setting the needs of capital over and against the needs of the local communities. The pragmatic and reactive response of the state was to cut public expenditure in areas like social welfare, thus reducing the social wage. Reductions in expenditure and investment by both state and capital led to further increases in unemployment. And there was pressure from capital for access to profitable areas of state provision – privatisation – expanding the logic of commodity circulation.

It is the issue of public expenditure and social welfare costs that needs to be addressed first. Under the Conservative government of Margaret Thatcher public expenditure has come under close scrutiny both in terms of the relationship between such expenditure and the public sector borrowing requirement (and thus rates of taxation) and in terms of the government's ideological antipathy to the economic and social role of the state. '... the present Conservative leadership's economic strategy as well as its political philosophy combine to make reduction in public expenditure and rolling back the "frontiers of the state" complementary top priorities' (Grant and Nath 1984 p.157). In fact, however, the idea of cuts is really a crude and limited way of looking at Conservative policies with regard to social policy spending. As important as the effects of cuts, are the effects of new regimes of organisation and evaluation being required of social welfare systems. Welfare and public service expenditures are being subjected to new criteria for effectiveness. Thus, policies based upon the imperatives of social distribution are increasingly marginalised and derided. Issues of inequality and social justice are no longer seen as worthwhile bases for policy making. 'There is a fundamental contradiction between the imperatives of capital which require the priority of profit and the imperatives of social justice which require the priority of social needs' (Harvey p.104 in Grace 1984). However, to some extent the full impact of reductions in public expenditure have been averted by shifting the logic of social welfare provision (collective comsumption) closer towards the requirements of capital.

In effect, in terms of the sorts of policies outlined above, I want to argue that social welfare has been significantly *restructured* and *repositioned* in response to the crisis in capital accumulation. In education we can see this restructuring and repositioning occurring via three aspects of Thatcherist policy.

1. Controls over and the redirection of spending and expenditure cuts.

2. The attempt to reorient and redefine the meaning of education itself, 'what counts as education'.

3. New forms of control over the professional workers of education.

The result or effect of the policy and ideological work done on education in these ways has shifted education out of its firm location within the sphere of reproduction into a closer relation to the sphere of production. Costs which were seen to be a drain upon the profitability of capital can as a result be presented as directly enhancing profit. The strong classification which Bernstein argues has existed, between education and production, which 'creates the condition for the relative autonomy of education, the division of labour between those who are located in production and those who are located in cultural production (education)' (1977 p.175) is, as a consequence, significantly weakened.

I do not propose to discuss cuts in educational expenditure in any detail here, partly because such cuts are so difficult to specify with any precision (limited increases must be set against the effects of inflation) and partly because, as noted already, an emphasis on cuts tells only part of the story of the restructuring of education. What money *is* spent on is as important as what it is not spent on. A perusal of Government White Papers on Public Expenditure can be illuminating. Mace (1986) in discussing the 1984/5 White Paper makes the point that as well as indicating cuts the White Paper also gives some guidance as to government priorities, those areas marked out for protected or increased expenditure. The two worth noting here are expanded vocational provision in Further Education and increases in the science budget. Mace notes:

> As to external efficiency, the government clearly considers that education can promote economic developments, provided that it is of the right sort. The government's emphasis on vocational and science-oriented teaching suggests that this is where it perceives the education system can best serve the needs of the economy.
>
> (p.126)

A further point needs to be made about a 'cuts' analysis. The nature of educational provision does not lend itself to quick and thorough-going changes in expenditure. The use of limited increases, below the level of inflation, has a slow, cumulative effect. The continuous nature of educational provision does not lend itself to drastic cuts. Unlike, say, building projects, educational activities have no clear begining or end. Changes have to be planned well in advance. Furthermore, less than 5 per cent of annual education spending is on capital goods. Large scale cuts require significant reductions in the workforce. Even so, it is possible to identify cuts in spending on education and to find particular programmes or areas where such cuts have a major impact – nursery school provision, adult education, school meals, etc. But clearly these gross changes in funding do not explain or illuminate the general thrust or direction of education policy. More important are the ways in which expenditures are moved around within the system, the ways in which cuts in some kinds of provision are off-set against increases elsewhere, and the ways in which control over funding is changed (particularly the increases in direct, ear-marked funding, and the switch of expenditures between different agencies). Monies spent in the same sector by different agencies may have very different kinds of impacts and effects. Also, in general terms, the climate of cuts has its own effects; budgetary control is a way of asserting discipline and bringing about changes in organisational emphasis. Thus, the ideas of value for money, effectiveness and accountability imported into education in the 1970s and 1980s are more than just mechanisms for good housekeeping, they provide ideological as well as financial control, they are indicative of discursive shifts in the meaning and governance of education. Again the point is that expenditure policies must be seen in relation to broader policy shifts and priorities. The financial agenda can provide a powerful vocabulary of motives for the work of repositioning and restructuring education in relation to the sphere of production.

Repositioning and restructuring

Crucially, the repositioning and restructuring of education involves changing the nature of its relative autonomy, with 'the specification "relative", as in relative autonomy, primarily . . . to be understood in the qualitative sense as referring to a particular *kind of relationship*' (Fritzell 1987 p.24). In particular, I want to argue that this repositioning involves extensions of aspects of the commodity form, 'the dominant organizational principle of exchange in capitalist societies' (Offe 1984 p.39) into education, that is the previously de-commodified manner for the delivery of education is changed. Education is made more subordinate to and less autonomous from the commodity form, and the nature of its relative autonomy is thus changed. In Fritzell's terms the *potential* for autonomy is closed down as the 'functional imperative' of accumulation penetrates the form and content and delivery – pedagogical and organisational – of schooling. This change, I am suggesting, is multidimensional and affects the experience of students, teachers and parents. (Fritzell's own discussion is limited to the students' experience.) But this change is not uncontested and it is not untrammelled, as I shall try to indicate.

As Fritzell suggests, the nature of relative autonomy in or for education rests upon the tensions which arise between 'the functions of efficient accumulation and legitimation' (p.27); or, in other words, the kind of relative autonomy enjoyed by education is embodied in the particular ways it fulfils the function of the reproduction of the economic foundation of society. Fritzell outlines two versions of such autonomy.

The first is positive correspondence; here the structuring of schooling is both structurally and functionally tied directly and harmoniously to accumulation and legitimation. (Structural autonomy relates to the correspondence of significant properties and internal relations between systems, here education and the economy. Functional autonomy relates to the adjustment in terms of social consequences between systems. In very simple terms structural autonomy is a matter of similarity of forms and processes; functional autonomy is a matter of outputs. In a broad sense the former relates to social reproduction and the latter to technical.) Seen in terms of positive correspondence, school is a competitive, formal and hierarchical process, knowledge and social roles are fixed, teaching is standardised and is directed towards formal examinations. This provides the framework for what Offe (1976) calls the 'achievement principle'. Examinations serve as personal qualifications providing access to particular occupations. The ideology of merit legitimates this access in terms of individual ability.

The second version of relative autonomy is negative correspondence; this 'concerns functional contributions by means of the *exclusion* of critical tendencies and the *prevention* from destructive developments' (Fritzell 1987 p.30). Here the process of schooling are distanced from the commodity form; functionally school remains tied to the needs of the economy but structurally *it may appear* to be autonomous. Social education and the personal development and individual capacities of the pupil are given emphasis. Self-realisation and expressive competencies are used as the basis for the evaluation and ranking of students, and access to the labour market is emphasised in terms of social competencies as much as cognitive ones.

In the latter case the character of the relationship of education to the commodity form has shifted, though it is not necessarily less corresponding to or more destructive of the basic commodity form. Fritzell (1987) makes the following important point:

> while the systems of schooling under modern capitalism have tried to adapt their internal structures to the conjunctural adequacy of different forms of correspondence, the general tendency in the development from liberal to advanced capitalism has been and is a continuously growing relevance of the negative form of correspondence. Traditionally, that is to say, the system of schooling within the capitalist State seems to have pursued its functions related to efficient accumulation and legitimation predominantly in the positive form of correspondence with the external commodity form. With the developments of capitalist society, however, this form of internal structuring seems increasingly hard to maintain as a general principle. To point only to a few relevant aspects here, the developments have included an ever growing social division of labour, a trend towards service production, expansion of the State and transformation of its forms of intervention.

(p.32)

Indeed it may be that negative correspondence is a reflection of restructuring within aspects of capital itself and the emergence of new forms of work and work relations and new expectations of labour as well as an adjustment to high levels of youth unemployment and the preparation of significant numbers of young people 'for a status somewhere between work and non-work' (Pollard *et al.* 1988 p.5). That is to say, negative correspondence may turn out to be not negative at all, but rather a form of positive correspondence with new forms of commodity exchange, particular services and information. And it may also be positively related to the need within capital for an orientation to continual change.

Negative correspondence is realised very clearly and directly in the educational projects of new vocationalism. And clearly the new vocationalism has made significant headway in its impact on school-age education in recent years through courses like TVEI and CPVE and the adoption of City and Guilds and BTec courses. However, two important corollaries have to be added to these general comments. First, in some respects the inroads of negative correspondence have been general. For example, the Records of Achievement movement has made considerable headway in many schools and LEAs and has received strong support from Keith Joseph during his period as Secretary of State. Aspects of the new GCSE examination may be seen as take-up of the shift towards more motivational forms of learning and assessment. And the growth in courses of PSHE (personal, social and health education), and ATW (Active Tutorial Work) indicate the spread out of 'pseudo-concrete' activity in schools –courses, that is, which celebrate self-realisation and personal awareness but which display 'lack of interest and awareness as to the deeper structures of individual development in a social context, and in particular the ignorance or bracketing of the individuals' dependency upon the economic structure' (Fritzell 1987 p.30). Second, however, the sponsorship of negative correspondence has been aimed particularly at the lower two-thirds of the ability range. Courses like CPVE, TVEI (despite the intentions of the MSC), City and Guilds' 365, and BTec's First Award basically service students who have failed at some point in the traditional subject route through school, for whatever reason. In part this can be seen as efficient in correspondence terms – such students are likely to be the earliest entrants into the labour market, and most susceptible to periods of unemployment; they need to be best prepared for interrupted occupational careers – however, this kind of specialisation of the negative correspondence form can also be seen as a deflection. The penetration of new vocationalism has been sponsored by a variety of groups and agencies associated with schools/industry relations and vocational preparation and it receives strong support from many representatives of big business, the industrial trainers. But the inroads of negative correspondence are opposed, particularly in relation to high-ability students, by the supporters of traditional, absolutist forms of curriculum, pedagogy and assessment, the cultural restorationists. The result of such opposition is evident within education policy in terms of limitations imposed on the expansion of the ideology of new vocationalism (see chapter 5). Remember, I am suggesting, extending somewhat beyond Fritzell's own argument, that the changes in the internal structure of the schooling process are only one aspect of the penetration of commodity forms into education. The experiences of parents and teachers also need to be taken into account (see below).

I want to discuss the processes of restructuring and the development of negative correspondence in more detail by suggesting five aspects of policy which have been and are acting in and upon the education system as a whole: privatisation, marketisation, differentiation, vocationalisation and proletarianisation.

Privatisation

Privatisation, in the form of selling-off assets and nationalised industries, has been a key feature of Thatcherite economic policy. In education the effects of privatisation have been, thus far, more subtle and piecemeal.

1. Perversely in economic, if not ideological, terms there are various channels for the provision of state aid to the private sector of education – the Assisted Places Scheme is one, and the purchase of LEA and Armed Forces places in private schools is another. Payments are also made to private schools for children with special educational needs. From the point of view of the Conservative government the existence of the private sector provides an example of the possibilities of the market form in education, and the private schools also offer a powerful benchmark of excellence for the state sector to aspire to (Robson and Walford 1989).

2. There has been increased reliance on parental contributions in state schools both in the form of payments for things like music lessons, swimming lessons and school trips (now the subject of charging policies) and extra-curricula activities and in the increase in parental contributions through covenants, PTA fund-raising, and cost-savings like redecoration. Pring (1986 p.72) gives the following examples.

(a) Department of Industry financed computers to LEA schools on a 50:50 basis, but one authority insisted that the parents find the 50 per cent and running costs.
(b) Esher Sixth-Form College launched a £20,000 appeal to raise money for computers and library books.

(c) Parents of Churchill School, Avon, pledged to covenant £60,000 in four years to establish a charitable trust for spending on such 'extras' as library and text books and on scientific and laboratory equipment.

3. The use of private managing agents for YTS courses based on employers' premises is based on government preference for private enterprise. In some cases private managers have been awarded contracts which would otherwise have gone to Further Education colleges. The private sector is used to encourage competition and to push state provision towards greater efficiency. The increasing use of short-term contracts in Further Education by the MSC for the delivery of courses is intended to have the same galvanising effects.

4. Similar to the above is the putting out to private tender of school cleaning and other support services. Again the private sector has been used to break the direct labour provisions of local authorities. The economic, political and ideological purposes of policy are tightly interrelated here.

5. The increased use of industrial sponsorships and attempts to draw in contributions from business, for example in the funding of City Technology Colleges (CTCs) (see chapter 5). Schemes like the CTCs, COMPACT, the London Business Partnership, etc. are intended, in part, to draw in direct funding, in money or equipment, from business, for specific programmes in state schools and also to increase the influence of the business community in educational affairs.

6. In the run-up to the publication of the Education Reform Bill in 1987 Bob Dunn, Under-Secretary of State for the DES, floated the idea of what he called Crown schools and Company schools. The former are represented in the Education Reform Act in the guise of Grant Maintained schools, schools which opt-out of LEA control and become directly funded by the DES. The latter have yet to appear in formal policy proposals but, as outlined by Dunn, companies, encouraged by tax relief, would tender for a 'package' of schools and, after five years, their results would be compared with other schools which had remained under Local Authority control. Teachers' wages would be set by competitive tendering and related to performance measures (i.e. examination results). Both of these possibilities are beginning to emerge from the recommendations of the Secretary of State's Advisory Committee on the Pay and Conditions of Teachers.

Marketisation

That is the introduction of market forces into education.

1. A series of measures since 1980 have strengthened the possibility of parental choice and have increased the importance of competition between schools for enrolments. This began with the requirement for schools to publish examination results and culminated in the Open Enrolment provisions of the 1988 Act. The creation of an education market has already been discussed in some detail in chapter 3, but, to reiterate, LEAs will no longer be able to protect less popular schools. Schools will be able to admit students up to a standard number, fixed at their 1979 intake. The DES see some closures as inevitable.

> Yes, and the government would recognise that and say, well so be it, if that's the way it is . . . if a school really does produce poor performance, maybe that school should lose its clientele until it has to close.
>
> (senior civil servant D)

Schools will survive or not on the basis of their reputation and their ability to sell themselves to prospective clients. They will be judged by 'output measures' applied to their 'products'. This also has implications for the nature of teachers' labour in the school (see below). The Hillgate Group, in their pamphlet *The Reform of British Education*, urged that:

> HMI's role should be redefined, so as to assign to the inspectorate, as its principal duty, the investigation of schools or Local Authorities which fall below the national attainment standards. They should make much more use of the quantitative indicators, which have been and will become available
>
> (p.18)

Under the provisions of the 1988 Act Local Authority Inspectors will take on a more direct monitorial role.

2. The Open Enrolment provisions of the ERA are given teeth by being linked to per capita funding arrangements. Schools will be funded primarily in terms of their numbers: more pupils more money, fewer pupils less money. Here again is an indication of the restructuring of educational provision and funding according to the commodity form. A very direct input–output system is being inserted into the process of schooling. In effect pupils are reduced to a form of exchange between parents and schools: 'In exchange a definite quantity of one product changes places with a definite quantity of another' (Bottomore *et al.* 1983 p.86). Here is a version of the confusion of relations between people with relations to things which Marx called 'commodity

fetishism' (Marx 1968 Ch 1. Sect. 4). The relation between teachers and parents and teachers and pupils appears as a relation between intake numbers, capitation payments and examination results. The educational process is obscured. Moreover, the ideology of commodification, the confusion of social relationships with exchange relationships, so basic to the philosophy and culture of Thatcherism, is reconfirmed by its introduction into a fundamental aspect of human development. The social roles constructed out of these exchange relations also act back upon both parent and teacher – the former is confirmed as a consumer, the latter moves closer to classic wage labourer.

3. We can add to the other restructuring aspects of the ERA, Local Management of Schools (LMS). By making schools into independent spending units with much greater control of their own budgets a number of things are achieved. First, the possibility of diversity – an important basis for the New Right conception of an education market – is increased. In the way they make choices about the use of resources, within the constraints of the National Curriculum, differences between schools are likely to increase. Second, and concomitantly, the idea of a common or universal provision of education is broken. Third, the devolution of budgets is likely to lead to the introduction of institutional and regional variations in teachers' pay and variations based upon scarcity (more for shortage-subject teachers) and performance (the use of merit awards). (Both of these were flagged in the 1986 Audit Commission Report, *Towards Better Management of Secondary Education*, and the report also noted that: 'Local accountability is lacking, The Commission agrees with government's view . . . that effective local accountability is the key to securing economy, efficiency and effectiveness in authorities' use of resources' [p.50].) It is likely that in order to maintain market flexibility schools will be tempted to increase the use of temporary contracts for some staff. Fourth, this brings the model of school organisation closer to that of the industrial organisation with head as Chief Executive and governors as Board of Directors. Good management is thus brought closer to the rigours of profit and loss. The school as an organisation takes on a structural (see Fritzell 1987) correspondence to the organisations of accumulation as the discourses of management and profit take hold (see proletarianisation below.)

Taking these points together, ideologically there is a neat and powerful package for reworking the meaning of the educational process, shifting education into a structural relation to the basic commodity form of market exchange.

4. As already discussed, the further, and logical (for many New Right Conservatives) extension of these procedures is the introduction of vouchers. The argument and push for vouchers emerged first in the

Black Papers (Boyson 1975) and has been an ever-present possibility in Conservative education policy since. Rhodes Boyson, Arthur Seldon and Stuart Sexton have been the major proponents, and one attempt to introduce vouchers during Keith Joseph's period as Secretary of State proved a close-run thing. The voucher is the embodiment of commodified education and the apotheosis of a Hayekian, neo-liberal free-market state. Stuart Sexton, discussing the Education Bill in interview in early 1988, outlined the neo-liberal argument for vouchers:

This bill is only a step on the road, it's not the end of the road by any means. I have tried to sketch out the next steps in *Our Schools* and I still think that is the way we are going. What we have got is the first timid steps down the road to Utopia. My Utopia is when we have a system of all of the schools independently managed by their governors and their heads in the same fashion that the best independent schools are, but in which you have tax payers' money to pay for the education on a per-pupil basis. Now whether that has to be something called a voucher or whether that is something done by the taxation system is a technicality, but the principle that we are working towards is a situation where the funding of the school is in direct relation to the parents' choice of that school, as with the independent sector. The only difference being that your maintained school would not be able to set the level of fees that would be set by the government on behalf of the tax payer. So there is never going to be total freedom. We are talking about ten or fifteen years.

Describing his period as Minister of State at the DES, Rhodes Boyson also bemoaned the failure of the voucher initiative and links it also to Keith Joseph's attempt to introduce a student loans scheme for Higher Education (which resurfaced controversially in 1988). Reviewing his own successes and failures as a junior member he said:

It's (a) what you've done and (b) what you've been stopped from doing. On the first was the increase in parental choice plus the Assisted Places scheme, that was good. Then I moved on to two other areas. I moved on to the voucher and to loans and I produced a great loans scheme. I visited all the relevant countries about this. And I still think now that it will have to come in, certainly if you are going to have education for all, as I would like, on that I am quite radical. I developed a scheme which is still in my loft somewhere, which I thought was the best ever done. And it fell, the party wasn't ready for it. It fell at a cabinet sub. It disappeared. I spent six months on that. Now Keith was working on the voucher, but it was obvious to me that nothing would happen. Then, apart from encouraging schools to do sensible things, like bringing discipline back, there was no other radical thing I could do and I don't waste my time. There is no purpose in kicking against the bricks, you know, I knew after that loan system, it fell just like that 'bang', there's no point in slogging your guts out. I realised that one would have to go back again arguing about the ideology. By that time we had won against the comprehensive school. We hadn't won to the extent that they wanted the selective school back. But at least they knew it was a bad thing that the party hadn't got to the extent that there must be a better thing somewhere else. It had moved to parental choice. I hadn't got the voucher but I'd got parental choice and an extension of freedom and Kent was seeing what it could do. But it wasn't ready for the voucher. Every one of us once you become a politician and not the evangelist outside is controlled by the climate. And the climate wasn't ready.

Here again, parental choice, selective schooling, discipline and vouchers are tied into a neat and powerful ideological package.

5. Finally, here I would draw into this ensemble of policies, developments and possibilities, the work of effectiveness research and the *effective schools movement*. The ideological work done by effectiveness research, linked to notions like accountability, school review and school improvement, should not be under estimated. Again these concepts draw upon industrial metaphors and practices and link ideologically with the key notions of efficiency and value-for-money. Such terms operate judgementally within the input–output logic of the commodity form and displace and exclude other criteria of judgement. The cruder manifestations of accountability floated in the *Black Papers* and the Great Debate have been reworked into versions of surveillance and monitoring which fit into the preferred teacher discourse of professionalism. In effect, teachers are entrapped into taking responsibility for their own disciplining through schemes of self-appraisal, school improvement and institutional development. Indeed teachers are urged to believe that their commitment to such processes will make them more professional. Thus, Young (1985), writing on the implications of school effectiveness research for management in education, argues:

What these studies and others cited elsewhere in this chapter underlined is the considerable autonomy that exists for the individual teacher that can in some instances deflect from the achievement of known and approved goals. They also point up the need for an effective headteacher to ensure that the school community as a group functions well and that known and agreed goals are reached to the satisfaction of all.

(p.185)

Here the control of teachers is seen to be the major problem and the major issue – schools need to be made teacher-proof. Also embedded here is the assumption of the possibility of unequivocal consensus about good schooling and good teaching. Professional debates about education are reduced to 'what we all know to be best' or 'what management decides'.

Effectiveness researchers both construct a concept of the ineffective or sick school and draw upon the use of confessional techniques (an admission of transgressions and a ritual of atonement) as a mechanism for the return to health or to a state of grace. The school is to take responsibility for its ailments and its own cure. The confession 'is a ritual of discourse in which the speaking subject is also the subject of statement' (Cousins and Hussain 1984 p.212). The secular confession is founded on the notion of normal as against abnormal transposed from the religious opposition of sin and piety (Foucault 1978).

As with the notion of consensus the thrust of effectiveness is the limitation of the range of possibilities for normal education. Once established, such norms can be used to compare and divide and stigmatise. When normalising judgements are turned upon whole schools, each school is immediately set in a field of comparison. This again articulates with the commodity form of education and the educational market place. An artificial order is laid down, 'an order defined by natural and observable processes' (Foucault 1979 p.179). The definition of behaviour and performance embedded in the order and the norm are arrived at 'on the basis of two opposed values of good and evil' (p.180). Thus, also where there is illness there is also cure, models of effective practice. If self-examination fails, the expert, the authority, the consultant, the moral disciplinarian is at hand to intervene. And in this role the scientific and the moral are tightly intertwined. In effect, given the logic of management, ineffectiveness is seen as a disorder of reason and, as such, susceptible to cure by the use of appropriate techniques of organisation; or, if all fails, the market will render its judgement and the weak or sick school will close. The disciplines of the market produce dual, contradictory and concomitant effects – diversity related to competition and conformity related to comparison. Here then academic research speaks the discourse of the market and of the commodity form.

Differentiation

Briefly, linked to the above, it is possible to identify, by putting separate policies into an ensemble, a further aspect of Conservative Party ideology at work in current policies, that is differentiation, by ability and by specialization. Differentiation is the basis for *diversity*. Again the main issues were introduced in the previous chapter.

1. The private sector is held up as a model for the rest of the education system and, as noted above, has received considerable direct and indirect financial support from the state. The sector has an ideological significance in the discourses about standards and markets which allows for questions of real independence to be glossed over. The Assisted Places Scheme ramifies the ideology of selection and privilege in the private sector by offering an escape route for high-ability students from state schooling. These pupils are creamed off from the comprehensive sector.

> The Scheme has been justified as an extention of parental choice, a restoration of academic opportunities to many children who would not be fully stretched in schools which have to cope with a full range of ability, and as a protection both for those individuals and for the nation's resources of talent against the levelling-down effects attributed to comprehensive reorganisation.
>
> (Fitz *et al.* 1986 p.xx)

2. Grant Maintained status for opted out schools has added a further element of diversity. These schools (twenty-nine have been approved as of February 1990) are funded directly by the DES as semi-autonomous units. They are no longer subject to LEA strategic planning decisions and have reaped significant financial advantage from their new status in the form of building and equipment grants from the DES which are five times higher per pupil than grants available to LEA schools. The majority of schools thus far approved for grant-maintained status have opted out to avoid LEA schemes of school reorganisation.

3. The next layer of schools in the emerging hierarchy of differentiation will be the star schools in the LEA sector, those which are over-subscribed and which turn away pupils and have steady-state or rising budgets. This leaves below them in the pecking order the 'sink' schools – those which are unpopular and under-subscribed. The rhetoric surrounding the parental choice process and its effect on schools is often couched in terms of a standards raising mechanism, but the expectation, as we have seen, is that some schools will lose out.

'Sink' schools will take some pupils deflected from star schools and will also have a captive population of pupils whose parents are unable or unwilling to meet the demands and costs of arranging travel. They may even choose as a survival strategy in the education market to specialise, say, in responding to the needs of pupils with learning difficulties. Reporting the findings of a research study on the effects of parental choice in Edinburgh and Dundee, Alder and Raab (1988) note that:

Large outflows have, in a few cases, combined with declining
school rolls and a small catchment area to produce very small
intakes. Coupled with low staying on rates and poor examination
results, this can only exacerbate the problems faced by these
schools and make them less effective. All in all, the evidence in
Edinburgh and Dundee suggests that the Parents' Charter is leading
to the emergence of a number of 'magnet' and 'sink' schools and
thus to increased inequalities in educational provision.

(pp.176–7)

In addition, some authorities, notably Wandsworth and Bradford, are
proposing to introduce American-style magnet schools – specialist
schools with staff and courses geared to pupils particularly interested (or
gifted) in science, languages or the performing arts. Reporting on the
Bradford scheme the *Observer* (20 June 1989) indicated that Bradford
City Council was 'planning to divert State education cash to help
establish a group of rival schools which would then bid for extra funds'
(p.4). The article went on to note that 'Mr Baker, the new Conservative
Party Chairman recently held private talks with Bradford leaders about
the concept. Behind the scenes Baker is also encoraging a similar plan
by Wandsworth Council' (p.4). The Draft Education Plan for the
London Borough of Wandsworth states the following:

It will be important that permanently [sic] surplus places are
removed from the county system for educational as well as
financial reasons. Before final decisions are reached, a number of
varying kinds of schools and colleges and patterns of education
will be examined in addition to existing types, including city
technology colleges, campus models, sixth form, tertiary and
community colleges, encompassing Adult Education work, and
magnet schools – schools encouraged to specialise in a number of
particular strengths while continuing to offer the National
Curriculum .... All schools, colleges and AEIs will have the
opportunity to see how they can become attractive centres of
excellence and performance within a system committed to this
principle and purpose.

(Wandsworth 1988 p.ii)

4. Into this stratified pattern, although it would seem in small numbers,
comes the City Technology College (CTC). Based in part on the rhetoric
of the grammar school and inner-city provision for high-ability pupils,
in part also modelled on the American magnet school system, and in part
a hybrid, business-oriented response to industrialists' complaints about
shortages of technologically skilled workers, the CTCs are less significant for their numerical effect than for their symbolic one. They are yet

another skim from the comprehensive school pool of ability and from the pool of funds for normal state education. In the period 1989-92 the DES expects to spend £126.6m on CTCs (and since sponsors enjoy tax relief on covenants the cost to the Treasury is even higher) (*Independent* 20 June 1989). Their organisation, working conditions and ethos are deliberately fashioned on industrial models. Teacher unions are not recognised and staff have to sign contracts agreeing not to strike. The National Curriculum does not apply in these independent schools. The school day is longer. They were intended, but did not turn out, to be funded directly from industry, weakening again the principle of welfare education.

Taken together this emerging stratification of schools not only rests upon a competition between schools, it also creates the basis for a large-scale return to competition for places between pupils. The competitive self-interest of families is underlined and the logic of Thatcherist individualism is ramified in the education system. The education market will tend to weaken social bonds (the social engineering project of comprehensive education is anathema to conservative thinking) and encourage strategies of exclusion and social closure; that is the generation of boundaries of positional hierarchy.

5. Lastly, it is worth indicating (but I would not over-estimate) the differentiation of routes *within* schools. There is, more clearly than for many years, the possibility of early separation of life chances and occupational entry. Two increasingly distinct routes are emerging. TVEI, CPVE and YTS (Youth Training Schemes) have sketched out a worker-pupil, pre-vocational/vocational route which could be embarked upon from age 14, separate from an academic, subject-based, GCSE, A-level and Higher Education route. Some research evidence already exists which demonstrates a tendency for working-class pupils to follow pre-vocational courses, while children of professional groups tend to take academic courses (Dean and Steeds 1981). Afro-Caribbean pupils may also be over-represented on the pre-vocational courses (Atkins 1982). Atkins (1986) also makes the point that 'Those students who are tracked into the pre-vocational curriculum are led to see this process as a reflection of their personal inadequacy for academic work, as 'proved' by their poor showing in school examinations and tests' (p.48). There is an ironic inversion here in relation to the critique of anti-industrialism which has been so strong in the Conservative educational offensive, an inversion that the MSC has tried to avoid in TVEI courses – that is the identification of pre-vocational routes with failure, as being second-class alternatives for students unable to sustain progress in the academic route. The defence of the academic curriculum (by strident cultural restorationists and the DES) continues to relegate practical, applied

knowledge and skills to low status and the pre-vocational credentials continue to be measured against the existing academic benchmarks by parents, teachers and many employers.

Vocationalism

By drawing upon the developments outlined at the begining of this chapter and some points already made in this section it is possible to identify, as might be expected, a crucial vocational element in the restructuring of education. As suggested already a primary aspect of the process of making social expenses productive is to establish direct links between expenditure on social needs and the needs of industry. Thus the orientation of education has begun to change from being primarily one of collective consumption to one which ensures that school leavers are better prepared for work roles. This is what Fritzell (1987) calls functional correspondence. As already discussed, this kind of correspondence operates in a number of different ways in different sectors and at different levels of education. Simply put these might be: technical training or know-how, teaching skills or familiarisation with labour processes; producing particular attitudes and demeanours – deference, punctuality, subservience, etc.; teaching knowledge about wealth creation, and encouraging entrepreneurship and the skills of business.

1. One part of this vocationalism is the general development of the skills of, and a positive attitude towards, production and wealth creation. A whole range of policies and programmes are relevant here. TVEI and CVPE, with their vocational elements and work experience components, are obviously relevant; so too are more general schemes of work placement. But the Mini-Enterprise in Schools Project (MESP) is a specific example of this sort of development.

> In contrast to the classroom based teaching about industry that
> remains common among vocational courses, MESP involves
> students in the actual production and realization of value . . .
> although student activity is still based at school, they are taken into
> the market place to sell a good.
>
> (Shilling 1989 p.115)

The Economic Awareness project, the Schools Curriculum Industry Partnership (SCIP), and the Understanding British Industry project (UBI) are other examples of the dual strategy of attitudinal and cognitive socialisation. Thus, part of the process of establishing schools/industry links is the fostering of a commitment to the idea of work, and positive attitudes towards industry and enterprise. However, attitudes, knowledge and skills are distributed and targeted very differently within each of these initiatives. Sometimes these different concerns may actually be in conflict. For example, the development of initiative, decision-making and marketing skills appears to have little relevance to many jobs requiring no more than the routine repetitions of general labour. Here work in mini-enterprises may create a disjunction between the capabilities of future employees and the needs of employers. Analysing the development of the Education for Enterprise movement generally, Rees (1988) points out that:

> There is ample evidence that the work ethic is alive and well among the young unemployed. The current concern of the state, the industrial sector and community groups is to change the expectation that they will be expressing that commitment to work as *employees*. The particular model of alternative employment promoted varies according to who is doing the promoting. As the state becomes increasingly involved, it is the self-employment and small-business version, the capitalist mode, that will be presented to the exclusion of others.
>
> (p.16)

The point is that there are many different forms and contexts for work. Work is not a unitary category.

2. Within school-based pre-vocational courses, considerable emphasis is given to forms of assessment which are intended to motivate pupils while at the same time providing a broad profile of their attributes and abilities – cognitive, affective, social and psycho-motor. Viewed positively, profiles of this kind can give some status to achievements and qualities outside the academic domain, and by discussion and negotiation involve pupils more fully in deciding their own educational needs. While for the pupil these profiles may be justified in instrumental terms – job-getting – they also serve employers' needs of job selection and worker preparation. The whole of the pupil is opened up for assessment and surveillance. As Hargreaves (1987) suggests, they can 'be used as instruments of social control; as ways of securing conformity to the system, heading off deviance before it starts, of prying into and keeping track on emotions and feelings that might have disruptive consequences for the school' (p.22). The person rather than the performance is on the line in such assessments and thus in the search for employment. Failure is personalised and individualised. This perpetuates the view that the burden of adjustment to the labour force lies with the individual. The role of motivation is discussed further below.

3. Pre-vocational courses like TVEI and CPVE also carry with them a learning message which some employers see as better attuned to the

realistic needs of high-tech industry (and self-employment) – flexibility and adaptability. The FEU, on whose work, particularly ABC (A Basis For Choice), the CPVE was based, have been very consistent advocates of the flexibility hypothesis. But while acknowledging the role of these elements in pre-vocational courses, not all commentators see them as related to the actualities of factory life.

> TVEI aims to disseminate ideas of transferable skills, to accustom pupils to ideas of technological change requiring them to move across job demarcation lines and to change jobs continually throughout their working lives. These may well be desirable objectives, but I would hypothesise that British employers and employees learn attitudes which inhibit effective technological change in Britain *after* they leave school.
>
> (Senker 1986 p.298)

Doubt is also cast upon the real degree of the matching between national policy imperatives in employment training and the demands of working life and expectations of their workers held by the majority of employers (see Rees *et al.* 1989). If the mismatches are serious then this strengthens the argument that education is being used as a scapegoat for other kinds of failure, and that the disciplining and restructuring of the education/production relation has other purposes, for instance those suggested by Stronach.

4. Possibly the most common feature of schools/industry relations is the work experience placement, although different agencies and schemes view its role and intentions differently. Work experience is described by the DES (1984a) as 'an insight into the world of work', as 'part of an educational programme', whereas the MSC see it as an 'early' and 'permanent bridge between school and work' (MSC 1984) and thus as providing skills and familiarisation, an initiation into the 'truth' of work (Stronach 1988). But again intentions may not be borne out in practice, some outcomes may actually be counter-productive. Shilling (1987) makes the important point that 'the dominant *view* of work-experience as held by the MSC alongside many schools and industry, often stands in a problematic and contradictory relation to the *practices* experienced by students during their work placement' (p.419). For a number of pupils work experience is a disappointing, alienating or sometimes combative first engagement with the world of work. The burgeoning COMPACT schemes are a highly-developed form of this kind of schools/industry accommodation.

5. Control and policy making in education are now more overtly and directly influenced by the business community. It is now normal for the

government to nominate representatives of industry to key committees and decision-making and allocatory bodies concerned with education. A number of industrialists have also been appointed to significant posts in educational bodies.

Proletarianisation

As noted already, the insertion of the commodity form into education is not limited to the experience of pupils; teachers too are becoming subject to new relations of production. The nature of the school as an organisation, as a workplace, is being steadily transformed.

1. The DES clearly see forms of industrial management as the necessary and appropriate method for school organisation. Significant amounts of money are being committed to the management training of heads and deputies, through local INSET schemes and the setting up of a National Training Centre at the University of Bristol. A specialist cadre of school managers is being formed. The attempt is being made to model headship on the Chief Executive role in industry, as noted above.

2. Management techniques, based on a separation of policy from execution, have the effect of further delimiting the professional role of the teacher and have tended to encourage the development of 'them and us' attitudes similar to those in industry. This latter will be enhanced by the devolution of teacher employment from LEAs to schools in the LMS provisions of the ERA. Local Education Authority policies on employment will no longer apply. Schools will not be bound by Equal Opportunities policies or by arrangements for the protection of the jobs of teachers made redundant. There will be no schemes of redeployment to safeguard teachers from the uneven or unexpected effects of falling rolls.

In the near future schools may also have the choice of employing teachers of different types, with different kinds of experience and training. It may be cheaper to employ Licensed or Articled teachers than to go for the fully trained and qualified variety. Indeed, in some circumstances a school might consider it worthwhile to opt for fixed capital costs, a micro-processor network or new laboratory facilities, rather than take on board additional salary commitments.

The employee, as opposed to professional, perspective and commitments of teachers is further underlined by the introduction of a formal contract of service with fixed hours of work (imposed August 1987 by the Teachers' Pay and Conditions Act). Pay and promotion is increasingly tied to performance by the award of incentive payments. These developments can also related to the introduction of schemes of Teacher Appraisal.

97

3. The LMS provisions of the ERA also carry with them implications for changes in school ethos. I have already made the point that the key factor in establishing a market in education is linking competition to reward. Schools are to be put in a position of having to make strategic planning decisions about maintaining or expanding their market share – their pupil numbers. Time, effort and money will have to be devoted both to the running of devolved budgets and to policy analysis and planning – most large secondary schools will be dealing with more than £1 million per annum. Schools will either have to spend money on employing bursars or accounts clerks or the like or existing staff will have to take on such responsibilities. Whatever decision is made in a school the role of senior staff is likely to undergo considerable change. Heads and deputy heads will more than ever be in the business of business. They will have day to day responsibility for the budget and for the management of their staff. The gulf between teachers and the senior management team is again likely to increase. It is also possible that school governors will begin to consider employing executive heads who are not or have never been teachers, but are good managers. In other words, we may see developments like those brought about in recent Health Service reforms.

The question of costs and responsibilities also extends into the area of marketing. Some schools are already beginning to appoint teachers or give posts of responsibility for marketing. Some teachers will be spending good parts of their time on developing or maintaining the image of their school in the market place. And there will be a scramble for sponsorship and business support for school activities.

In all these ways the nature of teachers' work is being changed and constrained. To be added to all of the above is the introduction of the National Curriculum and National Testing, and the reduction in teachers' scope for decision making that they entail. Teachers will have much less responsibility for deciding what they teach, when and how.

All in all, these changes amount to a significant change in the labour process, ethos and conditions of work of teaching, a process of *proletarianisation*. What we have is a massive interconnected policy ensemble, a complex of projects, initiatives, schemes, agencies, imperatives and legislation, which is pushing education in new directions and is affecting the way teachers work, the way schools are run and organised, and the nature and delivery of the school curriculum. But this ensemble is not always coherent or co-ordinated. The actual relations between school activities and the world of work are not always clear or logical. Grand intentions are not always realised in practice and may actually be contradicted. The concerns of schools, of industry (and of different schools and different industries), of the state (and of different sectors of the state) rarely come together unproblematically. Thus, the effects of restructuring are general and piecemeal rather than precise and total. Further, the relationship of vocationalism to capital and the economy is complex because capital itself is changing. Nonetheless, the evidence for a general restructuring/repositioning of education in relation to production, and the 'requirements of work', is compelling.

5

Towards the post-Fordist school?

The structuralist account presented in the previous chapter is both abstract and materialist, and rests on the identification of a theoretical chain which logically links and articulates the elements of society into a social totality. It gives causal precedence to the economic. However, the process of the restructuring of capital 'has economic, political and ideological dimensions, each of which has significant implications for the basic relationship between capital and labour' (Sharp 1980 p.169). It is possible to trace the logic of connections between crises within the economic and changes in consciousness within the ideology, to realignments of influence in the political. The mechanisms of restructuring and the policies which facilitate and legitimate change are actually brought about through the actions and interactions of a whole variety of particular people and groups. But at the level of social action these mechanisms and the formation and implementation of policies are neither smooth nor neat.

Essentially, as I have argued elsewhere, education, as a field of discourse and practice, is an arena and an object of struggle. The promulgation of a particular definition of what is to count as education is central to the vocational impetus with which we are concerned here. And the vocational is clearly set over and against other 'regressive' definitions of education (see Dale 1985, Gleeson 1989, Jamieson 1986). But, as already indicated, the discourse of vocationalism is not entirely coherent in itself neither does it align unproblematically with other influential discourses inside government. In this regard I would reiterate Williams' (1962) distinction between both old humanists and industrial trainers and my own sub-division between the reformist old humanists and the conservative, cultural restorationists. It is also necessary to acknowledge the emergence within the educational establishment of new progressivism (see chapter 6). On a whole range of issues the industrial trainers (at least those involved in or who have influence over education policy) have supported and encouraged changes emanating from within the educational establishment which are bitterly and vehemently opposed by the cultural restorationists within the New Right (like the introduction of the GCSE). Indeed it has been suggested by some New Right commentators that TVEI and the education wing of the MSC were 'captured' by the left-liberal, educational establishment (North 1987). Both elements, the vocational and the new progressive, are enemies of tradition; and on some issues, like a mass *v.* elite system of education, the industrial trainers support with enthusiasm public educator arguments. Further, on some specific matters of policy (like CTCs) there are significant numbers of industrial trainers, especially those who represent major multinationals, who reject what the government is trying to do. It is also evident that there are significant differences in emphasis with regard to the nature, scope and content of the school curriculum between the industrial trainers and the DES curriculum planners (the reformist old humanists). There are significant members of the industrial lobby who see the concerns of the DES as antithetical to the schools/industry movement.

In other words, I want to introduce a degree of messiness into the neat account of restructuring outlined above. There is a whole series of specific matters which could be dealt with here but two issues in particular need attention. First, I want to examine more closely the industrial trainers' views on curriculum, pedagogy and assessment in schools, what I shall call vocational progressivism. This will also provide a way of considering the industrial trainers' assessments of the Education Reform Act and its National Testing and National Curriculum provisions in particular. Second, there is the question of CTCs and the issue of elite *v.* mass schooling which this raises. In looking more carefully at these specific issues it will be possible to identify some aspects of the mechanics of restructuring. But these issues also serve to underline the point that what is at stake here *is* the basic relationship of capital and labour.

Vocational progressivism

Many recent accounts of new vocationalism have clearly been based upon a root and branch opposition to and a worst-scenario analysis of, anything which attempts to relate school experience to the world of work. The combination of political dogma and industrialists' special pleading, which lies behind many of the initiatives in the schools/ industry movement, and the apparent hostility of some vocal industrialists towards state education and teachers, has understandably stimulated suspicion and resentment. Thus, Maurice Holt, writing in 1982, described TVEI as likely to produce 'a divided curriculum perpetuating Victorian views of knowledge and social class' (p.11). It is perhaps perverse, then, in a political analysis of educational policy making to describe the schools/industry movement in terms of vocational progressivism, although clearly progressivism is always a complex and paradoxical form of educational ideology (see Sharp and Green 1975). I use the term somewhat in the way that some Marxist writers have referred to the progressive effects of capitalism. The use of the term here serves several purposes. It highlights the vocational challenge to the liberal-humanist, academic domination of the secondary school curriculum. It also indicates the basis of common cause that exists between some members of the industrial lobby and new progressives in the educational establishment on matters of curriculum structure, assessment and pedagogy. 'Here radical teachers join with industrialists in claiming that "real world" problems do not fall neatly into academic subject divisions' (Jamieson 1986 p.37). But Dale (1988) sounds a note of caution: 'the superficial progressivism [in new vocationalism]' he argues 'conceals a harsh industrialism' (p.57). This is evidenced by industrialists' concern with the need for education to adapt itself to the realities of production and business. The argument here, then, is that the potential or effect of some forms of vocationalism is progressive, sometimes despite the intentions of its progenitors. Thus: 'One of the effects of the schools/industry movement then is to crack the edifice of didacticism in some schools' (Jamieson 1986 p.37). And, in a discussion of TVEI, Gleeson (1989 p.100) argues that, 'there is certainly potential for curriculum change, changes in teaching styles and for a better deal for many young people in schools and colleges'.

Clearly the schools/industry movement cannot simply be reduced to the position of advocating a narrow and divisive form of vocational training. In several respects, and clearly in a spirit of enlightened self-interest, the industrial lobby has nurtured, supported and defended a series of innovations in schools and Further Education which are a reaction to the narrow, abstract, academic, elitist nature of the forms of knowledge and teaching predominant in British schools since the nineteenth century. We have a situation in which attempts at change arising from particular theories of learning and philosophies of knowledge (which I call new progressivism), which were intended to enhance the learning experiences and increase the motivation of students, have coincided (for want of a better word) with technological changes in industry, affecting the labour process and modes of production, which require new kinds of attitudes and competences from employees. This is no crude reductionist 'back to basics'. Dr Ray Peacock, Research Director of Philips Laboratories and member of the National Curriculum mathematics working party, puts the progressives' position very clearly and indicates some basic disagreements with the cultural restorationists of the New Right.

Nobody ever does long division. I mean it's ludicrous . . . my son
doesn't know his 16 times table. The only reason anybody ever
wanted to know his 16 times table was because some berk invented
ounces and pounds. There 's no other reason for wanting the 16
times table. Now I want instant recall . . . I want people to say nine
7s, but I can't see a lot of point in much of the repetitive rote practice of long multiplication, long division, extracting square roots,
that sort . . . because you never do it, damn it. I mean it's a bit like
when people say well . . . I know you do it on calculators . . . but
what happens if the batteries go flat. Well that's a bit like arguing
that you've to learn to ride a horse in case you run out of petrol.
You don't learn to ride a horse, you stay with the car don't you?
And all the 'declining standards' seems to be based on tests of that
sort . . . if you can multiply six vulgar fractions, well yes, but
whoever does?

However the other bit that I do want out of education seems
unquestionably to improve. The bits I want, and I think the bits that
kids need desperately for the modern world that they're in . . . is
certainly to be extremely flexible, because I know of no job,
whether you're in a travel agents or whether you're in a shop or
whether you're in industry or wherever, where what you do now is
the same as what you were doing 5 years ago. The travel agent
doesn't look it up in a book any more, he runs it on the screen of
his machine and he calls it up from a database. Your salesman, he
may go out in his car but he gets all his information over his
telephone line at night, onto his screen at home . . . And there's a
distinction between knowledge and ability here. Lots of people
think knowledge is what we want, and I don't believe that, because
knowledge is astonishingly transitory. We don't employ people as
knowledge bases, we employ people to actually do things or solve
things . . . knowledge bases come out of books. So I want
flexibility and continuously learning. And again in the schools and
the universities, you are individually assessed throughout the whole
of your education career, and the first thing that happens whether
you leave school at 15, or whether you go and do a PhD at 24 . . .
the first thing that happens, you roll into where you're going to
work and they say, by the way, you're in this team over here. And
nobody has any vision about whether you're any good at working
in a team. We are never told in industry, whether anybody's any
good, so we ask damn fool questions like, do you organise the
scouts and things like that, to try and find out. So I need flexibility
and I need team working. And part of team working is
communications, of course, and I think kids are much better at

communicating than they were. Most people when they're taught communication, only talk of transmitting . . . and there's an obligation in communications to be able to receive . . .

And the third one that I see kids better at, although that's very patchy, is just sheer persistence. Because educational tasks usually come in 45 minute dollops max, 5 minute dollops, about 30 second dollops max . . . When you are out doing any job, in any business . . . the tasks are not 45 minutes max, they're usually 3 week dollops or one day dollops, or something, and the guy who gives up, oh sod it, you don't want him. So the things therefore are the flexibility, the team working, communications and the sheer persistence, I think kids have come out of schools and they've come out of universities a hell of a lot better at that than they were 20 years ago

Here are a complex set of expectations of schools and universities which embody a critique of rote and fact-based learning, individual competition and a highly classified, subject-based organisation of learning. What is required of students is a set of social skills and transferable competencies. And, as Dr Peacock sees it, schools are responding effectively to these kinds of expectations and in these terms the standards being achieved are higher than previously. It may be, of course, that Dr Peacock has been 'incorporated into the stage army of education' (Jamieson 1986 p.36). In part what lies behind this shift of emphasis, in pedagogical terms, is a shift from teaching to learning. This is reinforced by the Reverend Dr George Tolley, one-time Head of the MSC Quality Division.

It does seem to me that a very large amount of what goes on in education is teaching, and perhaps therefore teacher dominated, and in that view of education there's a sort of transfer process and stuffing-in process rather than a process in which the learner in fact ought to be in a position to exercise considerable influence upon the processes of learning. The effectiveness of education at the end of the day has to be determined in terms of outcomes for the learner, not in terms of inputs from the teacher . . . And that teaching/teacher dominated thing has been supported I think by the examination system, which has been very much testing of knowledge rather than testing of performance, and to the extent that education has been teaching and teacher dominated I think that that has underwritten the sort of separation between industry, viewed as part of the market, and education as part of the service of provision. And I suppose most of what I have been about in education over the years has been trying to formulate and to come up with some answers to that question, what is effective learning? . . . And asking questions about the way in which the processes of learning should be related to what we now call the market. A few years ago we wouldn't have called it the market, we wouldn't have been talking about clients and customers and specific sets of relationships. To the extent that one can get effective collaboration between provider and consumer then you are more likely to come up with effective outcomes for the people who are in fact making that transfer from the provider to the consumer. I see a sort of circle here and the learning processes figure very large, and over the years I have become increasingly irritated and deeply suspicious of a great deal that was going on in our examinations system, because it didn't seem to me to be assessing learning at all. It seemed to bear no relationship to the processes of learning. Neither did it seem in the vocational area to be assessing any outcomes that were sensibly related to what an individual student or graduate was going to need to take with him. Neither did it relate very much to what the customers wanted, in terms of customers as industrial employers.

Here Dr Tolley is pointing to the importance of changes in pedagogy and concomitant changes in modes of assessment. But Dr Tolley's comments also make clear the kind of framework within which vocational progressivism operates: it is within the framework of the market, of supply and demand. Industry is taken to be the consumer of education's products, and in this case the consumers are taking the lead and intervening in the market to make sure that they get the products they want. And, again, flexibility is at a premium in the market place.

The fact is that you're going into business as a 16-year-old or 18-year-old, and right from day one you're just not going to be stuck at the same machine, or in front of a typewriter, even if we are talking about that level . . . For one thing you cost quite a lot, as a 16-year-old. You certainly cost more than a 16-year-old in Germany would cost. Employers tend to bid up wages quite a bit for teenagers. I think that's going on and a lot of people are concerned about that. People in the education system . . . are concerned as to whether employers are actually training or they're just bidding up wages just to get bodies to do the jobs, which is obviously of legitimate concern with demands for flexibility. I don't think that employers are just going to be as crude in their use of young workers as they were, and certainly with the sort of demographic time bomb starting to go off now, youngsters are going to be at a premium, so their skills really are going to have to

105

be developed quite highly within the job context, and they've got to be able to approach the job context with a flexible frame of mind not just the basic three Rs.

(Robert Joy, Employment Research Executive: Institute of Directors)

Flexible competencies and a predisposition to change are set over and against basic skills. The labour market training needs and educational outcomes are again intimately related.

In interviews with representatives of industry, CPVE and TVEI were frequently quoted as providing models for the sorts of changes, in terms of teaching methods and student motivation, which the progressive vocationalists would like to see spread throughout the education system – particularly the emphasis on learning, pedagogy and new modes of assessment, rather than content.

All of those things are about method, aren't they . . . you think about them, CPVE brought in the method of regular monitoring, review, interviews, stuff like that. Alright, it brought in a new curriculum, but one of the things it's heralded for is really method. Because you know, for 16-year-old kids who are staying on at school they usually have to sit down and listen to some sort of path that leads them to A-level or perhaps another O-level, whereas as this was a kind of departure in the way we teach them, and it's quite exciting.

(Sherall Andrews, The Industrial Society)

In addition to TVEI recent developments in the teaching of science (since the Secondary School Science Review) and mathematics (since the Cockcroft Report) are also seen as crucial in establishing new kinds of relationships between school work and the realities of industrial work. New methods of science and mathematics were also seen as enthusing, and thus retaining more, students of science and mathematics.

I mean I do see a few young people as well, and I mean it's all about motivation actually . . . I can show prejudice here, because I am by background a scientist. And as a scientist I really know what a turn-off a lot of science is. My own kids are actually quite good at maths and physics, but they didn't want to go on, they've all gone into business administration. Physics was an absolute turn-off. It wasn't exciting, it was learning stuff . . . lenses . . . one over U plus one over V equals one over F type stuff. At the moment, looking at the skill shortage, we need to attract more people into Further and Higher Education. It's no good offering them a job in five or six years' time. They've got to be turned on when they come in.

(Brian Kington, Public Issues Manager, IBM)

As indicated already changes in teaching methods and in ways of motivating students are closely related to new forms of assessment, particularly profiling and records of achievement and graded assessment techniques. In part again this is related to the sorts of outputs that industry would like to have. Narrow academic assessments are no longer regarded as adequate or appropriate.

> I cannot see any value in measuring something because you can do it accurately, if it isn't what you want to measure. Now the things I want to measure are much more soggy and imprecise, but nevertheless industry has to make an assessment about it. When this guy comes for a job, and he is going to join your sales team, you've got to make a judgement about whether he can fit in with the team, about whether he is persistent, etc. etc . . . I would like people to come complete with a data sheet, just like an integrated circuit comes with a data sheet, to tell me what this guy would do.
>
> (Dr Ray Peacock)

> There's also a big debate going on about how do you actually test in a way which is fair. Again I think the CBI hasn't got involved in the details of all this, what we've tried to do is to define the outputs that we think the system should be capable of delivering. And I think our assessment of government policy has been on the basis of, will the changes make the likelihood of those outputs being achieved greater?
>
> (Tony Webb, Director of Education, CBI)

The new modes of assessment provide the information and reflect the sorts of developments of competences that big industry feels it needs. In particular, the introduction of the GCSE, with its emphasis on course work and project work, received a unanimous vote of support from those speaking for industry:

> If you have a terminal exam at 16 . . . in that case and I think, we'd say that GCSE is quite a good exam and certainly better than its predecessors. I think it's going to be easier for employers, once they get used to it, to understand the unitary systems. I think there were problems with the dual system and translating the values from one to the other was always a problem for employers, so I think the concept of a unitary system has more of the kind of skills and aptitudes that business would be requiring. I mean it's not just academic learning, I mean in history, for instance, it's more project-based and research-based and it's actually a question of finding things out. I mean I'm very interested in history, I studied history but we just read a book and regurgitated those answers in examinations. Local history and things like that would've

developed better methodology in me for tackling other problems that I came across at work. So from that point of view, I think we would generally welcome it.

(Robert Joy)

Equally there was a sense of disappointment that the Higginson Report (and its proposed reform of A-levels) was not accepted.

The linking of curriculum and assessment developments with the issue of motivation is itself significant. Hargreaves (1989) sees the 'crisis of motivation' in education and in the relation between education and employment (or unemployment) as a crucial factor in 'stimulating educational policy change' which 'can be seen very clearly in the development of pupil profiles and Records of Achievement' (p.55). Certainly the discourse of motivation draws together a set of inter-related teacher, employer and political concerns. The teachers' task in the classroom is facilitated when students are well motivated; employers welcome the positive effects of having well-motivated school leavers, and in so far as motivation is the alternative to alienation, problems of delinquency or social disorder may be reduced. Thus, a variety of interests can be welded together around the concept. However, in these terms the instrinsic educational benefits of graded assessment, profiling etc. may be less obvious. Hargreaves argues:

> Under circumstances such as these, the enhancement of pupil motivation shifts from being an *educational* process of positive disposition to learning worthwhile knowledge; to a *socio-political*, state-managed process of accommodation to the realities of economic crisis; of adjustment to diminishing prospects of employment and economic reward and to an educational experience that, for many pupils, can no longer promise social and economic benefits in adulthood. Motivation that is, becomes transformed from a process of educational encouragement, to a strategy of social crisis management.

(pp.56–7)

It is possible to take this argument one step further. Clearly the enthusiasm within the vocational lobby for assessment-led forms of teaching and learning cannot be accounted for solely in terms of absent effects, that is in terms of adjustment to *un*employment; this is essentially a political problem. The employers' view of these developments is based upon the positive effects of motivation in terms of *em*ployment. Arguably the assessment-led reform of education provides a response within education to the general establishment of a *new mode of social regulation* (see below).

However, as indicated above, these sorts of curriculum and assessment developments are not unproblematic or uncontested. To some in the industrial lobby the National Curriculum appears to be strengthening a more traditional subject view of school knowledge, somewhat against the developments brought about by TVEI and CPVE. *The principle* of a National Curriculum was generally supported by interviewees as providing the basis for a common system of education and a set of standards for testing and monitoring quickly in the system. However, Dr Tolley, for instance saw the National Curriculum and the vocational curriculum as being at odds.

> I think there are very considerable risks of an increasing lack of coherence at 16 plus, and one can see it in the mismatch I suppose, between some of the things that are emerging in the National Curriculum, and some of the things that are happening in the vocational curriculum. One can see it in what would seem to be almost the deliberate policy at the moment of trying to squeeze out vocational qualifications from schools . . . for all sorts of reasons.
>
> I find it disappointing that there doesn't seem to have been much in the way of radical rethinking of curriculum relationships. There's been an attempt to redefine content in certain new ways perhaps, here and there. But what's coming out still seems to preserve some of the undesirable aspects of the secret garden, in the sense of 'well we've got to preserve a certain purity of subject', and that becomes the touchstone by which the nature of the curriculum will somehow be judged.

In particular cases in the face of the National Curriculum, innovators clearly feel their work to have been devalued.

> Mini-enterprises are not part of the national curriculum and we are very disappointed indeed. As an organization we aim to put a lot of pressure on the working-parties to try to become included. If the worst comes to the worst, we'll have to aim to occupy some of the remaining time in the curriculum not covered by the National Core.
> (Sheila Holt, Deputy Director of MESP, quoted in Shilling 1988)

Clearly the non-core areas of the school curriculum are going to be hotly contested as competing claims for space are put forward, and vocational aspects may lose ground in this struggle.

It is evident, however, that even in its short gestation period the overt subject orientation of the National Curriculum has been weakened, at least to a degree. The original proposals outlined in the DES Consultative Document (the Red Book) seemed to leave little scope for the vocational curriculum. But Jack Peffers, of the Schools Curriculum Industry Partnership, sees significant changes emerging from the consultative process.

109

I think it's quite interesting to go back to the Red Book, and to see that there was hardly any mention of TVEI, and there was hardly any mention of cross-curricular work, and economic awareness and so on, and it was perceived that the subject-centred curriculum would occupy 95 per cent of the time . . . towards a situation now where we see in the science and maths final reports, a strong emphasis on infusing that curriculum with an industrial dimension. We now see the move towards 30 per cent cross-curricular time, with the inclusion of cross-curricular themes, like industrial and economic awareness, like PSE, like careers education. And there certainly don't appear to be any blockages to a modular implementation of the National Curriculum, where the attainment targets are there and the programmes of study are there, but the delivery could conceivably be in a whole range of modules infused by an industrial dimension. Whether many schools will go down that path is another matter, but in my view there is the prospect of a modular curriculum, there's the prospect of an industrial dimension in the subjects, there's the prospect of industrial and economic awareness as a cross-curricular theme.

Reaction to the strong subject base for the proposed National Curriculum came from a variety of sources. The SCDC, for example, made the critique of a subject base the main thrust of its response to the Consultation Document. This is a confrontation between antagonistic discourses.

First and most important the specification of the National Curriculum is in terms of *traditional subjects* throughout the years 5-16 and the recommendation of programmes of study will be the responsibility of subject working-groups. By contrast there has been recognition in recent years that traditional subjects alone are not an adequate vehicle for conveying the knowledge, concepts and skills and attitudes required by pupils who will be living and working in the last years of the twentieth century and the early years of the twenty-first. The consequences of specifying the National Curriculum in subjects rather than in the now familar areas of learning and experience or in terms of broad curriculum aims are a recurrent theme of this SCDC response.

(SCDC 1987 p.1)

The CBI also had its doubts about the subject-centredness, while supportive of the National Curriculum in general.

The particular area where we expressed doubts was economic awareness and the fact that it's a subject-centred curriculum. Would this mean that the themes which have been put across so

well by TVEI and similar sorts of initiatives would be lost, and
particularly the economic awareness thing? And we were told, well
no, that would be something that would run through the whole of
the curriculum. I think that's going to be very hard to achieve,
demanding a lot of the teachers and the head to ensure it happens. I
think, ideally, that we would prefer that there was some element in
the curriculum which dealt with economic awareness, as a separate
subject. But we do believe there are some immeasurable benefits
that will arise from the National Curriculum and the associated bits
of it, the GCSE exams. Because it will set standards, and it will
provide the testing, and the testing will not only provide for pupils,
but it will also, by implication, be testing the teachers as well.
Altogether this must lead to higher standards, provided something
can be done to get the morale of teachers up, which I hope can be
done in the next year or two.

(Tony Webb)

A member of the FEU also raised doubts in interview about the emphasis and clarity of the National Curriculum as outlined in the Consultation
Document:

We were mainly concerned about the process. We're not opposed
to the idea of a National Curriculum, but like most curriculum
bodies, we're fairly concerned that whatever controlling
mechanisms are applied by the Department [DES], are not so
restrictive as to destroy the quality of the learning process. And
obviously we are interested in the integrated curriculum, and we
are interested in new ways of teaching and learning. And on the
face of it, the document seems . . . to be advocating a somewhat
old-fashioned approach to the curriculum. There is a confusion
between objectives and content. There are some very confusing
sentences where it isn't clear whether the content will be described
in terms of curriculum objectives or whether it will be described in
terms of syllabus content. And I think that's the sort of fear that
people have . . . what the effects of nationally-imposed assessment
will have on the learning process. Whether assessment can be both
diagnostic and normative, for example. And if, as we suspect, you
can't actually achieve both in the same test, what will the emphasis
actually be in the long run? [see chapter 7]

(civil servant G, DES/FEU)

The question that is difficult to answer is whether the weakening of the
subject position, such as it was, in the published Education Bill, was a
result of the force of argument or the effect of more direct pressure being
brought to bear. One respondent indicated the latter.

I think that that's come in not as a result of the work of the DES and the civil servants in the DES but as a result of political pressures from the Department of Employment and the Department of Trade and Industry

However, the DES view is clearly that too much has been read into 'apparent' omissions. One civil servant (E) explained:

Can I just say that I think that TVEI wasn't the only thing. I mean there's no reference at all to careers in it, and I'm not sure there's any reference to economic awareness in it [the National Curriculum]. No, I think that there are a lot of things, that if we had realised the way in which people would home in on apparent omissions and read too much into them, it might have been worth Schools Three's while to put in an additional paragraph or two. I think they just weren't aware that the cross-curricular theme was likely to generate as much interest as it did.

It is still reasonable to ask, as some of the respondents did, whether the notion of cross-curricular themes is just a convenient escape clause, leaving the subject curriculum and its effects relatively untouched. (At the time of writing the NCC report on cross-curricular themes is already behind schedule.)

Of what vocational education is the DES has done nothing. And when it starts looking and people start singing the praises of TVEI, TVEI is all things to all people. It is something that's got a loose set of principles, but the practices vary from scheme to scheme. And that's not vocational education in the generic sense of the word, and therefore I don't know what vocational education is. And given the emphasis that the government has been making for this last five years, about increasing understanding of vocational education . . . one of the things that seems to me singularly lacking is the fact that we do not have an understanding of what vocational education is, what place it can have and should have. I'm mindful of the fact that if I look at the guidelines that Elizabeth House sent out in respect of the National Curriculum, there is no mention of vocational education. So I then conclude that Elizabeth House doesn't think much of it. So I then say what the hell is going on and what is the place of vocational education?
(Alan Ainsworth, Personnel Manager of Players, Chairman of the
FEU and member of the CBI Education Committee)

This view is echoed by Jamieson and Watts (*TES* 18.12.87)

The *dirigiste* nature of the national curriculum seems likely to undermine the trend in recent years towards more use of active learning in schools. Schools–industry links have themselves been a powerful force in promoting such learning. Moreover, some of the strongest sources of active learning have been work experience, work shadowing, residential courses and community-based activities. The national curriculum makes no provision for such activities.

(p.11)

And they go on to link this criticism to the policy struggles within the Conservative goverment.

The notion that the Government and its advisers are united behind a set of coherent reforms is a fallacy. A battle for the high policy ground appears to have been waged between two factions. The first – associated most strongly with Lord Young, the MSC and the Department of Trade and Industry – is concerned with developing an enterprise culture, with preparing young people for adult and working life, and with producing a skill-based curriculum focused on *doing* rather than simply on *knowing*. The second – associated particularly with the group which orginated with the Black Papers and which has now most recently manifested itself as the Hillgate Group – is preoccuped with academic 'standards' and a return to traditional subject-based learning. At the moment, the Hillgate Group appears to be winning.

(p.11)

This then restates the basic conflicts which exist between the cultural restorationists and industrial trainers, between the pure and applied, elite and mass. One is a discourse of competence and inclusion and response to change; the other is a discourse of sensibility and exclusion and fixed standards and qualities. These differences in emphasis and concern are summarised in figure 5.1 (p.131). To be clear, I am not trying to detail that which is vocational education, rather my intention is to illuminate the dynamics, at a practical educational level, of the restructuring of education in relation to the economy, the policy conflicts which this restructuring engenders and the struggle within the educational state to control what is to count as education.

CTCs

City Technology Colleges were originally announced at the 1986 Conservative Party Conference. These colleges, which are intended to provide a 'new choice of school', responsive to 'the changing demands of adult and working life in an advanced industrial society' (DES 1986b), can be set up by an agreement between the Secretary of State and any person who undertakes to establish and maintain such schools. They are legally independent and, as such, not subject to the National Curriculum. On the face of it such a proposal would seem to be a strong indication of the Conservative government's commitment to the schools/industry relation. Here is an opportunity for industry to make a direct input into the funding of education in order to provide technologically-oriented education. Kenneth Baker decided to follow up his conference speech with a CTC launch at the headquarters of the CBI. Alan Ainsworth describes what happened.

> It's two years ago now that CTCs were launched. They were launched, if my memory serves me right, the first public announcement was by Baker at the Tory Party Conference . . . and between the Tory Party Conference and the official launch, and the official launch happened to be at the CBI Headquarters, and the CBI can't have what I would term command meetings, but it can put the strongest possible emphasis that it wants people to attend a meeting, I mean there was the strongest emphasis to attend this particular launch. It was essentially a group of people who'd been involved with the CBI for a fair number of years in education and training issues and we were, all of us, in a position that said, for Christ's sake you brought us all here, you tell us that Baker is going to be launching this damn thing, are you saying that we have to stand up and support it, because if you are saying that, you ain't going to get it. And we had a most strange meeting with Baker, because I think Baker was led to believe that he was going to have a platform of friends, in which he could have very positive questions in which to launch it onto the media, and in the event he had more negative comments than positive comments. The subsequent week there was a CBI meeting to discuss the CBI position on it and, let's put it this way, the people who were deemed the opinion-formers were all negative. The CBI was not prepared to be negative right, ideally it wanted to send a message out to its members, 'Support this'. We were in my view highly successful in getting the CBI into a position that said that it was not going to give any advice. It was going to be neutral. And to give it its due, it adopted that neutral line and it has stuck to that. It will not give companies advice as to whether they should assist or not with the scheme.

Clearly the Secretary of State and his advisers had badly miscalculated. Big industry in general has shown little or no interest in CTCs. On the whole those companies which spend money on education projects do not see a great benefit in spending large chunks of that money in one or two flagship colleges. Brian Kington of IBM explains:

In fact George Lowe, in *Education* about 18 months ago, produced our position fairly succinctly. We have a structured education programme, which is partly based on money, but only a small amount of money, and partly on the donation of equipment, but most importantly on involvement of people particularly at the local level. Our donations, most of them, are not done centrally. What full support for a CTC would have done, would've meant that all our financial resources, unless we got extra ones, all and more would've gone into one school. It would've been somewhere where we might have had a base, Basingstoke, Southampton, Portsmouth, somewhere like that, but then all the other things going on in that area would have had to go by the board. And all the people up in Greenock would've said, "Why are you putting all your money up in Hampshire?". So for policy reasons we said no, we support them, we will support them, as we would any other school with work experience, careers advice, speeches, staff training because we do that for other schools as well.

This view was clearly understood and appreciated by one of the DES civil servants interviewed (E).

I think there is a feeling from a company's point of view, it's perhaps better not to nail all your colours to one particular mast but to spread it around some other ships. It's a question of finding what's most appropriate and what you as an employer, as a company, think it's going to do the most good. I mean CTCs, is one of the options, but it's one of several and I don't think anybody here would want to prescribe what companies ought to do. You can get involved as much or as little as you like. You don't have to put up x millions of pounds to be associated with the CTCs you may prefer to develop informed links with local schools.

The *Times Educational Supplement* (27 June 1987) provided front-page coverage of ICI's refusal to take part in the CTC initiative.

The massive UK-based multi-national spends more than £5 million a year on educational projects and is, in the words of Mr Alan Calderwood, the Cleveland chief education officer, 'one of the few good things we have going for us on Teeside'. Mr Kenneth Baker, The Education Secretary, and Sir David Hancock, his senior civil servant at the Department of Education and Science, have been wooing senior executives of the company and will be bitterly disappointed with their failure to gain its support.
  More than 1,800 firms have been approached to sponsor CTCs but only seven promoters have been named. Several commercial

giants, including Marks and Spencer, BP and Sainsbury's, the supermarket chain, have refused to help.

But the response of the big industrialists is not simply one of disinterest or ambivalence. There is clearly a strong current of opinion that sees the CTCs as counter-productive and potentially damaging. Alan Ainsworth explains:

> The CBI's view tended to be something like this. It had seen, in the whole field of the interface between education and industry, significant changes over the last ten years. It did not accept the argument that the educational sector was now remote from industry and commerce. All sorts of bodies and agencies – SCIP, TVEI, you name it – the impact of the whole of this was bringing about a better understanding on both parts. You have major organisations which have undertaken a lot of educational support work with individual schools. I'm thinking in terms of ICI up in Cleveland, BP in Essex and Cambridgeshire. Organisations which are really big opinion formers. They were on a route that said look we are supporting the education system that's provided by the State, we have major doubts as to whether in the total climate that it is sensible to go down this other route. It was all the negatives that were flooding out, that said, if you're going to put them in inner city areas and you're saying that there is an open door selection, there are not going to be the candidates for these particular schools. And they're going to be perceived by many people as being equivalent to grammar schools, and people are going to apply for them on that basis. And they're going to denude the State system of elements of teaching staff that are in short supply – CDT for instance. And you're going to pay differential salaries because they're going to get support.

Several points are at issue. First, that the CTC initiative fails to recognise the successes of the schools/industry movement across the system as a whole. It is a distinct, political strategy which fails to articulate with grassroots changes. Second, the CTCs threaten the supply of teachers, funds and materials to other parts of the system. Third, and in more general terms, the CTC approach, of targeting monies from industry, of introducing greater diversity and selection into the state system, runs counter to the view of many industrialists that emphasis should be upon the improvement and development of the mass education system rather than the encouragement of specialisation and elitism. George Tolley expresses this view when comparing the concerns of Keith Joseph and Kenneth Baker.

I think Keith Joseph, of the two, was the much more radical person really and the much more liberal person. By that I mean that it seemed to me what Keith Joseph was about was really trying to open up the education system, open up to ideas, to influence and attempting to improve the effectiveness of the system. But not to look for simple ways of determining that effectiveness which I think Baker is after. And I think what Kenneth Baker is also after, is that he's hankering after the old quality indicators and insistence on academic values. And it's not really good, frankly, in quality terms, because I mean we're concerned with international not just national aspects of quality, and there's nothing which convinces that our best education in this country is, as it were, outdistancing the best in other countries. I think it's struggling hard to stay up. And to the extent that we're trying to hold on to the old quality indicators, in academic terms, we're in fact tending to slip behind other countries, because what they found out, ahead of us, is that you've got to have a jolly good broad base right across education to cope with and cater for all your ability ranges.

I would like to think that the influences and inputs from the world of employment would bring about a demand for pulling up the floor. Not just a demand from industry saying we need better graduates, but also saying that the bulk of other processes is really dependent upon the quality of 85 per cent of our work force. Their educational standards are too low. I would like to think that that is one of the messages that will be coming through increasingly and will be making itself felt through governors from industry on school governing bodies.

And Tony Webb of the CBI also underlines this point while commenting upon differences of opinion among his members.

Where there are two firmly entrenched camps, those who say CTCs are a very good opportunity to experiment and ensure that we get foundation skills, there's another school also very entrenched that says the state should take responsibility for education, and the state should treat all schools in the same way, if a CTC is a good thing, then all the schools should be CTCs.

SJB: So, in effect, support for a comprehensive principle.

TW: So support for the comprehensive principle subject to the reforms which have been pushed through with the Education Reform Act.

SJB: Are those two camps finally balanced or is one dominant?

TW: Well we've never done a thorough investigation but it's quite clear that there are people with very entrenched views, and what we've done at the CBI is, when giving members advice, to say these are the arguments for getting involved, these are the arguments for not getting involved, but the decision is yours. It's not something that we have decided to take a pro or anti stance on.

And Sherrall Andrews of the Industrial Society pushes home the point. The CTCs are seen as an unnecessary diversion from the main business of schools/industry links, and as a piece of politics rather than sensible education policy.

It's a misunderstanding of the reasons why employers put money into education. There was this kind of notion that they would all be like Victorian worthies, because business was booming and they were making extra profits. You're always going to get the quirky industrialist who puts his money into a school but it's not a universal thing. Like Richard Branson, he wants to put his money into this performing arts thing, great, O.K. But in the general run of things that's quite quirky. But the whole thrust to CTCs, in our view, denies all the good work that's being done in TVEI, CPVE and we should be building on that.

This commitment to education for all was, as Raymond Williams notes, a basic concern of the nineteenth-century industrial trainers, but a commitment which 'led to the definition of education in terms of future adult work' (1962 p.162). In the discourse of vocational progressivism this argument is again being put, and again this is set over and against the elitist conceptions of knowledge proselytised by the old humanists. The CTCs provide one terrain for this struggle. Within struggles of this kind, inside the educational state, there are contrasting definitions of what it is to be educated and of the form, purpose and delivery of the curriculum. Also there is an opposition here between cultures and between political priorities and policy concerns. The economic, political and ideological aspects of policy making are in tension. One attempt to resolve this tension was to reverse the normal flow of influence and pressure in the relationship between the political and the economic. The government, or rather the Prime Minister and the Secretary of State, have sought to put pressure on potentially supportive industrialists to lend their weight and their funds to the CTC initiative. Off-the-record comments referred to a meeting held at No 10 Downing Street where 'arms were twisted'. One industrialist commented:

I know from its sins our company has been screwed. Because the Chairman is a Thatcherite supporter, he was screwed. He was screwed on the basis of goodwill to cough up a million pounds and it is not by conviction, it is by what I would term the need for some industrialists to cough up to ensure that Baker doesn't fall flat on his face with egg on it. And I think the speed with which things have got underway is evidence of the fact that there is no bursting out all over of support for these sorts of institutions.

Another added:

As a company which is very visible in this field and also very high-tech and of course the whole thing about this is that it's high-tech. I mean, Keith Joseph wrote to us, a personal letter to the Chairman, so we had to think very carefully what we would say, and we have had further approaches from Cyril Taylor and we explained to him what our position was, because obviously it was high on the priority list, especially with Kenneth Baker when he came in. I mean we don't want to upset things, quite important people are making decisions which affect other things that we do.

The last sentence captures another aspect of the industrialists' dilemma in this matter.

Kenneth Baker and his advisers also made the rounds of possible sponsors like the London Livery Companies. This particular initiative supposedly provided the basis for the proposal to turn the Haberdasher's Aske schools in south London into a CTC. Despite these efforts however, the weight of funding has now shifted considerably away from industrial sponsorship, even in the case of those CTCs which have got off the ground. The DES is now providing money for the vast majority of the cost of these new schools. Judith Judd reported in the *Observer*, 22 January 1989:

The Government last week promised £4 million to the Haberdashers' Schools in Lewisham, South-East London, if parents and governors agreed to turn them into a technology college. One parent opposed to the scheme described the promise as 'a bribe'.

Rosie Waterhouse, in the *Independent* (29 June 1989), added to the story under the headline 'Mounting Costs of Baker's Beacons' (p.19), noting that:

Many of the 14 main sponsors who have been named so far are major Conservative Party contributors: the Hanson Trust, Lucas Industries, Trust House Forte, the Argyll Group, and Harry Djanogly of Coates Viyella together declared donations of more than £1.1m to the Party between 1981 and 1988.

Forms and contents of change

In analysing the complexity of the effects of new, progressive vocationalism in education most attention is paid obviously to the impact on students. However, the vocational impetus also has significant implications for teachers and for school organisation. As indicated in the previous chapter the thrust to establish direct correspondences between school and industry also operates at this level. The insertion of commercial values also has effects here. Several of the key discursive concepts identified previously come into play again. Markets and competition are clearly identified as requiring and stimulating a drive towards greater efficiency and a more consumer-oriented planning. These are also linked to notions of quality control, which has implications for teacher appraisal. Local Financial Management is also seen as requiring new management skills from heads and their senior teachers. And also embedded in these imperatives is a sense of getting better value for money. In other words, schools are increasingly being viewed as commercial production units, the notion being, therefore, that schools can and must learn from industry. The Institute of Director's work-shadowing scheme for teachers clearly has elements of this. Robert Joy explained that:

> They regarded it as a management opportunity, for themselves. Some of them haven't worked since vacations when they were doing degrees and they really wonder what's it like in the business world now. Or some of them want quite specific things, they want to see how meetings are run. One of them wants to know how decisions are taken and implemented. So I think that's quite interesting, that some of the requirements are fairly specific. But in the main they regard it as a development opportunity, and I think they are quite enthusiastic about it, certainly the ones that came around here on Monday. I mean all of the teachers turned up and about half of the business men, so perhaps that reflects the fact that the businessmen aren't as . . . well I won't say they are not as enthusiastic, but perhaps they don't really think they've got as much to learn as teachers do.

He also outlined a clear relationship between the need for schools to compete for their market share and the need for good management.

> If you empower consumers, which parents are and children are, then obviously they are going to make choices, and that could be one of the results of the process of choice . . . so therefore the way the head needs to look at all of this is that they don't want their school to lose out and they'll institute the necessary management to prevent it happening, and the reputation of the school is going to

become more important than it ever was. Certainly the reputation of the school with employers.

Schools without good management were seen to be deficient. And, crucially, good management is linked with the ability to innovate successfully and thus to compete effectively and maximise market share.

> I think these things can be done, if you are really ahead of the game in a managerial sense. Probably 90 per cent of the schools in this country are not. And if we are honest they've not got the managerial ethic. We're trying to bring a culture in which has not existed before in education, and therefore it's going to be extremely difficult to get a lot of this through, without putting money into it. There's no doubt about it, Baker he's spending money on it, but he's going to have to put a lot more in it if he wants it to run like a Rolls Royce. And there is always this thing at the back of my mind that he is trying to do it on the cheap . . . That's what worries me because I think that with the entrepreneurial, enterprising head, with the person who is a good manager, with a person who's got the staff, they'll do it. But there are so few of them about. They're like gold dust. The great majority are going to sit and go, 'Oh God! Woe is me! What am I going to do now?' And that's not what they are paid for of course, they're paid to take on these challenges.

Management and entrepreneurism are tightly tied here to choice, to innovation and to value for money, that is management is seen as an effective vehicle for implementing reform, specifically the implementation of ERA. In describing the work of the Industrial Society with schools Sherrall Andrews draws the elements of change together.

> Another thing that we do is the transport of ideas from industry to education. We're now in what some people describe as a managerialist era, the fact that appraisal is a big issue, and the Education Reform Act is full of things like Local Management of Schools, managing your own budgets and all that that entails, and the imagery of the school. If you are going to opt out you've got to create the sort of image where people are going to want to send their kids . . . So what we've been doing is actually looking at what's happening in industry and saying, 'Can we relate it?' (we don't say it must be related), what's the best examples of things that can operate?'; and quite clearly appraisal sprung from industry. Now there are appraisal systems which are awful, we would concede they are awful, the ticking boxes and stuff, that's not on. But there are appraisal systems like, the first developed with ICI about fifteen years ago.

121

And arguments that attempt to differentiate the world of education from the world of business are seen to be spurious.

> Well, they're too cut off . . . not just from industry, they're too cut off from the realities of life. Things are changing, we used to have an uphill battle with some schools, about the notion of appraisal, or the notion of leadership. They'd say 'You can't compare education to making biscuits. We're not in the business of baking dough, we're in the business of developing minds.' And we'd say 'Yes, fine, okay'. And there are people who say 'You can't measure that', and we'd say 'But you do measure it, you examine them, you test them, you put them through all sorts of assessments to find out how much they've taken in'. And yet people turn around almost as a kind of knee-jerk defence, saying you can't measure what I am doing, it's too pure, too philosophical, they always wheel that one in when they get defensive.

Management is clearly and unproblematically presented as the one best way for schools to organise and compete. Other models of organisation, based on collegiality or professionality (however vague and untidy those notions might be) have no place in this vision of schools. The headteacher is the key figure in the management scenario. The classroom teacher becomes an off-stage subject of management, the to-be-managed, most often referred to in relation to schemes of appraisal, the to-be-appraised.

> If you are really going down the route of saying the person who we call the head or the principal, or whatever, is in fact expected to behave as the manager of that institution, then let him behave as the manager, and let him choose whether he requires a set of advisers or whether he is perfectly happy to put his own balls on the line. I think we have no clear perception of what actually management within the educational sector is. You see, I hear Banham [director general of the CBI] saying that he expects people who are looking after institutions to negotiate their own terms. I can understand that that is a possible model, you can't say it's impossible. But if you want to move from where we are, to that model, then you've got to do some bloody education and training and management exposure for the people who are now heads of those institutions, because they ain't yet fitted for it.
>
> (Sherrall Andrews)

The headteacher needs to be trained to manage; concomitantly the teacher must learn to be managed.

The establishment of management as a separate function, with
unique expertise and responsibilities, and with major and critical
claims to authority upon which the efficiency of the whole
enterprise depends, is a crucial first step to control over the
workforce. Because once this conception of management has been
accepted by workers, they have in effect abdicated from any
question of, or resistance to, many aspects of their domination.

(Littler and Salaman 1982 p.259)

As noted already the ERA clearly establishes a pattern of organisational
control, with the new responsibilities of governors and heads, which
parallels the Chief Executive and Board relationship of many business
organisations. DES Circular 7/88 *Education Reform Act: Local
Management of Schools* spells this out.

Local management will give head teachers power to match their
existing responsibilities. Head teachers are already managers, and
the Secretary of State expects that across the whole range of
decisions relating to local management the governing body will
consult and take the advice of the head teacher. The head teacher
will have the key role in helping the governing body to formulate a
management plan for the school, and in securing its
implementation with the collective support of the school's staff.

(p.6)

Straightforwardly, policy and execution is separated, in classical
management terms. In this structure of demarcation, influence over the
definition of the school is removed to a great extent from the hands of
teachers and placed into the hands of managers. As well as the values
shift that this involves and the organisational implications, the overall
effect of such changes is a reconstruction of the teachers' relationship to
their work, their claims to esoteric skills, and their sense of themselves
as professional practitioners. Robert Joy indicates the general approval
of LMS within the business community.

That's a change that we would welcome, because it does bring to
the staff a kind of business reality which you can't really bring to
the school in any other way. No amount of visits by industrialists
are going to be as salutory as realising that you've gone over
budget, because you spent too much on PE equipment and you
should've spent it on something else. Those kinds of realities of
management are very important, and you'll only change people's
attitudes if you can actually give them the power to run their own
budgets. Business men, of course, could help in that.

In a very basic sense schools are to become incorporated into the logics of capitalism and into the logics of Thatcherism – the extension of popular capitalism. But we must recognise these developments as a particular kind of adaptation to particular kinds of developments within capitalism. The school as a Fordist machine, as mass-producing common, educational experiences, as marked by authoritarian relations and centralised planning and rigid organisation is the wrong kind of image for these changes. ERA contains (at least in its LMS provisions) a very different kind of imagery, 'emphasis shifts from scale to scope, and from cost to quality. Organizations are geared to respond to rather than regulate markets' (Murray 1988 p.12). This is the post-Fordist school. As Jessop *et al.* (1988 p.142) note:

> The post-Fordist mode of accumulation places a lower value on mass individual and collective consumption and creates pressures for a more differentiated production and distribution of health, education, transport and housing.

The key point here is that the dominant mode of regulation within production, and perhaps consequently within education, is shifting from Fordist to post-Fordist.

Post-Fordist education

How, then, are we to understand the industrial lobby in British education? How does this brief account of the discourse of vocational progressivism illuminate the process of restructuring outlined previously? We would do well to consider first the scope of the vocational impetus. In effect, what is being undertaken is a thorough-going reworking of the realisation of formal educational knowledge via the four basic message systems of schooling (Bernstein's three and Bates' fourth) – curriculum, pedagogy, evaluation and organisation. Indeed a shift in the underlying principles which shape curriculum, pedagogy, evaluation and organisation is being advocated and pursued by the schools/industry movement. At the heart of this process of change is another shift, that is in the principles of social control, the mode of regulation, embedded within the processes of social reproduction in contemporary capitalist society. By mode of regulation is meant 'the ensemblement of institutional forms, networks and explicit or implicit norms which assure compatibility of market behaviour within a regime of accumulation' (Lipietz 1985 pp xvi-xvii). As we have seen, such an ensemblement is realised in the key discursive concepts which articulate the industrial lobby – the market, motivation and flexibility, and management. In effect, the processes of schooling are subordinated to the principles which provide organisation and social control within the economy. In Bowles and

Gintis's (1975) and Fritzell's (1987) terms a correspondence is established, or rather proposed, between the mode of regulation of schooling and the mode of regulation in the economy. That mode of regulation, I suggest, is post-Fordist. (Recognising still here that in fact the economy and capital are not of a piece, there is no single dominant mode of regulation. I shall return to this correspondence below.)

We should note, however, that theories of post-Fordism contain two distinct elements. In the first, more limited, usage post-Fordism refers to changes in production and consumption. Change, that is, from the mass-production, mass market, machine-paced production systems of Fordism to the production of specialist, luxury and niche market goods, and production systems based upon 'the application of micro-electronics and information technology to the operations of the firm. The result sometimes termed "flexible specialization" – is an integration of small-scale production with design, stock control, marketing and retailing' (Jessop *et al.* 1988 p.128). The question is whether such changes in consumption, flexible specialisation, and in production, flexible automation, describe real, large-scale, relatively permanent changes in the economy or are partial and epiphenomenal adjustments within limited areas of capital. The second usage of post-Fordism focuses upon the institutional regulation of economic growth and social conflict. Here what is being described is:

a decline in the scope and effectivity of collective bargaining; a shift from private to individualized forms of welfare consumption; a decreased role of the state in securing traditional social-democratic, or inclusive national, objectives; a growing polarization of the population along occupational, regional, ethnic and gender lines; and the consolidation of exclusionary, or two nations, forms of mass integration.

(Jessop *et al.* 1988 p.129)

I have already noted (chapter 3) the introduction of such forms of control and divisions into the consumption of education through the creation of an education market. There are at least two further indications of relationships between changes in industry and the economy and changes in the processes of schooling. First, it is tempting to view the use of techniques like graded assessment and profiling in terms of the development of a new, individualised (and generalised) consumption orientation. The consumption relationship in education that is, as being extended to aspects of the teacher–pupil relationship, and the pupils' acquisition of consumption habits and values. Second, as we have seen, flexibility clearly plays a key role in the educational discourse of those representatives of industry involved in the policy process. They are involved in describing a relationship, a correspondence, between the processes of teaching and learning and the labour process of industry (or at least some sections of industry). In policy terms, and in the practice of certain courses and innovations, like CPVE and TVEI, the correspondence is very real.

Learning plays a key role in post-Fordist production, 'Post-Fordism sees labour as the key asset of modern production . . . machinery becomes a cost, and labour [its] fixed asset' (Murray 1988 p.12). Production relies on multiskilled workers, capable of innovation and the improvement of products and processes. 'Workers are no longer interchangeable. They gather experience' (p.11). Thus, a 'high programmatic quality [is] given to education; training and research are functional for "progressive modernization"' (Rustin 1989 p.64). The post-Fordist organisation is marked also by informal and networked social relations and flat or lateral hierarchies. Skills, knowledge and attitudes are tightly enmeshed here in the formation of the post-Fordist worker. As noted already, co-operative, problem-solving, project-based methods which stress capability – knowing how rather than knowing what (see Jamieson 1986) – offer the best fit between school and the new work. Motivation by reward – intrinsic and extrinsic – and a continued positive orientation to learning is essential to 'the post-Fordist bargain which offers security in return for flexibilty' (Murray 1988 p.13).

Now a detailed exposition of the changes in the message systems of schooling, and their implications, is beyond the scope of our concern here with the policy process. The bases of these changes have been articulated in general terms in the comments quoted above. I will briefly reiterate the key elements in a more theoretical vein. Much of this has been anticipated and adumbrated in Bernstein's work on educational knowledge codes, and it is his original analysis which provides the framework for this exposition (the page numbers refer to his 1971 paper). The application of Bernstein's analysis also points up the degree of confluence and coincidence between educational progressivism and vocational progressivism. The key, in Bernstein's terms, is a shift from a collection to an integrated code in the organisation and relations of school knowledge.

1. The organisation of the educational knowledge code underlying the vocational curriculum is provided not primarily by states of knowledge but rather by 'ways of knowing'; evaluation also emphasises the latter (p.57).

2. The degree of boundary maintenance between contents, the primacy of the subject, is weakened, cross-curricular themes, open-ended investigations, and problem solving, and 'areas of experience' take precedence (p.54).

3. Subject loyalties and specific identities are de-emphasised in favour of generalised skills and competencies (p.55).

4. The vocational curriculum 'will require teachers of different subjects to enter into social relationships with each other which will arise not simply out of non-task areas, but out of a shared, cooperative, educational task' (p.62).

5. The degree of control teacher and pupil possess over the selection, organisation and pacing of knowledge transmitted and received in the pedagogical relationship shifts towards the pupil. Learning is emphasised over and against teaching (p.50).

6. The pedagogies and forms of assessment employed in the vocational curriculum (profiling, graded assessments, process assessments and records of achievement) enable a greater range of the student's behaviour to be made public and to be made subject to assessment (p.65).

7. Bates (1983 p.71) suggests that administration provides a fourth message system of schooling, 'administrative control of the central message systems of the school . . . ensure that constraints exist on the definitions of culture which are able to be reproduced through schools'. The adminstration and culture of schooling is clearly being shifted from collegial and professional forms to managerial (Ball 1987).

New managerialism as moral technology

Bernstein suggests that the mode of regulation, or, in his terms, the principle of social control, underpinning the vocational curriculum is that of conformity rather than submission. This articulates directly with the vocationalists' emphasis on the need for flexibility.

> Changes in the division of labour are creating a different concept of skill. The inbuilt obsolescence of whole varieties of skills reduces the significance of context-tied operations and increases the significance of general principles from which a range of diverse operations may be derived. In crude terms, it could be said that the nineteenth century required submissive and inflexible man, whereas the twenty-first century requires conforming but flexible man.
>
> (Bernstein 1971 p.67)

Furthermore, Bernstein also points to the crucial nexus of motivation which is embedded in the disintegration of previous, submissive forms of control, and the requirements for new, conformist forms: a push–pull of change.

I suggest that the movement away from collection to integrated codes symbolizes that there is a crisis in society's basic classifications and frames, and therefore a crisis in its structures of power and principles of control. The movement from this point of view represents an attempt to declassify and so alter power structures and principles of control; in doing so to unfreeze the structuring of knowledge and to change the boundaries of consciousness. From this point of view integrated codes are symptoms of moral crisis rather than a terminal state of an educational system.

(1971 p.67)

What I am suggesting here is, in Bernstein's terms, a crucial integration between the principles of education and the principles of work – an integration which, writing in 1975, Bernstein felt to be impossible.

There can be no such integration in Western societies . . . because work epitomises class relationships . . . Indeed, the abstracting of education from work, the hallmark of liberal education, or the linkage of education to leisure, masks the brutal fact that work and education cannot be integrated at the level of social principles in class societies.

(1975 p.135)

The point is that the changes outlined above are predicated upon crucial changes in the nature of work and in the nature of class relations which Bernstein had not anticipated. But Bernstein's analysis conjures up one further complexity in this field of change and proposed change. Bernstein's Open School (1967), and his 'invisible pedagogies' can be read either in terms of simply providing new, more subtle principles of social control, or as the basis for a more open and emancipated educational form, or, perhaps as he intended, as containing the possibilities of both. Clearly, some innovations advocated and developed by the new vocationalists *have*, as already noted, opened up spaces for positive change as well as introducing new modes of social control (Gleeson 1987 and 1989).

In policy terms, the industrial lobby, like the New Right, wants to shift the power of determination in educational provision from producers, the teachers, to consumers, but in this case they envisage themselves, as employers, as the consumers. As we have seen, the employers' representatives quoted above advocate a mass, common system of education, not in itself a post-Fordist vision. In this respect the interests of many teachers and many employers coincide as both are faced with the untoward effects of the warming-up–cooling-out dilemmas created by selective, competitive systems of schooling (Hopper 1971). Both parents and employers have been enfranchised to an extent by the provisions of the ERA. Representatives of local business now sit as of right on school governing bodies. The discourses of *choice* and *preparation* have both been pursued, as alternative policy projects, by the Thatcher government. The result in policy debate is both dislocation and incoherence, particularly in the expectations and criticisms being aimed at teachers. The teacher is caught between them; criticised on the one hand, by the cultural restorationists, for throwing out traditional practices and values in favour of progressive methods and curricular, for abandoning the academic (the pressure here is back to visions of the qualities and standards of grammar school education); and criticised on the other hand, by the industrial trainers, for being too academic, too conventional, too locked into traditional school practices and the perpetuation of an anti-industrial bias, reluctant to adapt to technological change, to innovate. The pressure here is forward to a vision of high-tech, state-of-the-art schooling, run like an efficient business, quick to respond to the changing requirements of the market. To some extent the resolution of these two discourses lies in the CTC-embodiment of high-tech, high standards and efficiency, and (in theory) funded privately. The existence of a handful of CTCs, and the attention they attract, provide the image of policy which the government would wish to pursue on a larger scale. But the symbolic role of the CTCs underscores the tensions between mass and elite visions of education. Too few CTCs, and the industrial lobby see them as an expensive irrelevance; too many, and the pursuit of diversity, standards, selection and choice is lost.

Let us now try to bring together the argument about structural crisis laid out in the previous chapter with the consideration of the discourse of the industrial lobby above. The general thrust of the argument has been that the beginnings (but not the origins) of the rise of new vocationalism were rooted in the structural crises of social reproduction which ran from the late sixties to the late seventies, and that these crises were both political and economic in character, the two elements tightly, organically, interwoven. The 1970s, in retrospect, appear as a watershed in the development of economic and social order. The crises and their effects in education, and elsewhere, as moments of uncertainty and chaos, produced claims and the articulation of visions about both what was being lost and what might be achieved. The old humanist vision (and both the neo-liberal and neo-conservative elements of the New Right, in their different ways) looked backwards to the nineteenth century, to Victorian values, to *laissez-faire* economics, to a moral, imperial curriculum, to authority, standards and order. In contrast, the industrial trainers' vision was forward-looking towards the twenty-first century, to meritocracy, to change, to an intelligent, self-directed, self-motivated work force, responsive to incentives rather than orders, to a technological, enactive and inductive curriculum, rather than fixed subjects. These are alternative hegemonic projects. The contrasting versions of education, of what counts as being educated, turn upon differences in economic and political structure. In shorthand terms they rest on the crisis of the Fordist state (Bonefeld 1987) and the breakdown of the post-war interventionist, welfare consensus and the institutionalised class struggle of socialised labour against local capital. The old humanists want to return to some kind of pre-Fordist idyll, based upon the public school and the grammar school and sponsored mobility (Turner 1960). The industrial-trainers are pushing towards a post-Fordist, decentralised, open, contest mobility (Turner 1960) and thus an education system compatible with the desocialisation of production and the individualisation of living labour, and flexible work practices and wages and labour markets. Nonetheless, there are also points of commonality between the two, in particularly anti-statism and an emphasis on self-responsibility. The struggle for influence over policy contains and reflects competing images of the ideal society (Prunty 1985) (see figure 5.1).

In analysing current policy and the policy-making process we must come to grips with the limits of the influence of the vocational lobby, and the divisions and differences within the state and the educational state. In one sense, then, restructuring must be seen as a composite process, the outcome of several distinct policy and political thrusts. The industrial lobby does not unproblematically translate into policy. While the social composition of the state ensures a sympathetic hearing for the interests of capital, the state also responds to other interests and has other concerns. There is no absolute relationship here between the political and the economic: the state develops and pursues its own independent purposes. Thatcherist education policies, in particular, are marked by a combination of the ideological, technocratic, pragmatic and popular. Also different elements of policy reflect the different concerns of elements of the state. Thus, the educational policies emanating from within the DTI and the DoE are very different in emphasis from those of the DES. The DES is much more insulated from the industrial lobby but more closely engaged with the educational establishment. This takes us back again to the conception of the state outlined in chapter 1, and to the position of the dual-polity thesis. What is crucial here is a view of the state which can accommodate 'both the prevalence of key economic interests and the practical effects achieved by less powerful groups' (Saunders 1986 p.217). Despite the attractions of structuralism it should be evident from this that the *outcomes* of policy formation remain to be explained empirically *and* in terms of the purposive actions of individuals. The state itself is not a thing with its own intentions. We need to develop:

	Industrial Trainers	Cultural Restorationists
Form of Analysis:	Schools are too staid, they are too academic and anti-industrial. National economic performance is under threat.	Schools are too progressive, areas of valued national heritage and academic standards are under threat.
Definition of Education:	The needs of industry and the economy. Applied knowledge, flexible skills, correct attitudes and material sensibilities.	The academic, the cultivation of literary and aesthetic sensibilities and the reproduction of heritage. Moral subordination.
Modes of Control:	Consumer control/influence over education, with industry in a position of critical influence. Schools to be made responsive to the requirements of the market.	Stronger state control and a mandated curriculum. The definition of a 'selection from culture'. Proscription of non-subjects and the 'politicised' curriculum.
Styles of Practice:	Innovation, shift of emphasis from teaching to learning. Formative assessments by grade-related techniques and profiling. More schooling based on common provision. Co-operation, groupwork and an emphasis on process and social skills, and ways of knowing.	Tradition, formal relationships between teachers and taught. Summative assessment by examination and selection by academic ability related to separate provision. Competitive individualism and an emphasis on cognitive skills and knowledge for its own sake.

Figure 5.1 'What is it to be educated?'

a mode of analysis which recognizes the crucial role of human agency in shaping state policy . . . but which also recognizes the potential and limitations of the different kinds of demands, interests and preferences which come to be expressed by different kinds of groups through different parts of the state.

(Saunders 1986 pp.217-18).

The processes of restructuring and repositioning education in relation to the economy are multifaceted, in some respects dislocated, and sometimes incoherent. The content and impetus of the new vocationalism needs to be read in subtle rather than crude terms, and against a backdrop of changes within the economy. The relationships of vocationalism to capital and to the economy are complex; capital itself is changing, and is itself diverse. There are significant variations within the vocationalist *oeuvre*: some versions can be seen as dynamic and progressive, some others as 'archaic' (Stronach 1988).

6

Curriculum plc: the ERA, policy, partnerships and the school curriculum

I have already provided some basis for an analysis of curriculum policy making. In chapters 2 and 3 I considered the impact of the New Right on curriculum policy debate and in chapters 4 and 5 the impact of the industrial trainers. Here, and in the following chapter, I explore the role of the state bureaucrats, the DES and the HMI, and the Secretary of State, and their relationships with the educational establishment.

The ERA is the product of a set of complex compromises and coercive interventions and its formation, writing, progress and, latterly, its implementation, constitute a field of dispute and conflict in which interpretation and control are contested. This kind of process of conflict and compromise, especially as regards the school curriculum, is not new. I shall argue below that the school curriculum, and crucially the question of its assessment, has been a long-standing matter of concern and struggle in the educational policy community.

As an educational innovation on a grand scale the ERA is a social process, a product of social and political interaction. Its interpretation and its implementation, both through agencies like the DES, NCC and SEAC and in LEAs and schools, were and are not fixed or foregone. Those who conceived of or inspired or agitated for the Act did not necessarily have much direct influence over its formulation. Bates (1989) points out that

> centralised curriculum change [takes place] within distinct
> *operational* contexts. This term . . . being used to refer to the
> various work contexts involved in the development, production and
> use of new curricula . . . Curriculum production involves not
> simply a dichotomous 'ideology' and 'practice', as is sometimes
> implied, but layer upon layer of social action, involving multiple
> and contradictory relationships.
>
> (p.221)

Duncan Graham, Chairman of the NCC, commented in a talk at King's College London: 'it [the National Curriculum] was set up by people who probably wanted to turn the clock back but it's opened up a rather different Pandora's box'. In other words, to an extent the implementation of the Act has passed into the hands of a rather different constituency with a rather different view of what counts as education. I shall give some examples of struggles over interpretation below. Also, as I have tried to show in examining its antecedents, the Act is in some respects internally incoherent and contradictory. As a compromise aimed to satisfy different interests in the policy community and addressed to different problems in the field of education, the Act clearly has aspects which are crudely cobbled together. For example, in his talk Duncan Graham commented 'in some ways the National Curriculum and the Local Management of Schools are difficult to reconcile'.

In the initial stages of implementation managed by the NCC and SEAC (that is in the process of filling in the empty boxes of the National Curriculum framework and the undefined requirements of national testing), the struggles over the three message systems of the National Curriculum – knowledge, pedagogy and evaluation – have become relatively public. A whole set of levels of struggle are evident.

1. The framework itself is still disputed in some quarters. The inclusion and exclusion of particular subjects continues to be debated and the advocates of excluded or aspiring subjects pursue their case: archaeology, dance and drama for example. As a humourous, but telling, aside, Duncan Graham commented 'people did not write them in when they were writing the Act because they did not have them in their own prep. schools'.

2. The nature and conception of subjects is also a matter of dispute. That which is to count as history or mathematics or whatever is again the basis of competition between groups and interests in and around the field of education. The National Curriculum Working Groups established by the Secretary of State are one forum and focus for these fundamental disputes. And in some instances the opportunity for this kind of semi-public process of formulation has allowed the displacement of established conceptions and the assertion of hitherto minority positions. But, as we shall see the freedom of interpretation available to these groups is very limited.

3. Closely related to the above is the more specific knowledge content and scope of the subjects, related closely to the Attainment Targets and Programmes of Study formulated in the Working Groups.

4. Again closely related is the question of the time allocations made to each subject and the accessibility of subjects to different groups of

students. These issues shade over into ones of both equity and feasibility. The first is the question of whether National means everyone. The second is the question of teacher supply and the ability of the schools to deliver all subjects to all pupils. Also of interest here is the issue of subjects as against cross-curricular themes; the report of the Technology Working Group is the most obviously radical example of a non-subject-based approach. This is a part of the Pandora's box effect referred to by Duncan Graham.

To be clear, I am not suggesting here that the effects of the ERA and the National Curriculum are as a whole progressive or even benign. But there is a degree to which the deliberations surrounding the implementation of the provisions and the Act have moved in directions probably unanticipated by the initiators or formulators of the Act. In particular, the constitution of several of the Working Groups and of the NCC has re-established a base for influence for the Educational Establishment and, more specifically, has allowed the possibility for articulation of what I shall call new progressivism. Certainly the appointment of Paul Black as Chairman of the TGAT Committee and Deputy Chairman of the NCC is significant. He has been a key legitimator for and enabler of new progressivist perspectives in key sites of decision making.

Prior to his appointment as Chairman of TGAT he had a long-term involvement in the development of new forms of assessment and curriculum. He explains:

> I was involved as Chief Examiner of Nuffield A Level [Science] which was part of carrying through the work I was doing as one of the two organisers of the Nuffield Advanced Physics Scheme, and I carried on with that examining for about twelve years . . . and there were other commitments. I had also worked as a member of the Joint Matriculation Board and as a member of their research committee . . . the other point that is relevant, however, is APU work, and the work with the Graded Assessment Scheme [with ILEA] which led to the development of quite different perspectives on the whole business of assessing pupils, and of tying that assessment in with curriculum development and rather radical new approaches, such as the one opening up graded assessment of cumulative credit to pupils, so that they acquired GCSE in stages, with no terminal exam, but simply a final level they had reached.

Clearly, from the point of view of the New Right, cultural restorationists – Paul Black, and others like him in the science and mathematics education communities – are part of the problem rather than part of the solution. Their work presents a severe challenge to traditional forms of curriculum, pedagogy and evaluation.

Politics and policy making in education

Before proceeding let me try to make clear the position and significance of new progressivism. In Williams' (1962) terms this can be
regarded as an influence 'on the very concept of education' (p.161) and
as related to the basic concerns of the 'Public Educators', a commitment
to 'a natural right to education' for all. But new progressivism also
relates to and expresses new interests, it has strong affinities with what
I have called progressive vocationalism. The new progressivist discourse has been most clearly articulated in the 1980s from within the
mathematics and science education communities, although it draws
upon methods and perspectives developed earlier within primary education and English teaching. While not totally unified and coherent, it
gives emphasis to skills, processes and methods rather than content, and
to applications and problem solving rather than abstract knowledge; the
teacher is facilitator rather than pedagogue. New progressivism is also
strongly imbued with several aspects of learning theory and psychology.
The emphasis is learner-centred and constructivist (the view that children construct their own knowledge of concepts and ideas over a period
of time in their own, unique ways, building on their pre-existing knowledge). The emphasis is on the child's active construction of meaning
and, in this, motivation is also a key aspect. The use of graded assessments is specifically related to constructivism and motivation in providing regular and positive, but also diagnostic, feedback to student and
teacher. The emphasis on problem solving, investigations and applications has resonances of Dewey's work. New progressivism in science
and mathematics also contains challenges to the separate subject curriculum. Practical work and investigations stress the need for skills and
concepts to be applied across subject boundaries. The concern with
process, with practical applications and with team work in investigations, and the attention to student motivation make it not too difficult
to identify parallels with the 'progressive' information-based modes of
production, flat hierarchies and lateral forms of communication associated with post-Fordism. But new progressivism, despite its team
work activities, is primarily oriented to individual performance and
reward, based on graded assessments, as opposed to the batch examination, mass, class-teaching approach of the liberal-humanist tradition.

The remainder of this chapter consists of what I have called a history
of curriculum control, a brief and schematic account of the changing
pattern of concerns about and struggles over the constitution and delivery of the secondary curriculum. In this history a number of specific
moments of particular import will be offered in the form of descriptive
and analytical vignettes. In particular, the relative influence and control
of the DES, HMI and Secretary of State over the School Curriculum in
the run up to the ERA will be considered. In the following chapter a
further set of vignettes will be presented in order to capture aspects of

the formulation and implementation of the National Curriculum and National Testing provisions of the ERA.

The long history of the National Curriculum

There are two inter-related points at issue here: first, the changing concerns of the DES and the Secretaries of State for Education with regard to the substance and delivery of the school curriculum, and second, the ambitions of the DES and Secretaries of State to have greater influence upon or control of the school curriculum. It is important to recognise in both respects that the DES is not a thing, an entity in itself, but rather a changing amalgam of particular civil servants and inspectors. So when I write of DES concerns and ambitions I am referring to the motives and beliefs of senior officials and inspectors, and the positions taken up within particular branches or groups. Also it should not be assumed that the DES is of a single mind; there are indications that factions develop around particular issues, like the idea of a National Curriculum (Ranson 1985). Additionally, while the struggles and ambitions described below are presented in isolation, they exist within and are affected by the broader political and economic concerns and 'solutions' outlined in previous chapters.

Salter and Tapper (1985) argue that the DES is driven by a 'bureaucratic dynamic', that it is an 'ambitious bureaucracy' and that 'the Department has succeeded in expanding its control over policy formation in the interests of greater efficiency in the education system' (p.24). But Salter and Tapper (writing in 1984) also see the Department as losing out in policy influence terms to the more dynamic and more flexible and politically fashionable MSC. 'In a period of rapid economic change when demands for new types of knowledge, new ways of organizing knowledge and new forms of certification are emerging almost daily, the DES has been unable to cope' (p.25). It is easy to be wise after the event, but clearly from the perspective of 1990 Salter and Tapper's conclusions were too hasty. As of now the MSC has ceased to be the power it was and the DES has in its grasp a National Curriculum and a programme of National Testing. But Salter and Tapper's analysis was not just too hasty, it was also too technocratic and too short term. That is to say, in my view the ambitions of the DES are not solely driven by bureaucratic concerns of efficiency and control, they are also driven by an ideology of education, a conception of what counts as 'good' education, and in particular what counts as an appropriate curriculum, what Lodge and Blackstone (1982) call the 'ironside traditions of the DES'. And the 'successes' of the DES in terms of the imperatives of control have actually been rooted in a critique of, and concern about, standards and quality. Also Salter and Tapper seem to have been mesmerised in their analysis of the economic and unemployment aspects of the policy context in the early 1980s, and they ignore almost entirely, apart from a belated discussion of the HMI, the very active involvement of the DES and HMI in commentary on, and debates about, the mainstream academic curriculum. When they talk about the ideological space created by the Great Debate they are thinking only of the impetus given to vocational education and the schools/industry movement.

As I have tried to indicate already the ramifications of James Callaghan's Ruskin speech and the Great Debate went well beyond the question of the relationship of schooling to the economy. For example, the notion of *accountability* and the re-enfranchisement of parents as a group to be 'spoken for' in policy making also emerged out of the Great Debate. Fundamental questions about the care of the curriculum by the Schools Council and the LEAs were also clearly crystalised at this time.

> We spoke of accountability then. I mean it's nonsense what some people say – that Callaghan prepared the way for the Tories. We wanted the house to be put in order in a genuine way, with a concern for the service, so that the Tories wouldn't be in a position to do anything, and it's because the service didn't react that they're getting their come-uppance . . . . Those were the issues that ordinary parents had, that schools should be run as much for the children as for the teachers or the Local Education Authority. There should be some accountability. There should be some provision for parents to make comments, and that some standards should be applied, and that teachers who didn't perform should be removed. There's no reason why, if children are suffering from incompetent teachers, that should continue.
>
> (Lord Donaghue, political adviser to James Callaghan)

And, crucially, the speech and the ensuing debate made it possible to talk publicly about the school curriculum and curriculum control in more general terms. The issue of where the control and determination of the curriculum should lie was made problematic. A former senior DES official (B), reflecting on the aftermath of the speech, clearly indicates the way in which the possibilities of determination were changed. In particular, the role of the Secretary of State was thence to become more active and influential with regard to the curriculum. The Ruskin speech and its reception provided a mandate for ministerial intervention.

> Callaghan said things which did outrage some teachers and education professionals, and ought to have outraged them all. It was very popular with everybody else, because (a) it was sensible, and (b) the public actually thought that the government settled

these things. The British public does not understand that hitherto the curriculum has been settled by the schools. One meets very intelligent, well-informed, well-educated people who actually think there are standard textbooks. People almost can't imagine how the thing could have worked relatively well, leaving it all to chance, as it were. Once Ministers said that the curriculum needed to be reshaped in some way, they were increasingly in the business of expressing their own views, and then trying to get people to adopt them, working with the teachers, working against the teachers. What was very clear was that Conservative ministers all had a picture of what a school should teach. None of them would be so foolish or so arrogant as to say, 'I can tell you exactly what ought to be taught'. They would all realise there are things they didn't understand. But I think they would all say, 'If nobody else could tell you what ought to be taught in schools, I think I can. There ought to be this and there ought to be that. And on the whole I wouldn't do much of that and I'd do rather more of this. And I would much rather really that well-intentioned and well-informed and thoughtful and professional and expert people did the thing properly . . . .' I've never heard them say this, but I think they would say, 'Deep down, we have a belief as to what makes a good curriculum'. And if you go around long enough with that belief, and if you are in the business of reforming examinations, you have already embarked on the path of trying to get your notion of the curriculum established in the system. The rest follows logically. The big argument against the Thatcher government going for a National Curriculum has, I think, been the political obstacles, the philosophical obstacles. Is it the business of big government to take on this power? The fear of centralism. But I think they simply nerved themselves . . . I don't think that they'd rejoice in the fact that it has to be done by the government, but I think they are willing to swallow that.

As this interview extract indicates, the interpretations, ambitions, personal concerns, personality and commitments of the Secretary of State are to become increasingly significant in the determination of curriculum policy, a point I will return to below. But he is also aware of the ideological tensions in the Conservative government involved in nationalising the curriculum. The voices of neo-liberal purity, the CPS, and eventually also Keith Joseph, spoke against a broadly determined National Curriculum. Pauline Perry (ex-senior HMI), throws further light on this, and also points to the extent to which the DES officials and the HMI were keen to take advantage of the window of opportunity opened up at Ruskin.

Actually it was very important to begin the exercise of public debate . . . A lot of what's happening now in the Education Reform Bill, I believe, were things which lead back directly to Ruskin, and all of that period of softening up, which I actually think ought to have been long enough for people to have been softened up, but which it now appears that they were not, because they are still shouting that it's all too quick. But if they're shouting now, think how much worse they would have shouted if what Callaghan had done, instead of making that speech and then sending Shirley Williams off to launch the Great Debate, had been to bring in the Education Reform Bill in that year. Perhaps it would have been better actually, the opposition wouldn't have had a chance to form, I mean the oppositon to the ideas, the professional opposition. But I really do see it in a straight line.

Pauline Perry also explains why it was that it was the HMI who initially assumed the pro-active role within the DES. This was a role that the HMI were eager to take on.

Once the curriculum ceased to be a secret garden, we ceased to be a secret army, from the Ruskin speech onwards, governments of both colours moved into the centre of the debate about the quality of what actually went on inside schools. The DES that I joined in 1970 was a very passive central operation. When I was promoted into the DES in January 1975, actually into the building, and I became a Staff Inspector, I was desperately frustrated by this, what I called the sort of 'not us' syndrome. Whatever topic came up, that Ministers would ask, the DES officials would say, 'Oh, that's not us, it's the LEA's', or 'That's not us, it's the validating bodies'. The fact of the way things were run then was that DES centrally was only concerned with what I would call structural matters in education, the structure of schools. Important things, the comprehensive structure in '65, the setting up of the polytechnics, they were very much external structure, and nobody stepped beyond that. The ATO's [Area Training Organisations] dealt with teacher quality; the validating bodies dealt with quality of courses in higher education; the LEAs were responsible for the curriculum in local schools, and so on. And then Ruskin called a halt to all that and said actually what people are really concerned about is not the structure, it's what happens to their kids when they get into school or into college, or whatever. The Great Debate did, for the first time, take those questions into the DES, and Shirley Williams and Gordon Oakes and that team, and people they began to bring into the Department from other parts of the country or at least other parts of Whitehall really did shift the locus, and of course in so

doing they shifted the locus right into HMI's territory. I suppose
the 'it's not us' syndrome inside the department had always
included 'Let them [the HMI] go and worry about it'. They were
concerned with the curriculum. They were concerned with the
quality of what happened in schools, and they were concerned with
teaching quality. And consequently our work was very divorced
from policy. Now I think what increasingly began to happen, as the
policy moved into those territories, the people who had the answers
were the HMI rather than the administrators. The kinds of
questions that Ministers were now asking . . . were questions that
the HMI could answer, and the administrators couldn't.

Two important points arise here. First, that curriculum is becoming a
policy issue where previously it had stood outside the scope of policy at
this level. Second, the HMI's eagerness was substantively based upon a
considerable degree of disquiet and concern about the state of education
– the view of the HMI being that all was not well, that something needed
to be done. Bernard Donaghue, adviser to James Callaghan, and
co-author of the Ruskin speech, provides a sense of the tone of the
disquiet within government. From his point of view, and the view of
many politicians, officials and the HMI, teachers were very much the
focus of the problem.

We oughtn't to have a common or National Curriculum, because
your schools and your teachers ought to be wanting to teach those
things, and I would much rather have a flexible curriculum that
enabled much more local adaptability than there is in the present
Bill, because the teachers and the headmaster are the only ones
who really know what their pupils are best suited for. But we had
reached the point when the hard subjects were being avoided, not
because the pupils didn't want to do them, but because the teachers
were either untrained, or too lazy to teach them, and I saw some of
that with my children. You only go to regulation when self-
regulation fails. One has no sympathy for those professions at all.
If they don't do their own job properly they shouldn't squeak if
somebody else comes in to do it for them. But it's the nature of life
that it won't be as good. Central regulation is never as good.

And Pauline Perry again:

The Inspectorate's messages, before our reports were published . . .
it's less easy to see, but the messages from us, that something was
rotten in the state of Denmark, so to speak, something was badly
wrong with the education system. This had been coming through
certainly from before '76. I would date it from '73, '74, when the
Inspectorate really were beginning to say pretty loud and clear, and

identifying the areas that needed attention. So when Ministers
finally decided, for whatever political and economic reasons, I
mean I don't think they listened to the Inspectorate in No. 10, and
said 'My God, we must do something about education'. And I
think it would have been wrong if they had. I don't think a group of
professionals should determine national policy in that sense. I think
it's right for a Prime Minister to say, 'There's something wrong
with the country, we're going down the nick, we're not keeping up
with our neighbours . . . I need to do something about industry,
something about transport, in the process of all that I need to do
something about education.' And at that point they look for the
people who are saying the right kinds of things, willing to pick up
the baton and run with it, and I think the Inspectorate was riding
high, and has continued to ride high, because we were there, and
there were enough of us around who were willing to pick up the
baton and run with it and do something. We were certainly in a
position to respond.

The other point of interest here is that Pauline Perry sees the issues of
educational crisis and educational change as arising out of public debate
and political and economic circumstances rather than from within the
educational state itself. It is my contention that the immediate
beginnings of the National Curriculum (NC) should be understood as
lying in this period of disquiet. But it is dangerous to re-write or
re-interpret history in the light of the present. While it is clear that there
was already discussion of some kind of prescribed curriculum (after all
Shirley Williams' 1977 Green Paper *Education in Schools* (DES 1977a)
proposed a core curriculum for schools) what was being considered was
minor tinkering rather than major reform.

The curriculum wouldn't have been as rigid or as extensive . . .
because the moment you go to the present extent of the
government, it's both too long and not long enough. It still
excludes subjects which may be emerging, and be very desirable,
and in three years' time we'll want them in. It's all right saying the
Secretary of State can put them in but he won't. So our view of the
curriculum would have almost certainly been that it must include
mathematics and science and literacy, I mean that's really what we
would have put. I don't know what would have emerged, because I
didn't think it was the job of 10 Downing Street to actually draft
the minutiae, it was our job to outline the strategy . . . to put things
on the right line . . . and then hopefully . . . the specialist
department would then get down to the job of making it work, well
they didn't. So I don't know what would have emerged.

(Bernard Donaghue)

The other point to be made about these beginnings is that exactly parallel debates were taking place in the Conservative Party's reformulation of their education policies in the late 1970s. The points of issue did literally shadow those of James Callaghan, Shirley Williams and the HMI. But again these discussions were couched in vague and shifting terms. Disquiet had not led at that time to firm conceptions of policy. Keith Hampson MP explains:

I think Shirley and Jim only played around with the issue of a National Curriculum. To say it shouldn't have been so wide and all-encompassing, it shouldn't have been so statutorily enforceable . . . is actually ducking out. I mean the first working papers, when Shirley started the Great Debate, had envisaged – as we had, when Rhodes [Boyson] was then our education schools spokesman, and I was Higher and Further – very much a core, which was English, maths and science, and it was 7, 11 and 14 testing. I mean we really have come full circle, and it was Shirley's follow-on to the initial discussion document which started sketching in, in inevitably vague terms, what education was, what is the definition, which immediately broadens you out in terms of what you expect to be delivered in terms of delivering the civilisation, the heritage. I mean to say, you're into history, perspectives on the world. You're into geography, and I mean it was Shirley that did all that, of course, driven by the Inspectorate and the traditions of the department.

There were always two views as to what a National Curriculum did, I mean Rhodes was, as indeed he is now, and I think the Prime Minister is, of the view that you're talking about a core, which is really reading, writing and arithmetic, the three R's, and we had ridiculous debates in the shadow cabinet about this, which ended up with Norman [St John Stevas] proposing a fourth R, which was religion. But he never knew anything about the nuts and bolts of his subject, despite seven years in it. So we had the fourth R, because the Prime Minister was very turned on by this, and I mean we get it all now, about worship in schools, daily assembly, all that in the Bill, was always there in '77, '78. And I despaired in a way because I failed really to get them to appreciate, until Keith [Joseph] came along, in the job, that you had to have a broad vocational programme. But when I tried to say that as part of that you needed to have a heavily beefed-up careers structure in the school, the Prime Minister, then Leader of the Opposition as she then was, just wasn't interested. This was the fripperies of education, these guys were parasites, they weren't getting down to the real basic subject teaching, back to basics. Why waste money on careers teachers? So that was the main thrust always, back to basics, and give parents more say. That's what parents want, back to basics.

Here again there are early indications of the disputes about the NC that would be fought out in the late 1980s (see 'Hand to hand fighting in the following chapter), and there are echoes of other rallying cries from James Callaghan's Ruskin Speech, 'Back to basics' and more 'say' for parents. (The Taylor Report *A New Partnership for Our Schools* was published in 1977 and proposed that the school governing body should be composed of representatives from teachers, parents, employers and representatives of the local community.) Another way of seeing this, a way which Bernard Donaghue rejects, is that Callaghan's speech was actually an attempt to steal the critique from the *Black Paper/* Conservative education offensive. Certainly Rhodes Boyson expressed himself pleased with the Ruskin initiative.

> For ten years I have been advocating a return to standards. There will be a great sigh of relief among parents and Black Paper writers everywhere. Let me say we don't mind which government does this and I welcome Mr Callaghan's initiative.
>
> (Quoted in CCCS 1981)

The other major curriculum issue identified in the Ruskin Speech, as we have seen, concerned 'preparation for work' and this was taken up in the Green Paper. Indeed CCCS (1981) somewhat dramatically assert that: 'The Green Paper formally set the seal on the school-work bond as the rationale for schooling: the subordination of schooling to the require-ments of industry was complete' (p.225). However, in and around the DES the debate about the curriculum was not preoccupied with preparation for work; indeed, as I argued in the previous chapter, there has been relatively little enthusiasm for a schools/industry curriculum. This was a particular point of Bernard Donaghue's comment quoted above that: 'the specialist department would get down to the job of making it work, well they didn't'. Inside the DES the focus was almost exclusively on the liberal–humanist mainstream. The senior DES official B again:

> I think you will find neither Keith Joseph nor Kenneth Baker are instrumental technologists. They have had little difficulty in assenting to the three propositions in the White Paper, *Better Schools*, that the objectives of education are: (1) to develop personal potential, (2) education for citizenship and (3) education for work. All three are there, but they're in that order. If you listen to the wilder voices in Whitehall, you'd think that education was only for work. I think there are two reasons why this sort of highly

instrumental view, of preparation for work . . . hasn't totally
prevailed, though I notice that the education world claims that the
National Curriculum is that as well. But both Joseph and Baker
would never conceal the fact that they are broad humanists as well.
They do think that the two worlds will come together, that you
can't be a modern person unless you also have a sense of history
and literature and art as well as science, of course, and maths, of
course, and technology. Baker is enormously keen on technology
– keener than Keith Joseph. I think that's one reason. The other
reason is that this extreme view isn't shared by industry. If you ask
the fellow who makes sprockets down the road, he just says 'I want
somebody who can make sprockets'. But if you asked a larger firm
that deals with difficult problems, whether it's RTZ, Unilever or
the oil companies or Marks & Spencers, they say 'No, we want
people who are adaptable and can be trained. We don't want them
to have special skills, we'll give them all that, but we want them to
be basically numerate, basically good at communications, we want
them to have all the nursery virtues.' By the time you've done all
that, you've gone through a very nineteenth-century view of
education. They believe that that will give them a much better
labour force. And of course they're right, because that's exactly the
sort of labour force their competitors have. The German, French,
Dutch and Swedish labour forces consist of people who've on the
whole been fairly roundly educated, who have not been
vocationalised at 12 or 13 or 14.

The argument is a familiar one, a defence of general or broad education.
As we shall see, the key documents emerging from the DES/HMI over
the ten-year period from Ruskin stick closely to this position.

The argument so far has been concerned with the increasingly assertive curriculum voice of the DES and particularly the HMI following
Ruskin. But it is important to be clear about the nature as well as the
substance of that assertion. It is crucial to underline the point that at least
in the first ten years – 1976–86 – of this new interventionist/pro-active
era the assumptions about curriculum change, curriculum policy and
curriculum control were still rooted in the prevailing discourse of partnership. What the DES, HMI and Secretary of State were attempting
was to be more influential. There may have been those in the DES who
were more avaricious but they were constrained by the discursive
possibilities for policy making in education operating at that time. Thus,
these policy muscle-flexings did not go unopposed at this time, and the
resistant voices, or some voices, sometimes, had to be listened to. But
resistance also has to be set against new more insistent voices being
recruited to the Department. (Particularly in the 1980s, those officials

recruited from the MSC.) The discourse of classic partnership was beginning to break down. Keith Hampson reflects on this period.

There were other people who came through who were very much strong interventionists. There's an understrata of DES civil servants who tended at the time, I think, of the Yellow Book [see below] probably about assistant secretary level, who fed on particularly the HMIs and what they were saying on the schools. They wanted to move into what was known in the Department, as the secret garden (the curriculum), and I think there's probably always been a tradition, which has been the minority tradition, to want to get their hands on it. But the overwhelming tradition of the DES was not to do so, and that dichotomy has always been there, but clearly it moved. There's a whole series of HMI reports, during the last Labour government, somewhere around '76, '77, I think . . . which seem to me to indicate this. The DES was suddenly very keen to produce HMI reports. Suddenly there was a great pub-lication spate on curriculum thinking, which there never used to be. And then suddenly they wanted to get all this out, because they were all in the business suddenly of trying to change the climate, and I think that's what's happened actually, the whole climate has changed. But at that point there was enormous hostility, the unions, the local authorities, the chief officers, everybody was against it. It is all a very interesting episode of the change of an intellectual cli-mate, over a decade and a half, well it's two decades actually, and that's the problem, it's taken a decade longer than it should have.

Two points then need to be established. First, the period 1976–86 is marked by a slowly increasing degree of active intervention in and determination of the curriculum by the DES and HMI. The possibilities for intervention were gradually being changed as the general discourse of policy making shifted and, particularly after 1979, as the Conservative government became more confident and assertive in its implementation of ideologically driven legislation. Second, in or around 1986 there is a decisive break. The discourse within the DES moved from one articulated in terms of influence to one articulated in terms of intervention and the need for legislation. The complex, slow and dif-ficult process of trying to create a new consensus about the curriculum by use of indirect means (see Campbell 1989) was replaced by an explicit commitment to impose a National Curriculum on schools.

Now I am offering here an analysis of the recent history of cur-riculum policy making through the reflections and recollections of some of those directly involved. In this two notes of caution need to be entered. (1) No single account can be taken to be definitive; each is an interpretation of events from a partial and self-interested perspective. It is the composite, cross-referenced, general picture that is important. The various contributions here (and the many more not quoted) have to be set alongside and against one another. (2) The self-interest of the parties involved and the individuals quoted has several effects on their accounts, not the least of which are a tendency to emphasise their own impact and influence and a need to render their own motives primarily in terms of rational and altruistic concerns.

In retrospect the period from 1976 can be seen in terms of a series of ratchet steps, each one based upon a firmer, more clearly-defined and more clearly-determined curriculum. Attempts are made to mobilise acceptance at each turn of the ratchet – a process of climate-building. One current DES civil servant (F) explains these changes and shifts in the following way:

Well it was very much the trad DES one of working with local authorities, going with the grain of what they were doing, but pushing them a bit further in that direction, trying to encourage the laggards to catch up, using HMI consultation papers. As I recall it then, it all seems a bit before the ark in a way but, we are thinking very much in terms of continuing the series of HMI publications on the curriculum, as a means of encouraging authorities towards better practice, building on good practice where it existed . . . I mean I've worked on the curriculum on and off and in one of the earlier periods of my career I did the analysis of replies to circular 14/77. And at that stage authorities actually had to construct their curriculum policy for the most part in order to be able to reply to the circular. And it was my impression through contacts with that area off and on, that the Ruskin College business and the Great Debate and the circular – I mean all in a very inefficient, uneconomical way – did cause quite a lot of work to go on in local authorities, discussion groups and so on, and that was the kind of rather Heath Robinson type machinery that we operated. But calling it by that name doesn't, in my view, denigrate it, because that may actually be the sort of way in which you really need to get people involved in change, in order to get it to happen in schools. Anyway that was the way we were operating then. It was much less top-down I would say, even in *Better Schools*, than it has become now. In *Better Schools*, Walter Ulrich, who was then the Deputy Secretary responsible, took the view, which we tried to follow, that you've got to define the curriculum somehow. If you're talking about it, you want to talk about it in a way that makes sense to as many people as possible, then you're rather forced back on to traditional subjects, although you have to make all sorts of caveats about a curriculum description not necessarily being a description

147

of a timetable. Anyway we did get quite a lot of flack on that and on various aspects of that, but it's interesting that in meetings I attended with outside people in which the National Curriculum proposals in the Education Reform Bill were discussed, people were taking *Better Schools* as it were a kind of model of consensus of where we were on the curriculum, and contrasting that favourably with the government's most recent proposals.

I was closely involved in the drafting of *Better Schools*. I did the draft of the chapter on the curriculum. I mean at that stage we were not particularly thinking in terms of legislating for a National Curriculum, so to that extent there was a break between the present proposals and what I think was pretty much of a continuum since 1975–6 really, in terms of government policy, and no very noticeable difference in national policy on the curriculum, despite the change of government, so there was a discontinuity there. But, nonetheless, one could say that the new proposals drew on a great deal that had gone on previously. So probably of all the bits in the Bill, from my perspective, it looked as though the National Curriculum had the deepest roots.

It's not so clear to me that some of the other aspects of the Bill had such a long track record. Financial delegation, I suppose, is something the Department's always been interested in, and they have been watching closely what's been going on in other authorities, so there is an instance where the history of the policy actually is not so much within central government, but rather more central government watching what's happening outside and then drawing on it. But as for things like grant maintained schools, and policy on ILEA, you need to ask politicians a bit more about the antecedents of that.

Three key points here: (1) That in DES terms the school curriculum is essentially made up of subjects. (2) The ERA is a decisive break from the existing view of curriculum policy. And (3) the speaker is distinguishing in his terms between political and non-political aspects of the ERA, those rooted in DES orthodoxy and thinking and methods and those not – in other words, the DES and non-DES bits. There is also an attempt here to render the National Curriculum into the terms of a new kind of partnership and a new kind of consensus, to reassert continuity. Kenneth Baker's successor, John MacGregor, put considerable effort into this kind of consensus building and reassurance work. In a speech to the Secondary Heads Association (2.10.89), he asserted:

I know that many teachers have been reassured that the National Curriculum will not be a complete break with the past. Everything published so far has shown that its feet are firmly planted in existing best practice. We know that great things can be achieved because we already see that happening in the most successful schools.

However, in focusing upon the DES and HMI, it is important to recall that they were not, and are not, the only agencies seeking to define the curriculum. The relationship of the DES with the Schools Council, the SCDC, the New Right think-tanks and latterly with the NCC, also need to be accounted for in an examination of curriculum policy. These are, or were, *competitors* in the curriculum arena. Thus, two chronologies or mini-histories need to be briefly outlined: one to trace the series of DES/HMI publications and circulars concerning the curriculum in the period 1976-86, and the responses to these, and the other focused upon the conflict between the DES/HMI and their competitors. Neither history can be told exhaustively in the space available here, and, of course, they are not separate histories.

Publish and be damned?

The publications emerging from the DES from the mid-1970s onwards were mainly but not exclusively penned by the HMI, and the positional/discursive role of the HMI is of particular significance in understanding the impact and effects of the flow of documents. McClure (1988) suggests that:

> There is no doubt that the Department [DES] responded to the opportunity which arose in the mid-1970s to take an active role, in areas where hitherto the DES had been obliged to tread carefully. Sir William Pile, the Permanent Secretary from 1970 to 1976, had already begun to prepare the ground by strengthening the Inspectorate and opening the way for it to assert its inspectorial role over that of friendly advice.
>
> (p.158)

Salter and Tapper (1981) add the view that to some extent the Inspectorate had in this period come to replace the role of the Consultative Committees, and in doing so had moved into a closer relationship with other parts of the DES. But Lawton and Gordon (1987) are careful to spell out the ways in which:

> the views of the HMI on curriculum issues are very different from those of the DES. We suggest that this is not a chance difference of opinion, but a fundamental question of educational as opposed to bureaucratic values. Within what is generally referred to as the central authority or the DES there are three competing ideologies.
>
> (p.113)(See also figure 1.1)

The sudden burst into public print by the DES and HMI from 1977 on is a fascinating and extraordinary manifestation of their new assertiveness. The Inspectorate sought to establish itself as the authoritative voice on matters concerning the school curriculum, articulating a curriculum discourse of some sophistication but rooted in the liberal–humanist tradition. In a language of consideration, reason, appeal and moderation, the HMI output quickly established a set of limits and possibilities for reasonable and acceptable discussion of curriculum matters. The process is classically Foucauldian, 'the extraction, appropriation, distribution and retention of' (Foucault 1981) knowledge about the curriculum, was based upon claims about an overview of school practice drawn from their inspection activities and was patently translated into an enactment of power, a process of centralisation of authority – the authority to speak about the curriculum, 'discourse is not simply that which manifests (or hides) desire – it is also the object of desire' (1981, p.52). Pauline Perry:

> The people who had the answers were HMI rather than administrators. The kinds of questions that Ministers were now asking were questions that we could answer, and the administrators couldn't. Now a new breed of administrator very rapidly grew up, I mean they're very bright and very intelligent people, who began to inform themselves, but they began to inform themselves very largely through us. We were suddenly leading them around the schools instead of occasionally responding to a question that they asked. And the focus I think did become very firmly on what the Inspectorate was doing and saying, and of course the great shift was when our reports began to be published, which, I suppose, meant that action was taken when problems were identified.

The HMI were able to provide a 'certain economy of discourses of truth' (Foucault 1978 p.93).

Here the power and the discourse are policy. Campbell (1989) argues that 'on my reading of the situation, HM Inspectorate have taken on a directly interventionist role in policy-formation, despite their constitutional position and regardless of the cautiously laundered language in which they write' (p.165). The possibilities of debate and determination, in substantive and practical terms, were being drawn into the centre. Other possible sources of authority in these matters – the LEAs, the teacher unions, and the Schools Council – were being excluded, drowned out by the concern and commitment, and the 'will to truth' of the inspectorial voice. This formulation of a new regime of truth about the curriculum parallels that other displacement of voices achieved by the New Right, as described in chapter 2. Part of the process of establishing discursive authority over the school curriculum lay in debunking, revealing the supposed inadequacies, of other conceptions and other sites of authority – from the Schools Council to the classroom. (This is a crucial precursor to the idea of a National Curriculum, conformity to the national being asserted against the effects of local variations.) Thus, in its gentlemanly and somewhat arcane fashion the HMI was also engaged in a campaign of derision and assertion. As Maw (1988) puts it:

> in the drive towards centralisation, a reorganised and more pliable HMI are to act as the organic intellectuals of the DES legitimating central intervention by providing justificatory information and by promulgating a correct curriculum message through their impeccable professional voice.

> (p.55)

The documents speak about curriculum but also fabricate control. I asked Pauline Perry:

SJB: Would you see then the origins of the National Curriculum being in those early HMI papers?

PP: Oh, very much so. If you think what Shirley Williams did do, she did launch Circular 14/77, she did begin to move . . . all of those things were necessary. Most of us felt, although we were frustrated and wanted it all to happen of course, they always told themselves, 'Well we've been at the heart of it, we've been working on it, we've been debating, we've been publishing the stuff and it seems old hat to us, why the hell can't the system just do it tomorrow?' But then we would remind ourselves that it's all very well for the middle of the wheel, but for the message to get out to the periphery takes much longer and we thought well, Shirley's not daft, she's giving them time to absorb the ideas and so on and it was a softening-up process, there was a great shock wave went through the education establishment, as you know, with the Callaghan speech. Then with the Great Debate people did realise that they were being hounded into a corner, that they had to do something. Circular 14/77 was a very necessary piece of groundwork because the mythology was that the LEAs were doing everything 'about the curriculum', they had it well in hand, and of course what it demonstrated was that they didn't. Nobody was managing the curriculum. The British education system had no curriculum, and there was no curriculum philosophy, no curriculum theory, the LEAs didn't even know what curriculum was going on in their schools.

Here we find all the elements of discursive shift and discourse management. The HMI were wanting to fill the vacuums of philosophy, theory and policy for the curriculum. They are articulating a *mission*, a professional goal, expressed in the form of ambitions for curriculum change (Bucher and Strauss 1961, Goodson 1983). The DES officials, as Pauline Perry indicates, were less well placed in the mid-70s to take on a proactive role; the 'not us' syndrome was still evident. As one civil servant (C) explains, with only weak forms of influence at their disposal, officials found it difficult to become interested in curriculum matters.

SJB: Do the DES aspirations for some greater say in the school curriculum go back to Shirley Williams' Green Paper?

C: I don't think so. I think the politicians were very much on the lead until very recently. My branch, for example, which had the whole school curriculum, used to consist of one Assistant Secretary, which is one grade down from me, covering all of the things that I now cover, plus one or two other things as well, and that was the sort of weight that was given to it in the Department. There weren't great aspirations. Until quite recently, the DES were happy to sit back and say, we are a small policy department, that's the responsibility of the LEAs. We think great thoughts, we put out guidance, which says the Secretary of State wishes and the Secretary of State expects, but we have no lever to make it happen. Now that has changed, as soon as you start legislating, as soon as you take powers to issue specific grants, the whole basis of the game has changed. DES administrators have started getting interested in the curriculum and taking a more active stand in the curriculum. But that's really only during the last six years and before that it was very much HMI themselves, beginning to get interested in the curriculum, and the Curriculum Matters series was, I suppose, the first evidence that they were beginning to take a stand on what the curriculum should look like, as opposed to going out and looking at it in schools. That's all fairly recent developments, late '70s onwards. Started by HMI, then the administrators coming in behind. Things like Cockcroft [Report] maths, response to a general feeling that maths was being lousily taught, and the Science Policy statement 1985, those were the first two things that showed the DES administrators getting in on the act and showing an interest. And also Curriculum Matters, too, which was the basic statement about the curriculum 5-16, from HMI, that I think was also 1985, so the manifestations have been fairly recent. Then there was a circular that went out to LEAs that said 'Look, shouldn't we try and get some more standardisation into the curriculum?' That was post *Better Schools*, which was another example of the interest beginning to show. So I don't think it goes back into the Dark Ages, I think it's an '80s phenomenon.

The process begins in earnest with the so-called Yellow Book (1976), the brief produced for the Prime Minister's Office by the DES in advance of the Ruskin College speech (*TES* 15.10.76) and the 1977 Green Paper. In the Green Paper, on the question of the curriculum, in the predominant tone of commonsense ablandishment, four major concerns are stated:

1. The curriculum has become overcrowded, the timetable is overloaded and the essentials are at risk;

2. Variations in the approach to the curriculum in different schools can penalise a child simply because he has moved from one area to another.

3. Even if the child does not move, variations from school to school may give rise to inequality of opportunities.

4. The curriculum in many schools is not sufficiently matched to life in a modern industrial society.

Even though these points of concern were never taken much further by the Secretary of State, Shirley Williams, the grounds of debate about and arguments for some kind of National Curriculum were now initiated. McClure says of the Green Paper: 'it summed up the administrators' approach to the restructuring of the education system to bring it, by incremental stages, from the 1960s into the 1980s' (1988 p.158). Significantly, also, the Green Paper provided an opportunity to restate a role for the Secretary of State in relation to the definition and control of the curriculum. Part of the discursive work of the Green Paper is the re-articulation of a hierarchy of responsibility for and authority over curriculum matters: in particular the role of the LEAs in reviewing the curricula of their schools, the role of the DES in receiving, analysing and articulating the outcome of the review, and finally the role of the Secretaries of State in issuing any appropriate advice. Despite the subtlety of the language some very significant repositioning work is being done.

Fowler (1988) says the 'initial curriculum signals from the DES and HMI were couched in a general and hortatory form, but a working party of the inspectorate had simultaneously been developing a more detailed document under the title *The Curriculum 11–16* (DES 1977c p.41). The introduction to the document, a set of working papers on individual subject issues, again dealt with the case for a common curriculum. The themes of disorganisation and unacceptable variety from the Ruskin speech and the Green Paper are picked up and elaborated. What is conjured up is an image of chaos and the absence of authoritative voice. The idea that schools and teachers might be operating according to their own well-thought-out theories and procedures is not considered, rather they are seen as being isolated and as learning from their own mistakes. Autonomy is cast as a problem and is set over and against 'partnership in curriculum planning' (DES 1977c p.2). The solution is obvious, rational and undeniable, 'some common framework of assumptions is needed' (p.2). By defining the problem in its own terms the document can also define the solutions in its own terms.

A common-core school curriculum is proposed which would occupy 75 per cent of pupils' time. But crucially this document develops in two significant ways from Ruskin and the Green Paper. The terminology has shifted subtly from a 'core which is common' to a 'common core' (p.3); while the previous core was modest in conception, the HMI describe their common curriculum as 'broad and makes substantial claims on time' (p.5). Further, a compulsory core is now seen as inadequate in itself, the contents and goals of the common curriculum also need to be defined, 'as a body of skills, concepts, attitudes and knowledge' (p.7). Thus, at this point there is no particular prescription of subjects. Indeed the idea of a subject basis to the curriculum is played down, 'it is not proposed that schools should plan and construct a common curriculum in terms of subject labels only' (p.7). In strategical terms this can be seen as a very interesting ploy, for the argument used to construct this ideal curriculum is not political but essentially educational, it is overlaid with a patina of theory. The HMI do not claim to speak about the curriculum solely in positional terms but from a basis of conceptual argument. Nonetheless, the text also speaks 'powerfully'; it argues but it also proposes. According to Fowler (1988) these curriculum papers are 'a landmark in curriculum debate' and 'marked a considerable step forward in the detailed consideration of national curricular aims and objectives' (p.48). The idea of a National Curriculum was firmly on the public policy agenda.

However, we need here another analytical caveat. Despite the comments above, what is being described here is not a simple history of desire, neither is it a history of progress. I am not outlining the unproblematic assertion of desire for or untrammelled progress towards a National Curriculum. While there were undoubtedly some voices in the DES speaking for greater prescription and intervention the key actors in this drama of power were not subtly and strategically in control of history. I asked Sheila Browne (ex-Chief HMI):

SJB: Would it be far-fetched to see the start of the public process [in 1976] as being the origins of the Education Reform Act? That it was the beginning of a process of the shift of power and influence over the curriculum towards the Department and the HMI?

SB: No, I don't think it ever crossed our minds that that would be the result or would be desirable . . . It would never have occurred to me that what I was doing would generate anything like the crude formulation of the Reform Act.

Nonetheless, the production of curriculum discourse, indeed any discourse, is the play of power. And the 'effects of power' in this *oeuvre* rest heavily upon the inscription of truth, objectivity and reason within the texts. Thus, some representations of school knowledge and the school curriculum were authorised while others were blocked and silenced. The documents operate within a stance of omniscient rectitude, and the unstated claims to knowledge and skills in relation to curriculum matters by the HMI are crucial in this. The documents *did* have the effect of moving the grounds of debate and *did* have the effect of reconstituting the roles and relationships of the speakers and listeners in matters of curriculum. Teachers would listen while the DES and HMI spoke. The possibilities of the National Curriculum were being forged in these publications.

This discursive process is also cumulative and *ad hoc*. It cannot simply be reduced to the intentions and ambitions of a few key actors. Each contribution, from whatever source, ramifies and re-articulates existing concerns and assumptions. In a sense, the discourse speaks for itself and policy makes itself, as new documents are added to the *oeuvre*. It is not a process of fine strategic, political control.

Four key documents were published in 1980 and 1981, that is during the early period of the Conservative government of Margaret Thatcher. They are *A Framework for the School Curriculum: A Consultative Paper* (DES 1980a), *A View of the Curriculum: HMI Matters for Discussion* (DES 1980b), *The Practical Curriculum* (Schools Council 1980), and *The School Curriculum: A Recommended Approach* (DES 1981a). Again there are two basic points I want to make about these documents. First, they represent a further marked escalation in the language of intervention and assertion by government. Second, they are in some respects competitive documents and represent claims being staked for a say by three competing agencies in the curriculum field: the DES, HMI and Schools Council. I will return to this point in the second brief history below (p.160).

A Framework clearly extends the line of arguement begun by Ruskin and the Green Paper. It stresses a divided locus of responsibility for the school curriculum between central and local authority and reaffirms that LEAs should have clear and known policies for the curriculum provided by their schools. The paper also extends discussion of the 'core':

The difficulties and uncertainties attached to the application of the core concept do not mean, however, that it may not be a useful one in carrying forward the public debate about the curriculum to the point at which its results can be of practical benefit to the schools.

(p.2)

The basis for a common core has now gone beyond the point of argument and debate to the stage of practical necessity. Problems and objections are swept aside; alternatives do not even get any consideration.

A Framework (DES 1980a) moved the grounds of practical debate on in another sense; not only was the content of the curriculum being prescribed but so also was the distribution of time to be devoted to each subject. Fowler (1988) says of *A Framework*, 'The worm of centralist prescription emerged in the further declaration that the Secretary of State considered that all pupils should devote specific amounts of time to each of the common core subjects' (p.60). Another basic principle of the National Curriculum is put into place.

A View (DES 1980b), the HMI document, was referred to in *A Framework*. *A View* reiterates the concerns about untoward diversity and the basis of 'broad aims of education' underlying 'essential areas of understanding and experience' (p.1). Again 'there are sufficient grounds for unease to suggest a need to re-examine the rationale and organizational structure of the prevailing curriculum in many secondary schools' (p.2). It is proposed that science and a modern language should be part of the compulsory core for all pupils, leading to a substantially larger compulsory element.

The DES *The School Curriculum* neatly straddles the watershed of material influence which these documents are in part addressing. The conception of 'broad educational aims' (p.1) is outlined once again, but the principles that individual schools are to 'shape the curriculum for each pupil' (p.4) and that 'neither government nor the local authorities should specify in detail what the schools should teach' (p.5) are also included in the preamble. However, significantly, the role of school governors is emphasised, perhaps indicating a shift in the definition of that which counts as 'the school', and a 'Recommended Approach' to curriculum planning is presented. The work of the Cockcroft committee (1982) is also significant in this assertion of influence. The committee was under pressure from the DES to produce a definitive core curriculum for mathematics and did, in fact, outline a foundation course, to which few objections, of principle or content, were made. This was later adapted to become part of the National Criteria for GCSE mathematics.

Chitty (1988) discerns significant differences between the DES and HMI versions of the curriculum evident in these documents and others – that is an HMI 'professional common-curriculum approach' which 'reflects a genuine concern with the quality of the teaching process and with the needs of individual children' and 'seeks to undermine traditional subject boundaries and uses subjects to achieve higher level aims' (p.34) (this version interpellates a well-motivated, well-trained and skilled diagnostic teacher), and a DES 'bureaucratic core-curriculum approach' concerned with 'the efficiency of the whole system and the need to obtain precise information to demonstrate that efficiency' (p.35) (the interpolation here is of the accountable teacher). This latter version, whilst still imbedded in a liberal–humanist conception of content, gives some indication of the long-standing interest within the DES in an assessment-led approach to curriculum development and curriculum control.

The final document to be considered here involves a further shift in climate, and articulates very clearly the particular concerns of the next Secretary of State, Sir Keith Joseph (1981–86). Sir Keith shifted the grounds of curriculum discourse from entitlement and coverage to standards and quality, and from a content-led thrust for change to an assessment-led one. In his speech at the North of England Conference in January 1984, and in the DES White Paper of March 1985, *Better Schools* (DES 1985b), Sir Keith asserted that the dual aims of the Conservative administration were to raise standards of schooling, at all levels of ability, and to secure the best possible return from the resources which were being invested in education. He referred to the first of these in interview; he also indicated his frustration with the lack of a sense of urgency on these matters among civil servants:

> I think what I can claim to have achieved is to have shifted the emphasis from quantitative to qualitative, and I think that is now accepted across the House. When I arrived at the Department of Education, I found honourable and diligent civil servants who had scarcely had time to think about quality because they had been so preoccupied with roofs over heads, in the growth of the child population in the '50s, '60s and '70s, and I suppose I have to understand that. But I found them almost indifferent – no, that's unfair – almost unaware of the urgency of doing something about quality. And to the extent that I shifted that thinking and to the extent that my arguments in the House with my opposite numbers achieved a certain amount of agreement, it was that quality was top of the agenda . . . There's no doubt that the Prime Minister has taken fire about quality. She is passionate about this. There's no doubt that Kenneth Baker is. I don't perhaps go along with every one of the components of their Bill but I rejoice that we are going to try and do something about it. God knows how we will do it because I am far more impressed about the sheer difficulty of state

education and I think I made a number of blunders in some of the emphases I put.

In the North of England speech he announced plans to define levels of achievement for all pupils from 11 to 16, to make 16 plus exams into criterion-referenced measures of performance, and to bring 80–90 per cent of all pupils up to average levels of performance in the existing 16 plus exams. He offered examples of the sorts of attainment targets he envisaged in a range of subjects. In the White Paper it was claimed that the basis for a common curriculum, now set at 80–85 per cent of each pupil's time, had widespread agreement. What was envisaged was that 'The 5–16 curriculum needs to be constructed and delivered as a continuous and coherent whole in which the primary phase prepares for the secondary phase and the latter builds on the former' (p.1).

As Fowler (1988) notes:

> Much of the curriculum argument in the *Better Schools* White Paper will be regarded as treading on by now familiar ground: it must be observed however, that the overall stance of central government was becoming, perhaps ominously, increasingly definitive.
>
> (p.78)

Indeed some aspects of *Better Schools* found their way into the 1986 Education Act, but significantly the Act still envisaged the responsibility for 'determining and organising' the school curriculum as lying with the headteacher, although the Act also bolsters the role and changes the constitution of school governors. The headteacher was increasingly having to look to the Governors for approval on curriculum policy matters.

Better Schools can be seen as both the last of the first phase of the change in curriculum control and the first of the second phase. It would appear that full-blown curriculum legislation was still not being contemplated at this time, but the package of attainment targets – a broad common-core curriculum articulated in terms of subjects and cross-curricular themes – is complete.

Sir Keith did not envisage a legislative National Curriculum, indeed his political philosophy set him firmly against the idea. But clearly, Sir Keith was not averse to the use of indirect forms of intervention, as in the approval of GCSE criteria. It is evident that following his initiatives with regard to the secondary curriculum he was intent upon making similar inroads into the primary, again by using Attainment Targets (introduced in *Better Schools*). Attainment Targets, as a mechanism for defining curriculum and assessment, were to become a fundamental element of the National Curriculum. Keith McWilliams, Chief Executive of the SCDC, offers his view of this period:

> But you see I honestly don't think that that [a legislative National Curriculum] received much impetus until after Keith Joseph had gone. From all that I knew of Keith Joseph, and we spent quite a lot of time meeting at that period, he was chronically incapable of taking that kind of decision. It took the sharpness of Baker to really give the DES the green light to go down that road. I am sure that within Elizabeth House there were people who were thinking like that. I don't think whilst Keith Joseph was there, there was much chance of it. So that one only got glimpses from odd things that some civil servants might have said about it.

Keith Hampson, MP, supports this:

> I think the argument, when one looks at the official side, the HMI side, there's been a strong emphasis for the need of a National Curriculum. And the argument has only really been about how far that should be statutory, and how far you can assume that it could be carried out on a voluntary basis. And Keith took the latter view when he was Secretary of State. But I think that he was also culpable for not being able to make up his mind for several years. So I think it is ironic that he is now faced with a *fait accompli* and suddenly makes up his mind. But I don't think that's a basic dispute. I think that if you want a base curriculum you have no choice but to make it statutory. I mean the whole nature of the way British education works would frustrate the intent otherwise. That's not to say that we've still, these days, got the immensely powerful chief officers that we used to have, but some of them are still quite independent . . . I think we will move eventually to having education as a central grant which will be specific and will probably go as it used to, not to general purposes and finance of the Authority, but direct to education, as the system more or less used to be. But certainly the independence to a certain extent is there . . . and increasingly, as in Leeds, it's the [local] politicians that run the education service and not the strong, independent-minded chief officers. So it would be absurd in that sort of new world, to expect any voluntary fitting-in within guidelines that the government wanted. It would be totally productive of running friction.

Again Keith Hampson sees the curriculum issue as being tied up with more general aspects of control over education, and particularly the relations between central and local government. For many of those involved the idea of an Education Reform Act became a reality only with the arrival of Kenneth Baker as Secretary of State. A civil servant (F):

The rather more positive stance being taken by the Department on a number of issues is linked with his arrival personally. And from my own position I do feel that it's hard to over-state the extent to which this was Kenneth Baker's Bill. I would say that he, probably more than anybody, any single civil servant in the Department, knew the details of the Bill fully. Because I mean while obviously senior civil servants responsible on the schools side or Higher Education side knew their bits inside out, Baker was involved in every detail right across the board and he does have a great ability to tackle matters of detail and get involved.

I shall return to the role of the Secretary of State and the provenance of ERA in the next chapter.

Rivals at court?

Having arrived at the eve of the 1988 Education Reform Act by one route I now want to backtrack somewhat and approach the same point from a different route, a second mini-history. Here I want to consider the changing relationships between the policy rivals in the education field and their struggles for 'voice' and for influence in curriculum matters. Primarily this involves an examination of the relationships between the DES and its ministers, between the DES and the HMI, between the DES/HMI and the Schools Council, and the SCDC, and to a lesser extent the impact of New Right think-tanks and advisers. Significantly the representatives of the LEAs and teacher unions, except in so far as they were active through the offices of the Schools Council and SCDC, are almost solely absent in the account, although I will touch upon 'the problem' of the LEAs and teachers. I shall deal with these relationships fairly schematically here, given the limited space available, and the analysis will be indicative rather than detailed. (Again only a small proportion of relevant data can actually be quoted here.) In terms of curriculum policy the key question that is addressed here is not which curriculum prevailed but rather whose curriculum prevailed.

For a long time the DES was seen in Whitehall as one of the least prestigous and least interesting ministries from the point of view of both civil servants and ministers (see Hennessey 1989 p.427). In 1975 the OECD report on the DES had strong words on the style and effectiveness of the Department, arguing that the stance of the DES seems 'to preclude the possibility of interpreting the role of education as an agent for innovation and social progress' (THES 9 May 1978 p.10). However, the report also commented upon the Department's tendency to want to 'understate as much as possible the full role of government in the determination of the future course of educational policy and even minimize it in the eyes of the general public'. The subtle management of the status quo and the strategic use of indirect influence and manipulation by senior officials has often been underestimated. Kogan (1975) claims that 'the Department can itself act as an interest group ... [wielding] determinant authority and great power' (p.169). The ideologies of partnership and pluralism have tended to bolster the impression of far greater latitude and openness in policy debate than was actually the case (see Gerwitz and Ozga 1990). Lodge and Blackstone (1982) comment that 'an ad hoc, pragmatic pattern of consultation means that the process can be controlled by the DES, possibly in a way that protects the "departmental view" from orchestrated opposition' (p.25). And they go on to say 'arguably, the DES pursues a strategy that is designed to contain and manage the influence of outside pressures' (p.27). And, as argued by Salter and Tapper (1985):

> Like all institutions, the Department has over time developed its own momentum, and its own inertia, which means that its exercise of educational power runs in certain policy grooves. While on the one hand, the Department has succeeded in expanding its control over policy formation in the interests of greater efficiency in the educational system, on the other, it has shown itself less than adaptable in the face of new pressures for educational change.
>
> (p.24)

Some public evidence of internecine tensions associated with the expansion of control emerged through the publication in 1980 of the documents referred to above, *A View* and *A Framework*. Of course they can be read and are often represented as complementary, but their relative policy status, their claims to influence and to effect are at least ambiguous. For almost the first time the DES 'voice' on the school curriculum was being heard directly, separate from that of the HMI. By all accounts the documents were prepared independently. Lawton and Gordon (1987) argue that:

> on the question of a centralized curriculum, sharp differences between the DES and HMI emerged very soon. When the department's *Framework for the School Curriculum* appeared in 1980 it had not been scrutinized and commented upon by the HMI curriculum experts; this was a major technical blunder on the part of the DES. Instead of a united central authority front on the curriculum, there were two rival documents.
>
> (p.110)

Commenting in more general terms, Paul Black (TGAT Chairman) says:

I have to make sense of the fact that the way the HMI were talking about [the curriculum] was very different from the way the DES were talking. There was quite clearly a strong difference of approach, in terms of how HMI think in terms of whole curriculum planning, and broad curriculum aims and, after that, in terms of those aims, how subjects justify themselves. For the DES subjects are self-evident goods, and you put them down as obvious, and then you think about what's not been covered. Those are poles apart in their approach and that difference has been evident in all the documents that came out in the early 1980s.

Again the DES view of the curriculum as subjects is significant.

In the case of the 1980 documents the added spice in this concoction of voices is that the Schools Council also chose to write and publish a general document on the school curriculum, *The Practical Curriculum*. Sheila Browne commented:

I never understood why the Schools Council felt obliged to do that. We were asked to write *A View of the Curriculum* and we wrote it. And the interesting thing was that it was the HMI that was asked. It wasn't, as I remember it, in the first instance, the Department. But the Department, because of its relations to ministers, felt that it needed to write. But the Schools Council could never write for the political system.

Whatever the degree of latent or overt rivalry between the DES officials and the Inspectorate, both appeared to regard the Schools Council as an awkward, unnecessary and unruly third force in influencing, speaking authoritatively about, the curriculum. For some in Elizabeth House, the Council was clearly an expensive and inefficient disappointment; for others it was a power base for trade union and Local Authority influence when such influence was increasingly unwelcome in the sphere of policy making (of any kind). Whatever the analysis, from the mid-'70s on the Council was to be subject to greater and greater pressure and criticism from officials and inspectors. The 1976 DES Yellow Book described the work of the Council as 'mediocre' 'because of this and because of the influence of the teachers' unions this has led to an increasingly political flavour – in the worst sense of the word – in its deliberations . . . '. This provoked a stern response from the then Chairman, Sir Alex Smith, who expressed his displeasure in a letter to the Prime Minister. Nonetheless, in 1978 Secretary of State Shirley Williams amended the Council's constitution to reduce the effective influence of the teacher unions and put financial control in the hands of the DES and LEA representatives. In the early '80s the DES found in Keith Joseph a minister equally if not more antagonistic to the Council.

An inquiry was initiated, to which DES officials gave evidence, reportedly strongly negative (see Plaskow 1985), but which recommended the continuation of the Council. Keith Joseph did not accept the recommendations of the inquiry and in 1984 the Council was abandoned and replaced by the SCDC and SEC, whose members were directly appointed by the Secretary of State.

Not surprisingly the two sides in the Schools Council saga tend to see the processes of critique leading up to abolition in different terms: as logical, rational and justifiable on the one hand; as malicious, manipulative and calculated on the other.

The latter view is offered by Alan Evans, Education Officer of the NUT. He sees senior officials in the DES as engaged in deliberate and careful strategies to undermine the position of the Council.

> They may have been in favour of abolition because they thought that teacher unions were stroppy, bloody-minded, and they were prepared to tell lies. They told Keith Joseph that the reason that the Schools Council had to go was that the teacher unions were particularly unimpressive. They were a destructive force. One in particular did more than anybody else to kill the Council; he was the arch, pernicious, mischievous, propagandist. He was quite disgraceful. He saw it as a political exercise and a propaganda exercise that would then leave the Department free to influence curriculum structure. There were one or two people in the mid-'70s onwards and they grew in number. But they didn't have the skills. I mean the document they drafted *A Framework for the [School] Curriculum* in '79 was pathetic. And I dubbed it *The accountants within the Curriculum*. Some 17-year-old could have written it. It was awful. The reason why their *School Curriculum* document is much better is that HMI must have written chunks of it.

Keith McWilliams, Chief Executive of both Schools Council and SCDC, was in a unique position to witness the end of one body and the beginning of the other.

> For four months I was functioning as Chief Executive of a body that was to be created, and supervising the last rites of a body that was to be annihilated. And it was worse because it took place in an atmosphere of a lot of bitterness, acrimony and controversy. The Schools Council did not not lie down and just expire quietly. The unions in particular felt pretty strongly, and within the Local Authorities Associations there were some strong views. So that there was a fair level of distrust and a feeling that the new body, the SCDC, was going to be, well you may have heard the phrase, a poodle under the control of Keith Joseph, so the atmosphere was

pretty grim. That is the political atmosphere. In-house you had all the problems of a group of people feeling threatened, not knowing whether you had a job or not because the SCDC was to be a smaller and a different organisation. It was not automatic or axiomatic that you would appoint people from the Schools Council. Indeed there was a lot of political pressure to say that that was not acceptable. The SCDC had to be seen to be different and that was not just the view of the DES and the ministers, it was to some extent shared by the Local Authorities Associations. So it was not an easy decision to identify people who would fulfil a job in the SCDC and other people who wouldn't.

The changed basis for the new body, the SCDC, is clearly important in the politics of the school curriculum. So, too, was the DES attempt to impose on the Committee a highly restricted brief.

One of the very earliest meetings that Roger [Blin-Stoyle, SCDC Chairman] and I went to with Keith Joseph to talk about the possible work of the SCDC, and Walter Ulrich [Deputy Secretary] was there. He enunciated this policy that your job is to fill the gaps and don't you worry about the broad curriculum. It didn't come from Keith Joseph's lips, it came from his lips and I don't think Ulrich was ever positive about the SCDC. I would've thought he tolerated us and I think he saw that some sane and sensible things could emerge from a body like that. And in my view one of the reasons for what happened in '83 was the need to get the GCSE show on the road. The DES people were obsessed with the SEC. They had a much more high-profile Chairman and Chief Executive and the money was going in that direction. Now possibly in retrospect one could see that we could keep our head below the parapet and get on with the new stuff and therefore we weren't the focus of earnest attention from people like Ulrich, provided we didn't do anything daft.

(Keith McWilliams)

Again there is indirect evidence of the DES interest in an assessment-led mode of curriculum change and control. This is now in the period when, in effect, the DES and HMI have staked a firm claim for having the sole (or dual) authoritative view of the school curriculum. Having dispensed with the Schools Council the emergence of another different, or dissonant voice, speaking to the Secretary of State or with his authority would have been discomfiting. The Chairman of the SCDC, Roger Blin-Stoyle, explains:

To begin with there was suspicion and a degree of hostility because we had Schools Council's projects and the DES had great fear of bodies that were to some degree independent, and we were independent. Half our members and half our finance, and that's the important point, came from the local authorities. So we had to walk a tightrope of independence from DES and LEAs, and to begin with our relationship with the DES was slightly prickly. They were terribly afraid of a body saying things that they didn't approve of. And, for example, in our first meeting we decided that we must look at the curriculum as a whole and have views on that.

The SCDC were not, in Keith McWilliams' phrase, 'to rock the boat'.

This began to come to a head with the infamous filling-the-gaps definition of our role that Keith Joseph enunciated – that we would fill in where there was an odd gap in the curriculum. That we were nothing to do with curriculum policy, that was a departmental responsibility, therefore whole curriculum issues were supposed to be off the agenda and we were to concentrate on doing bits. We were not to start getting involved in the whole curriculum . . . I can well remember in the first board meetings that the civil servants who came constantly warned the board off those general broad curriculum issues, and that went down very badly. It went particularly badly with the local authorities who were still smarting that they were not constitutionally recognised as full partners. They didn't see that this new body should be limited and confined. In the curriculum sense how do you know the individual needs of small parts of the curriculum unless you have an understanding, a picture of the whole? You can't do your job, you've got to have a concept of the curriculum, and Roger Blin-Stoyle certainly subscribed to that view. So that was one of the very early tensions that came up and I think we were pretty skilful at not making it an enormous issue because if we had we'd have been slapped down. After all the DES were now in an evolutionary sense more and more in the driving seat . . . And it is not surprising that you find early on tensions because on the one hand you have people who wish to maintain the autonomous, free, independent virtues as they were seen by the Schools Council against central government, who were pulling in the reigns and wanting to have a much more direct body. So although the SCDC was called independent, as far as the DES ministers were concerned it was not to rock the boat . . . So I think given that we started from a low level of resourcing and low expectations and very restricted freedom what we have achieved has been good and I would rate it a success in that sense. I believe that the SCDC has contributed far more than people thought it could initially, and it has done far more controversially than some people wanted it to do.

In effect by 1984 the DES/HMI had succeeded to a great extent in clearing the ground for their own discursive control of the education policy field by marginalising or muting the possibilities for voice available to the teacher unions and the LEAs. With the abolition of the Schools Council they no longer had a position from which to speak with authority on curriculum matters. Indeed a whole variety of routes into the arenas of policy formation were being closed down. Alan Evans again:

> The really significant change in style came with Keith Joseph. There are two things they've been trying to do: take away power and influence from Local Authorities and [take away] power and influence from teachers. It started with the 1980 Act, it is the manifestation of taking power away from Local Authorities and giving it to parents. And then you get the curriculum document of the department in 1981, *The School Curriculum*, and you get Sheila Browne's document *A View of the Curriculum*, which was a much better, more professional document. So that process started although we were still consulted a lot, we still had the Schools Council, and the APU was meeting regularly and so on. Then Keith Joseph came in and gets rid of the Schools Council . . . And now people sit on the various bodies, CATE, the Steering Group on Records of Achievement in 'their personal capacity'. And under Keith Joseph it gets into its own, the marginalisation of teachers' unions, the reduction in their power of influence. And of course the unions played into their hands by not establishing their own curriculum body. The LEAS should have said 'Right, fine, we'll have our own'.

It was a mistake in Alan Evans' view for the unions and LEAs not to establish their own curriculum organisation, an alternative place from which to speak.

Update: Early indications suggest that relations between the DES and NCC and SEAC are not without their problems. The division of responsibilities and authority with regard to curriculum and assessment have produced at least a degree of tension. Particularly in regard to the NCC, the question is 'Who advises the minister?' The NCC official remit, 'to provide independent professional advice on the school curriculum' to the Secretary of State, can be seen as an interference in the traditional relationship between minister and officials. Senior NCC officials have not been happy with what they see as DES attempts to 'mediate' their advice. This has been interpreted as an attempt by certain senior DES officials to impose constraints on the scope of NCC activities. In substantive terms the DES have continued to push hard for a subject-based approach and are suspicious of NCC's work on cross-curricular themes. The TES (29 October 1989, p.4) reported that:

A tense battle involving civil servants and top officials of the National Curriculum Council was fought earlier this year over a report which should have played a key role in the introduction of the new curriculum.

Mr Kenneth Baker, the Education Secretary, is understood to have liked the report but was prevailed on by civil servants not to publish because it would have undermined the policy of seeing the national curriculum as consisting of 10 foundation subjects . . .

Tight-lipped NCC officials present at the launch of the annual report this week would say only that the delay was a technicality and that publication was now imminent. The council sees this as a crucial victory in a much longer battle over its right to publish without interference from civil servants. Senior DES officials had demanded that the council should not be allowed to consider reports unless they were cleared by civil servants.

In part at least the exclusion of the unions and LEAs from the educational field can be seen in political terms as reflecting a more general ideological commitment within the Conservative government to insert market economics and market discipline into the public sector. One senior DES official (B) certainly saw this to be the case:

There is amongst senior ministers a distrust and dislike of local government, which is at its most extreme when you get left-wing, or apparently left-wing, authorities. But they are not necessarily well disposed towards local government even when it's Conservative. To take an example, the whole of the inner cities' policies, working deliberately with private enterprise, that is obviously very sensible, but as far as possible working so as to cut out the Local Authority is based on certain preconceptions. It stands to reason, that if you wish to take away power and influence from local government, you have to ask yourself whether all that power and influence goes entirely to the private sector, or whether, it has to be retained in government, if it has then to go to central government. The bill [ERA] squeezes Local Authorities from both ends. I mean, they undoubtedly lose a great deal in the scheme of delegation, and when that's worked through the world will be different. They undoubtedly lose some of their institutions to central government. Although the local authorities have been very slow in seeing that they had a responsibility for the curriculum, they were just beginning rather sleepily to play that part and now it has suddenly been taken away from them. England is finally modelling itself on the rest of Europe including Scotland . . . I suspect when you look back on it as a historian this is just the maverick English getting slightly nearer to European practice.

Clearly also within the DES there was a long-term sense of frustration among civil servants stemming from their inability to direct educational spending. The block grant is a blunt instrument when it comes to education policy. An ex-deputy secretary (A), explained:

> It was absolutely idiotic, there was no power to make grants to local authorities from DES . . . We could not fund any experimental pilot schemes, we were completely hamstrung, people were very frustrated.

Sir Wilfred Cockcroft sees the ERA in more general terms as a product of such frustration.

> The background to the Bill is one of frustration. I think I would want to argue that it's frustration in many different ways. There's the frustration of not knowing how to judge a school, and can you be sure the local authorities know how to do it? There's the bigger frustration of central government versus local government in terms of expenditure, but those have been there since, well you can go back as far as Harold Wilson.

In education the construction of 'blame' for supposed shortcomings, building on the discursive foundations laid by Callaghan's Ruskin speech and the Great Debate, identified the quality of both teaching and local administration as root causes. Such a construction could both distance the DES/HMI from blame and justify their claims for greater intervention and influence. Both the quality and the mechanisms of Local Authority management of education were being indicted.

However, many of the provisions of the 1988 Education Reform Act, in dismantling great parts of LEA responsibility for the processes of schooling, can be seen as stemming from the more general Conservative offensive against Local Authority powers. While Alan Grunow, Secretary of the AMA, rejects the idea of an 'attack' on Local Authorities by central government, he certainly sees the provisions of the ERA as unfair.

> To describe it as an attack is to use the language of the politicians and I try not to. I think what this government has done has been to challenge a number of assumptions about the role and place of the local government. Its motives for doing so I am sure include distaste, horror in some cases of what they have seen happening, although I have to say that most of the things they quote are London based and that really does make northern politicians cross . . . The government sees local government as having a place in the governance of the country and it is a place with far less discretion than perhaps was previously accepted, and they would

argue that discretion is not consistent with the government's responsibility for guaranteeing provision of essential services. It is about being much more enablers of services to be delivered than direct providers, which is consistent with the competition proposals, it's consistent with the opting out proposals.

He went on to say:

And the opting out business, whether it's decentralisation or privatisation. I think that the bill has prejudged the value of LEAs, found them wanting. Or the Secretary of State has found their value below what he believes it should be, but he hasn't actually attempted to say there should be a different value. I mean if they are good enough to be able to reflect what the community wants in a variety of other services, what was so sacred about education? And I think the Bill does badly, too badly, by LEAs.

The ERA presents one solution to 'the problem' of Local Authority control over and national co-ordination of education, and the possibilities of policy making are shifted accordingly. But this was not the solution envisaged by Keith Joseph. Phillip Merridale, Chair of Hampshire Education Committee and Conservative Leader of the Employers' Panel within the Burnham Negotiating Arrangements (which dealt with teachers' pay negotiations until abolished in 1987), explains:

And, of course, in those days, nobody dreamt of the present Baker Act, and Keith Joseph was a constitutionalist to his finger tips and would never have contemplated, in my judgement, the present Education Act. But what you are trying to do is to bring about the state of affairs in which, within the concept of partnership, you can actually get us to do your bidding. Now what we've got to do is to find some way in which that can be rationalised, and his idea of that was that we should have a series of agreements. He had the idea of a National Curriculum to which we would all subscribe. He had the idea that there would be an agreement that the Local Authorities would be bound by, to teach, within the structure of the National Curriculum and whereby they could be held to account by the HMI if they didn't. He had a view that we should come together for the organisation of the structure of the teaching profession – how many people should be trained and so on – and that we should jointly agree how schools should be managed, and in what manner we would control the problems of falling rolls, and all the various other things. All the problems of management could be settled by agreements entered into between the government, as

an active partner, and the Local Authority, as the executive arm
that carried out the work.

Now I did explain to him when he put this proposition to me that
the difficulty with it was really that it would be like negotiating
with the Holy Roman Empire. You might get the emperor, which
would be me, to sign the treaty, but when he came to tell all the
electors, dukes and whatever, that that was what they were going to
do, they would raise two fingers and tell him to get stuffed because
he had no executive control over them, and therefore we had a
problem of the autonomy of Local Authorities. If he was going to
seek to bring about by agreement an enforceable and formal
agreement, I doubted whether we could go as far down the track as
he wanted to go because there would be individual free-standing
sovereign authorities. And you can think of a few without much
difficulty that would say, 'No, that is not for us'. He thought we
could probably get a good way down the road. In the event, of
course, his chances of doing so were hamstrung by the heightening
political tensions between left and right in national politics.

This was, in effect, the last attempt in the period 1985–86 to construe
education policy making within the framework of the post-war partnership. Increasingly the LEAs were seen by government as unreliable
partners. The ERA, as Allan Grunow explained, rode roughshod over
the sensibilities of local government, Conservative as well as Labour.
Central authority would now be the focus for curriculum policy.

To some extent, at least, this shift, in both determination and
definition, has to be seen in relation to the effects of the teachers'
1984–86 industrial action and Keith Joseph's personal and political
exasperation with the teachers and their Local Authorities. The action
clearly turned on more than pay (see Pietrasik 1987 and Ball 1988) and
the introduction of proposals for managing the workforce as part of an
attempt at a productivity deal (November 1984) can be linked to a
concomitant move towards managing the curriculum. The status of
teachers as workers is very much related to the degree of indeterminacy
available to them in construction and delivery of the curriculum (Jamous
and Peloille 1970). The introduction of some form of National Curriculum would reduce indeterminacy considerably. Phillip Merridale
clearly indicates the link between the specifics of the pay dispute and the
more general issues of education policy.

I think, impatience with our inability to get a permanent structured
settlement of these two basic defects, the administration – agency
or partnership – and the salary question. That is, how do you
provide an agreement, a working agreement for a professional who
must, if he is to be successful in doing his job, enthuse? How do

you legislate in a salary agreement for enthusiasm? Those two paradoxes, which lay at the heart of the difficulty, surfaced to such an extent that the present Cabinet said, 'We can't go on like this. There must be a really radical solution to this problem'. And you have thus the Education Act, which still shows traces of the genetic origins of the work of Keith Joseph . . . the National Curriculum, the call for quality, the search for teachers in shortage subjects . . . all manner of elements of that Bill clearly show the groundwork that was done by Keith Joseph in his search for a complete solution to the problem, but overlaying that and very much more visible to the general public, are the structural and contractual changes.

To spell out Phillip Merridale's first point, the issue is one of control over teachers and their work. Should they be regarded as autonomous partners, making key curriculum decisions in the staffroom or classroom, or must they be reduced to agents of policies which are decided elsewhere? Phillip Merridale sees the 1985–86 industrial dispute as precipitating the shift from the former to the latter. This too is fundamental to the formulation and implementation of the ERA, it is based upon a new conceptualisation of the role of the teacher. What we have here are the structural and material counterparts to the interpellations referred to above. Part of the change in the policy process under analysis here is a change of means as well as of ends, a matter of new roles and forms of control as well as a new definition of education. In Phillip Merridale's terms the teachers are no longer partners in policy formation and instead they have become agents of policies determined elsewhere. Furthermore, part of the new definition of the teacher was to be a new set of formal expectations and conditions of work – a contract, a revised pay structure and systems of appraisal. Keith Joseph's concern with *Teacher Quality*, the title of his 1984 White Paper (DES 1984d), and his sponsorship of appraisal and new forms of school management can be seen as the culmination of a long political campaign waged against teacher autonomy.

Pauline Perry again:

It was part of his [Keith Joseph] conviction, which I wholly share, that all the attempts to improve education founder, unless you get the teaching force right. You can change the examinations system, you can change the curriculum structure, you can change the schools structure, but if you've still got the wrong people standing in front of the class, or looking around the class, whatever they're doing, you're not going to actually impact totally on the pupil. Put yourself for a moment in the policy seat. If you were a Secretary of State tomorrow and you wanted to do something to help the kids of this country, how do you do it? How do you get better teachers?

171

Well you can do something about selection, you can pay them more, you can put in appraisal, you can put more in-service, you can improve the quality of the initial training, have bonus incentives, or make it easier to fire them; all of these levers are there, but a combination of any one or two of them and you can make things worse, not better. Joseph certainly, I think, returned to that as the central issue in education. I think he really did deeply believe that getting that part of the formula right was crucial. And he was willing to pay more money, he did recognise that paying more money was an important part of the equation. But he was determined not to pay more money without something, some assurance that it would be tied to quality, and that's where you run into all the deep waters that caused that horrendous three years of confrontation and so on [teachers' industrial action 1984–86], and yet it's right.

Thus, the run up to the ERA has to be seen in relation to the reform and displacement of the teaching profession. The ERA is predicated upon an entirely new relationship between the state and teachers. Philip Merridale also makes the crucial comment that the decision to embark upon radical legislation was taken at Cabinet level. The teachers' industrial action, concerns about teacher quality, the hostility toward local government, the influences of the New Right critique, and frustrations within the DES seem to have provided a powerful impetus. The new Secretary of State, Kenneth Baker, would take office with the specific task of bringing education under control. It was clearly also decided that education would be made into a major issue for the 1987 General Election.

Fairly briefly again I have tried to trace the development of the DES and HMI roles in curriculum policy making up to the eve of the ERA. But, as mentioned several times already, there are other positions in the changing politics of curriculum in this period which have to be accounted for. One, of increasing importance, is that of the Secretary of State; another is that of the New Right, and a third is that of the education professionals, particularly those I have identified as new progressives (these are discussed in the following chapter).

7

Colouring in the boxes: the struggles over a National Curriculum

In some of the general commentaries on the origins and construction of the National Curriculum, the curriculum itself and the process of formulating the curriculum are seen as a simple translation of political ideology into subject knowledge. Things are not that simple, as I hope to demonstrate here.

The Secretary of State and the school curriculum

As noted already, in the 1980s the Secretaries of State (and their respective Ministers of State) began to play an increasingly significant and high-profile role in the field of curriculum policy. I want to look here at some aspects of that new role and also, more specifically, to compare the concerns and interventions of Keith Joseph and Kenneth Baker in curriculum matters. I will take opportunity to look again at the decision to introduce a National Curriculum by legislation – the interplay of ideology and politics is complex.

Curriculum policy has clearly become a political issue in the 1980s, but at the same time it has increasingly been subject to the personal preferences and beliefs of the Secretaries of State. While Keith Joseph may have shifted his ground significantly at a later stage, all of my relevant respondents saw him as the originator of the concept of the National Curriculum. But it is important to make the point that Keith Joseph's view of education policy was very strongly value-led. His reflections upon his work in the DES, and his attitudes to DES officials and the HMI, indicate several of his key concerns: his orthodox neo-liberal commitment to minimal state intervention and non-compulsory schooling and the concomitant critique of policy as unhealthily dominated by a producer lobby; a suspicion of the untoward effects of compulsory schooling; his belief in standards, in the academic, and in particular in the role of grammar in English teaching, and a belief in the need for curriculum differentiation – a specific and relevant curriculum to the 'less able'. He said in interview:

Yes, I'm sure I should have. I should have fought against
flabbiness in general, more than I did . . . I thought I did, but how
do you reach into such a producer-oriented world? So far as HMI
are concerned, I think that they have only slightly improved their
performance as guardians of standards. Only slightly. They're
imprisoned by the system they operate – a system that tends to
discount motivation. You compel children to go to school, you've
got them as prisoners and if some of them truant, too bad. Now that
system is the one the DES has to operate. They're unlikely to say
'Let's jettison the whole system', and politicians who reach that
position are unlikely to go along and say, 'Let's go back to 1870'.
And short of going back to 1870, one is very limited in what one
can do. Very limited. I tried to escape from that constraint by way
of an examination reform, judging that if you can . . . require
standards on a differentiated basis, that you're not being unfair to
the people who don't happen to be academic, on the other hand
you're stretching the academic and you're stretching the
non-academic in appropriate ways. Stretching was my favourite
word; I judged that if you leant on that much else would follow.
That's what my officials encouraged me to imagine I was
achieving. I invented the GCSE, I invented the differentiation. I
said I'd only agree to unify the two examinations provided we
established differentiation, and I now find that unconsciously I
have allowed teacher assessment, to a greater extent than I
assumed. My fault . . . my fault . . . it's the job of Ministers to see
deeply . . . and therefore it's flabby. And if you have a flabby
examination system, and a compulsory attendance, you can't
guarantee benefits and results.

Keith Joseph's personal sponsorship of the final introduction of a common 16 plus examination, the GCSE, and his direct involvement in
setting National Criteria for the examinations was considerable. Sir
Wilfred Cockcroft, Chairman of the SEC, explained this and indicates
the extent to which the ministers at the DES were together becoming
involved very directly in detailed aspects of the school curriculum.

The Joint Council were to produce the criteria in draft form.
They'd been out, they'd been consulted, and the department also
had a view which had obviously been formed over quite a time
before we were set up. There were clearly Inspectorial views and
Sir Keith Joseph, as he was then, had views himself about what
should be there, witness the empathy in history. You know the
mind boggles when you think of four Ministers of State and a
Secretary of State sitting down to consider a science syllabus, when
there wasn't a scientist among them. When the Secretaries of State

sat down, that's when empathy came into history and social
responsibility went out.

This level of scrutiny of and involvement in curriculum matters by the
politicians foreshadows the detailed interventions of Sir Keith's successor. But Keith Joseph's ideological position clearly differentiates
him from several key aspects of his successor's Education Reform Act.
In particular, he set himself against the idea of a common, standard,
National Curriculum

> Look, the most important word in my GCSE initiative is the word
> 'differentiated', which isn't widely understood. Namely that you
> test people according to their potential, not by a common standard.
> And for that reason there are meant to be differentiated papers and
> differentiated questions, as you know. Now I'm not convinced
> about the 'national' word in the phrase National Curriculum
> because I want more breathing space, as I say, more air, more
> variety, but you don't find me defending either myself or the
> Conservative Party, but I reckon that we've all together made a
> right old mess of it. And it's hurt most those who are most
> vulnerable.

It was on these ideological grounds that later, in the House of Lords,
Keith Joseph actually found himself in opposition to his successor's
Education Bill. In collaboration with Labour Peer Maurice Peston he
moved an amendment to reduce considerably the scope of the National
Curriculum. The idea of a broad fixed curriculum would certain not sit
well within a Hayekian vision of an education market.

A civil servant (C) commented:

> He [Keith Joseph] still wanted to have a broadly-based curriculum
> for all pupils, but at the same time he wanted them all to have
> flexibility to do other things in the fourth and fifth years at
> secondary school. And I think he recognised that this was an
> inconsistent and untenable position. And he tried to put it in terms
> of not legislating but exhorting, that's the line that he'd taken in his
> White Paper [*Better Schools*]. He was heavily got at by the Centre
> for Policy Studies and that also showed up in putting down
> amendments which said 'Let's go for a core only' and then further
> amendments that said 'Let's add history and design and
> technology', because he was got at by other people.

Keith Joseph's period as Secretary of State displays a number of paradoxes. Not only is there the move away from formal examining towards
greater use of course work assessments in GCSE but in other ways his
administration provided official validation for a new wave of

educational progressivism. In effect, the exclusion of educational intellectuals begun by the blunt commonsense of Ruskin and the withering criticisms of the New Right and culminating in the closure of the Schools Council began to breakdown. Those I have called the new progressives were being given a voice within curriculum policy making. One respondent explained:

> Keith Joseph was totally convinced that you had to motivate the young, you had to teach them the right applications . . . and that the one-off exam was not the best way of doing either of those two things and so I don't know who talked to him. He talked to a lot of people outside the Department, and used his own brain . . . I think that it was the political network which on the whole was pushing him in that direction, because my impression is that he was under quite a lot of pressure to stick to some pretty academic practices. Of course the *Secondary Survey* was about and he did read that, and that has some sad things to say about the waste of time in the later secondary curriculum . . . but I mean Philip Halsey, of course, when he was knocking around, before he got to his present position [Chairman of SEAC], he brought a lot of knowledge of schools, and what it was actually like . . . *Cockcroft* of course, the Cockcroft Committee reinforced it. Though the funny thing was that they were in advance of their own constituency, because they were saying that industry didn't need [arithmetic], or that it needed it in a certain form.

Keith Joseph's approach to curriculum change, based on exhortation rather than legislation, wherever possible, was evidently not shared by his Cabinet colleagues or the Prime Minister. Even so, the White Paper *Better Schools* (1985b) continued with the principle of devolved control over the curriculum. Sheila Browne and Pauline Perry explain:

> SJB: *Better Schools* sort of slipped a bit didn't it? I mean there's a large gap between the Education Reform Act and *Better Schools* . . . I don't think it's intentional . . . it's just different hands.

> PP: It was he who really put the National Curriculum on the map. It was Keith Joseph who said, we are going to have a National Curriculum, and started all that. That's what the White Paper *Better Schools*, says: 'We are going to have a National Curriculum', and describes what it will be. And it was he who started the discussion documents on the National Curriculum, and what he said was, 'We will have a discussion document on each of the building blocks of the Curriculum'. I think the fundamental difference, although he now believes he is wrong, since his intervention in the Lords, between him and Baker is that he would

have been prepared to express the eight building blocks of the
Curriculum in words other than subjects and Baker would not. And
you know I think that it is an ideological thing which probably
divides a lot of the way the two of them [Joseph and Baker] see the
world.

The final point to make about Keith Joseph as Secretary of State again
relates to the point of transition noted already between reform of
education based on influence and radical change based upon legislation.
Several respondents made the point that most of the elements of the
ERA were well established within policy debate before the run-up to the
1987 General Election, but that the bringing of these together into a
single piece of legislation was not being seriously contemplated. If
Joseph laid the groundwork of ideas, Baker provided the political will to
carry them through (as well as bringing a few ideas of his own). Pauline
Perry commented:

> These things aren't new with Baker. The DES put a lot of money
> into the experiments in Cambridgeshire and Croydon and so on, in
> its devolvement in school finance. It wasn't being done perhaps as
> visibly and publicly as Baker was doing it, because it's now in the
> Bill, but the Bill couldn't have happened without all those things.
> There's nothing in the Bill that hadn't already been tried, except
> opting out. Opting out is Baker's own thing. At no point in
> Joseph's time was there ever any talk about opting out. There was
> [the matter of] vouchers of course, vouchers was very much on the
> agenda with Keith Joseph, which would effectively have been total
> opting out, every school would have been opted out under that. So
> in that sense Baker is less extreme than Joseph.

And a civil servant (B) who worked closely with Keith Joseph said:

> I think what was done on exams and on the curriculum (after all
> GCSE is in a way a curricular reform) what was done on teacher
> training and teachers' pay, and a number of other things that were
> done in Keith Joseph's time, are lasting things, and we can be sure
> that they will last. We don't yet know how the Education Reform
> Bill will go, but to a historian I would've thought the evidence was
> fairly clear, that Joseph had little to do with it [the ERA].

Despite the travails of the teachers' industrial dispute and the closure
of the Schools Council, Keith Joseph's ideology of reform remained
embedded in the last vestiges of partnership.

> At that time, with Keith Joseph, there was still a view which he
> epitomised, that education was still a partnership. It wasn't entirely
> a devalued notion that central and local government and schools,

that is the teachers, were still a partnership and that there were still curricular needs. The filling in the gaps principle, wasn't totally wrong in the sense that if you can identify some needs then you still need some means of undertaking some curricular development. And that's still persevering into the NCC.

(Keith McWilliams)

DES civil servant D attached to Keith Joseph's office also explains:

If you look at *Better Schools* you will see I think that it does not come over as a document where the department is trying to grab a power base. I think it comes over as a document that is honestly attempting to go back to the balance of the partners of the '44 Act and to say that for various reasons the Secretary of State's role has just never been what the '44 Act originally imagined it to be. I thought *Better Schools* was seeking to begin to fill a vacuum and to establish the Secretary of State and the Department, and I wouldn't like to divide between them, back as one of the partners in this business. I think I've seen an exorable recognition by the politicians that the centre does have something to say about the curriculum, and always from the '44 Act on it was acknowledged that it did have a part to play, and a gradual feeling of its way to playing that part.

The dramatic shift came when Kenneth Baker replaced Keith Joseph. Baker's brief as the new Secretary of State clearly included the preparation of a major education bill. Alan Evans of the NUT sees this shift as reflecting the direct concerns of the radical right in the Conservative Party and probably as being the result of advice flowing directly to the Prime Minister.

If you look at Joseph's *Better Schools* and you look at the Conservative Party's policy even four or five months before the election, which was on a par with *Better Schools*, and then look at the Manifesto, a coup takes place. There was a coup somewhere, Central Office, Thatcher's office, or wherever, because the social market and the contradiction between the National Curriculum and the rest of the Social Market package doesn't tie up with *Better Schools*. If you look at those phrases about 'the Curriculum should properly lie with the Local Authority' and so on, there are a number of key phrases in that. There was a coup, and these policies come from the radical right.

They don't come from the civil service and they don't come from the main stream of the Conservative Party . . . The assumption is that if you fundamentally weaken the LEA and appointments are made at school level and sackings take place at school level, and the head teacher becomes more the Managing Director and an agent of the employer, and that neither the LEA nor the unions will have power in that unit then there will be some sort of umbilical link between central government and the school which will be more conducive to the philosphy and structure of the Reform Bill and the Conservative Manifesto than previous arrangements.

Raphael Wilkins, Special Adviser to the Commons Committee on Education, Science and Art, also throws some light on this shift:

This, in a sense, is one of the things that has put the Select Committee out on a limb. Most of its work during the '83–'86 Parliament was conducted in a way which assumed that the old consensus was still at work: that central government and local government were partners, and that the broad education lobby, the teacher unions, interest groups, and so on, were all really pulling on the same side and just discovering the best practice here and the best policy there in an incremental sort of way. And what tended to happen was that the government simply ignored the reports . . . The extreme right-wing influences on the Secretary of State were not really manifesting themselves all that much until almost the end of the '87 Parliament. I think it wasn't until the City Technology Colleges that we had the first sign that that view point was actually breaking through, beginning to influence the Prime Minister and the Secretary of State. But from the point of view of the Select Committee, the scale of that influence was certainly not apparent until the spring of 1987 when really its work was more or less completed. Certainly the Select Committee itself was never lobbied by extreme right-wing elements.

Clearly it is a mistake to dwell over-much on the significance of personality differences when comparing the policy making done by and under different Secretaries of State, but the style, the political standing and the personal concerns of the incumbent have been of increasing importance in understanding changes in the way policy is made and implemented. Political ideology is also important in making sense of the forms of influence and control which were predominant in each case.

One former senior civil servant (B) compared Joseph and Baker (and Mark Carlisle) in the following way.

I think the one thing they had in common was that they regarded themselves as being in charge. They were, none of them, the type of Minister that we have had in the past in this country, and no doubt may have again, a Minister so feeble and so irresolute, or so limited in his or her interests, that policy vacuums occur and officials run round and in the end finish up by either making policy or allowing events to make policy. Carlisle was not as thrusting a person as Keith Joseph and Baker, nor was he in a way as much of a front-rank politican. In fact it was his only Cabinet job. He came, to a greater extent than the other two, from the consensus tradition. Though, by 1979, when he came in, Conservative ministers had very different ideas from their predecessors. Nevertheless I think he was not concerned primarily to change the system radically. His starting point wasn't, 'What a frightful system, could we have a different one? Could we make it very different?', whereas I think both the other two, as their actions have shown, are ready to have something different if only they could. I think that's the big difference.

Another (C) offered this comparison.

Yes, what has changed is the political environment, in which education has become a much more important thing. You will get that kind of cosy relationship going on in a policy area where basically the government isn't too bothered about what's happening. You won't, as soon as they accord it any kind of priority or as soon as they're looking at expenditure cuts and so on. So the whole environment has changed from that point of view, on the profile that education has nationally . . . a hell of a lot of money being spent, questions being asked about value for money and that education is actually being seen as an important aspect of economic performance [for example the work of Professor Sig Prais (1985 and 1987) – see below] so given those two kinds of thrusts . . . you are going to get more interventionist policies from ministers. And given a go-ahead Secretary of State, that also makes a lot of difference. Never underestimate the impact of a particular minister on a department and a department's policies . . . [Kenneth Baker] is much more of a politician, much less of an academic, which is not to say that he's not an intelligent man, he is. Keith Joseph failed to make the kind of progress, if you want to regard it as progress, that Kenneth Baker has made, basically because he did engage too much in dicussion and not enough in decision . . . and because having made up his mind, which it took him a long time to do, he wasn't then as able a person in going out and fighting for it, with his colleagues and with the world out there, as Kenneth Baker is. They are two very different styles of politician and you can argue both ways round. If you take the sort of view that you won't actually get to change if you discuss it forever, and that any decision is only marginally more right than another. In other words . . . there is no absolute right, then.

It was thus Kenneth Baker who left behind the doubts, worries and hesitations and to push on towards a large-scale, radical and reforming Education Act. One civil servant said 'He came with a harder heart . . . He may not have it 100 per cent right now, it may be 80 per cent right, but we'll have to tidy it up'. Another commented:

> The Baker style of approach, which is also the Thatcher government style of approach, I don't mean in terms of right wingers or whatever, but let us press on, let us make things happen, because that in itself will produce other beneficial results. That's very much his style. He knows roughly where he wants to get to, not in sort of any great detail, not worried about the great detail, let's press on and get there. You don't make omelettes without breaking eggs.

Kenneth Baker's successor, John MacGregor, has pursued a similar line.

> Uneven progress is a matter of serious concern. More worrying is the perception that we are doing less well overall then other countries . . . compared to some of our European counterparts and the Japanese, the evidence suggests that we are failing to bring out the best in pupils of average and below average ability . . .
> (Speech to the Secondary Heads Association 2 October 1989)

Clearly others outside the DES were convinced by 1985–6 of the need to legislate. A DES under-Secretary (C), recalls the run-up to legislation in the following exchange.

> (C): [Two years ago the National Curriculum] was beginning to be discussed in Conservative Party circles and with No. 10. I think it is something that had been on the stocks for some time. Its beginnings were manifested in the 1970s and certain thoughts coming out of the Centre for Policy Studies, certain thoughts coming out actually from Keith Joseph as well, bearing in mind that there was a White Paper in 1985, *Better Schools*, which actually said quite a lot about the curriculum and the nature of the curriculum, and I think that inevitably led into thinking about a national curriculum. So there was the beginnings of discussion about the time I arrived and that was first publicly floated, I suppose, in early January. In 1987 the Secretary of State went and talked to the North of England Conference, and said that he was contemplating legislation.

> SJB: Would you see it as foregone by that time, that there was an inevitability of moving towards a National Curriculum or would there still have been the possibility of some doubt?

(C): I think that needs to be formulated in terms of was it inevitable that there was going to be legislation, as opposed to something else, that's point one . . . and was it inevitable that the National Curriculum would be in the form in which it is, that's point two.

I think it was inevitable that there was going to be some kind of strengthening, of a central push, on what the curriculum should look like, and that was a very clear desire, it was a very logical follow-on from *Better Schools*. Whether that should be legislated or achieved by some other means, I don't think was at all settled in autumn '86, and certainly the nature of it was by no means settled. By National Curriculum, incidentally, I think it's worth making clear that we are talking not just about having a list of subjects which everybody should study, but also about having assessment. That was very much part of the thinking, and indeed in some ways it was the driving force from, for instance, the Centre for Policy Studies . . . that assessment or testing had to be something that you had, and the add-on that came from here and from the Secretary of State in particular, was, 'Look, if you're going to have assessment, you actually need to know what the objectives of your curriculum are, rather than just assessing in a blank', which is what had been happening in the States, with some fairly disastrous results. I think the other major factor was actually having a new Secretary of State who wanted to do things actively, and wanted to legislate more generally, and wanted to put a much firmer imprint on the curriculum. So that was quite a big push, and he of course arrived in May–June, something like that, '86.

The final Act is an amalgam of influences and voices and interests, from both within and outside the DES. It contains compromises, assertions and some vagaries. In particular, the effects and influences of policy borrowing are evident. Both Keith Joseph and Kenneth Baker have been keen to learn about and draw upon the experience of education in certain other countries – particularly France, Germany and the USA. The final linking of a National Curriculum with National Testing seems to have been firmed up in this way. The following account by a civil servant (C) captures this pot pourri effect.

C: There was a very strong push for testing based on some United States experience . . . this is sort of Chester Thin, and people like that and William Bennett, saying we must find out what kids know and can do, because they're a bunch of incompetents when they leave school. So fine, that was a sort of political marker. I suppose the other thing that happened significantly in 1986 was that HMI visited Germany, did a report on what was happening in West Germany, and in particular their form of assessment, and the relationship between that and a fairly prescribed curriculum [see Prais and Wagner 1985]. I mean it wouldn't be right to say 'national' curriculum, because of the federal structure of Germany.

But the relationship between assessment and a prescribed curriculum were the clear objectives, and a broad curriculum. It isn't just that you have objectives for each subject, but also the kids up to age 16 were covering a far broader range of subjects which were common to all schools and all pupils than in this country, and that was closely integrated with the assessment and testing. So that yes, I think the curriculum push did come from a separate place, from the original assessment and testing push, though there was also a core curriculum as opposed to a National Curriculum movement, which said we must make sure that everybody is competent at least in maths and English, literacy and numeracy, to which the enlightened added science and then the even more enlightened started adding other subjects, and that's why I say the argument about the nature of the curriculum, National Curriculum, was very far from fixed in the autumn of '86, and indeed it took a lot of thrashing out for a year following that.

SJB: So presumably those positions, in terms of testing and National Curriculum legislation . . . were actually being, so to speak, fought out within the DES in terms of different people holding up different positions and different ends.

C: Yes, it wasn't just within the DES, it was within the DES and within Centre for Policy Studies, No.10 Policy Unit, and Cabinet, and all the usual people that are involved in policy formulation . . . which is nothing unusual, nothing different from normal policy formulation.

But, as I stressed in chapter 3, while the Act is a composite it can also be read, and was intended to be read, as a systematic whole. The main elements of testing, curriculum, opting out and open enrolment provide a neat and effective balance between consumer choice on the one hand and central control on the other. As civil servant (C) explained:

There is a relationship which I don't think is conspiratorial, but I think it's overt and declared . . . the government has argued all along, 'Look, if we set the framework for what is to be taught, in other words the National Curriculum, then there is far more scope for local management, both in the sense of financial management and local management in the sense of parents opting school out from LEA control, because we've set a firm framework with expectations . . .' and that is overt. And the second thing which I think is overt is that by having a National Curriculum and assessment you provide a basis for information to be given to parents about what is happening, and that again, fully declared, nothing conspiratorial, which can be used either to help decisions about whether schools should opt out or decisions related to open enrolment, about where parents wanted to send their children. In other words, they would be able to look at how a school was doing and base their choice of where they wanted their kid to be educated on that. So it relates to open enrolment just as much as it relates to opting out.

Space here does not allow consideration of the passage of the ERA through parliament. There were some significant debates in both Houses and some interesting detailed scrutiny in the Committee stage, but very few amendments were passed or accepted by the government. Nonetheless some of the interested parties did devote considerable time and effort to the work of lobbying during the passage of the Bill. The National Association of Headteachers employed professional lobbyists, the AMA deployed their Parliamentary Officer, the AMMA contributed half the cost of a research assistant for Liberal education spokesman Paddy Ashdown, the NUT, NATFE, CASE, NCPTA and NAGAM were also regularly represented in the lobby. Most effort on the part of lobbying groups was directed at the Lords rather than the Commons where it was felt that there was more likelihood of carrying amendments. Damian Welfare, AMA Parliamentary Officer, commented:

> Given that if one's looking for real changes, they tend to come in the Lords, not exclusively, but they tend to. In many ways I see the Commons Committee particularly as a dry run for the Lords stages, because one is testing the arguments, seeing what the government's saying about particular worries, seeing whether it's a real worry or not, and if it still is, as it were. Then you've got some measure of the strength of feeling on both sides, when you come into the Lords with the issue.

In fact, the significant changes to the Bill affecting schools came from the government side and were marginal to the main concerns of the Bill – the Tebbit/Heseltine amendment in the Commons which brought about the abolition of the ILEA and the pressure in the Lords from Lord Thorneycroft and Baroness Cox which produced a stronger statement in the Bill concerning the status of a Christian act of worship in schools. (The former was discussed in chapter 2).

I want to take up a different aspect of the development of the ERA. As one civil servant explained 'the ERA is essentially a framework to be filled in'. I will examine this filling-in process, that is the translation of the legal framework, particularly matters relating to the school curriculum, into a set of more detailed requirements to be addressed by schools. Specifically I want to explore the attempts of the New Right cultural restorationists and the new progressives within the educational establishment to influence the process of defining the National Curriculum. And the role of the Secretary of State continues to be important. I will also attend to the emergence of the National Curriculum Council (NCC) and their relationship to the DES.

Hand to hand fighting

As I have indicated earlier, I am not trying here to present policy as a thing, as something that happens and then is over and fixed. Rather I am working primarily with the idea of policy as a discourse, a construct of possibilities and impossibilities tied to knowledge and to practice. Control of the discourse and thus of its possibilities is essentially contested in and between arenas of formation and implementation. As texts, policies can be subject to a variety of readings, they will have a different effectivity in relation to different groups of readers: 'readers are interpellated by a whole range of intra- and extra-textual discourses that prevent even the most closed of texts from absolutely determining its reading by readers who bring different knowledges, prejudices and resistances' (Whitty 1985 p.43). Particular readings can be asserted and the texts captured for particular interests. In effect, the ERA is a half-written text, a story outline; its detail, meaning and practice lie in on-going struggles related to the interpretation of its key components.

Here I want to explore some of the contestation which took place over matters of detail within the production of the ensemble of documents making up the proposed National Curriculum. Within this exploration the complexity of policy as text will be evident. The initial realisation of the National Curriculum as an educational entity began not with the ERA as such but in the activities of the various working parties set up to report on the core and foundation subjects within the National Curriculum and latterly in the interpretational, organisational and commentary work done by the National Curriculum Council. The National Curriculum Council (NCC) and the Curriculum Council for Wales (CCW) were officially established on 16 August 1988.

> When he set up the NCC in August 1988, the Secretary of State for Education and Science sent a letter to the Chairman and Chief Executive setting out some of the tasks which he expected NCC to undertake in its first years. Many of these NCC will share with the Department of Education and Science, with Her Majesty's Inspectorate, with SEAC (The Schools Examination and Assessment Council) and with the local education authorities . . . .

185

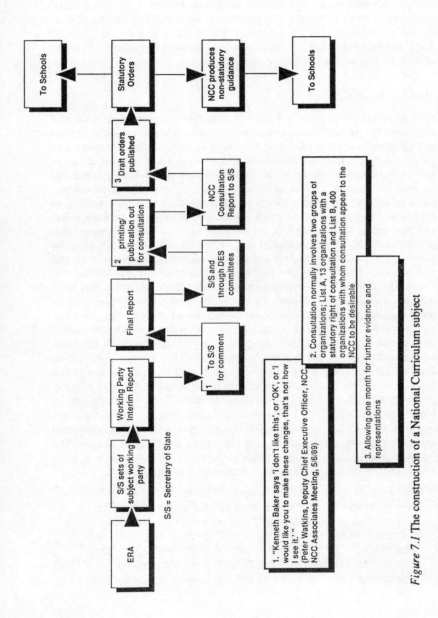

Figure 7.1 The construction of a National Curriculum subject

ERA → S/S sets of subject working party → Working Party Interim Report → Final Report → 2 printing/publication out for consultation → 3 Draft orders published → Statutory Orders → To Schools

Statutory Orders → NCC produces non-statutory guidance → To Schools

1 To S/S for comment

S/S and through DES committees

NCC Consultation Report to S/S

S/S = Secretary of State

1. "Kenneth Baker says 'I don't like this', or 'OK', or 'I would like you to make these changes, that's not how I see it.'"
(Peter Watkins, Deputy Chief Executive Officer, NCC NCC Associates Meeting, 5/6/89)

2. Consultation normally involves two groups of organizations; List A, 13 organizations with a statutory right of consultation and List B, 400 organizations with whom consultation appear to the NCC to be desirable

3. Allowing one month for further evidence and representations

The Council exists to provide independent professional advice on the school curriculum. It has responsibility for the whole curriculum, not just the National Curriculum.

(NCC 1989a)

Once the NCC was up and running, the complete process for the construction of a National Curriculum subject was as presented in figure 7.1.

The Secretary of State is the key point of reference in the process. He sets the membership of the working parties, comments directly on their interim and final reports, receives the Consultation Report from the NCC and approves the Statutory Orders (specifying attainment targets and programmes of study). Clearly, in practice a lot of the detail and routine of these contributions is done by civil servants, but, as we shall see, the Secretary of State was often personally involved in quite detailed scrutiny and re-working of the earlier reports. In any case the focus of formal control is clearly within the DES, although the basic subject texts are thrashed out inside the working parties. However, the NCC has a crucial input in its interpretation of the consultation exercise and at the very end of the formal process, in providing an authoritative interpretation and reading for schools of the Statutory Orders – Non-Statutory Guidance (NSG). The Non-Statutory Guidance has been much in the hands of subject experts and practitioners rather than politicians and civil servants, although HMI have made inputs into the writing. The NSG for mathematics, for example, certainly maintains a 'progressive interpretation of the Statutory Orders with emphasis given to "problem solving", pupils' use of calculators, open ended tasks and pupils' own methods of calculation' – all very much in the vein of post-Cockcroftian mathematics.

TGAT

Much of the conceptual framework for the subsequent filling-in of the National Curriculum by working parties and task groups was established by the Report of the Task Group on Attainment and Testing (chaired by Professor Paul Black). The TGAT report provided a structure linking the National Curriculum subjects to the proposed system of National Testing. The package consists of four main elements.

1. Attainment targets and profile components
These are the knowledge, skills and understanding which pupils of different abilities and maturities are expected to have achieved in each subject area.

2. Levels of attainment
The ten levels of attainment within each attainment target reflect differences in achievement related to pupils' abilities. The levels define progressive stages of attainment (supposedly) independent of age. (The ERA describes a pupil's years of compulsory schooling in four key stages, at or near the end of which assessment must take place. Key stage 1 [5-7 yrs], 2 [8-11 yrs], 3 [12-14 yrs], 4 [15-16 yrs].)

3. Statements of attainment
These are more precise objectives within each of the broader attainment targets. Generally there is a statement of attainment for each of ten levels defining what pupils should know, understand and be able to do in order to achieve that level in that attainment target.

4. Programmes of study
These are matters, skills and processes which have to be taught to pupils of different abilities and maturities during each key stage in order for them to meet the objectives set out in the attainment targets. The programmes of study are detailed but do not specify particular materials or teaching methods directly. Together with the attainment targets they should, in theory, provide the basis upon which teachers plan their schemes of work.

It is worth noting that 1 and 4 are embedded in the ERA, 2 was invented by TGAT, and 3 jointly by TGAT and the early subject working parties. As already noted, attainment targets emerged during Keith Joseph's time in office, as he attempted to introduce an objectives-based framework for the curriculum and associated criterion-referenced assessment. The term 'attainment targets' was first used in *Better Schools*. But the provenance of 'programmes of study' is less clear. Alongside attainment targets they would seem to leave little room for teachers' discretion. Brown (1989) suggests that 'programmes of study':

> seem most likely to have been included at the behest of right-wing pressure groups which were then particularly active in persuading the Prime Minister, via her Central Policy Unit, that our lack of industrial competitiveness was due to the weak mathematical performance of our pupils (e.g. Prais and Wagner 1985, Prais 1987). The decentralised nature of our school curriculum was contrasted with the tight central control exerted in Japan, in particular.

(p.2)

I am not particularly concerned here with the substance of this framework, but a grasp of the language and structure is important in making sense of some of the struggles touched on below. Also TGAT is important in itself in establishing an assessment-led approach to the design and conceptualisation of National Curriculum subjects. Again the constitution and orientation of TGAT is significant in indicating the readmittance of professional educationalists into the formal corridors of policy making. At the same time other representations, particularly those of the New Right, were being spurned by the Secretary of State. The TGAT report in all its complexity and sophistication represented an educationalist interpretation of the demands and requirements for a National Curriculum and National Testing laid down in the ERA. The following long extract from an interview with Paul Black, the TGAT Chairman, makes clear the high level of relative independence allowed to the Group in their deliberations.

> I was aware that there was a lot riding on the success of the report. I would doubt whether, except in a very general sense, the DES had a strategy, and that I fitted into that strategy. They wanted a set of good people who had a track record, were respected in education, and were prepared to think positively and creatively about this opportunity . . . In that sense, they presumably chose me because when they chatted to me about assessment I produced ideas and seemed to them more likely to make sense of it than other people they might have had in mind; but all that is a presumption. I don't think they had much idea of what TGAT could come up with any more than the rest of us did in some ways . . . And I think the feeling was that the Secretary of State was unclear about it, and I remember an initial discussion with him before the group was firmly on the table and he did ask several questions and expressed some concerns, but in many ways they were not central, nor did they indicate any desire on his part to give a very strong steer. I really got the impression that he wanted this to stand up, but was really giving a lot of freedom. And that was consistent, of course, with the sort of people they were getting on to the group, as it was with the sort of people who were getting on to the subject working groups. They were trying to hand that to the professionals. His only anxiety was a logistic one – we must have the answer by early New Year because the subject working parties would need the assessment framework. There are a lot of people in the DES who care about education, and who don't believe that they understand it all sufficiently well to control it, or that everything out there is rubbish and needs kicking into shape by some simplistic formula. I think the DES would resist all of that and would realise that you can only really make changes if you get professionals involved and carry them with you. So what happens is a tension between giving the professionals the say, or, crudely,

kicking them, forcing them to work to new constraints, and as I
discern it, the former is the strategy. You force on public
accountability and other constraints and then you say, 'Now make
sense of that lot. You are the professionals, you are supposed to
know how to do it, get that to work well'. And that seems to me a
sensible strategy. It frays at the edges, of course, particularly when
you are working things out in detail. I mean obviously all sorts of
things have to be done in the office and a lack of understanding of
the professional realities may produce bits of nonsense in the final
legislative drafting orders and all the rest of it, but the general issue
seems clearly in that shape.

I did not know, during the TGAT exercise, how, and to what
extent, we were going to be interfered with, and to what extent we
were going to be nudged and lent on and told, 'He doesn't like the
way this is going' and called in to talk to the Minister and all the
rest of it. And there was hardly any of that. There were some
pressures put on, but they were indirect and mainly through the
HMI route. There were concerns amongst some HMIs but those
were things that we could tease out and go and talk about, but
politically there was no pressure at all ... It was always evident
that there could be political problems *vis-à-vis* anybody in the
Cabinet when we had produced the report. We had very little idea
what was going to happen to it or how it was going to be received.
We knew vague outlines I had sketched to Baker and specific
points I had made to him in discussion which made sense to him,
but that was very different from presenting the whole grand plan.
Of course, the DES officers would have been briefing him all the
time, about how it was going, so he would have seen the
emergence. Therefore the lack of coercive feedback may either be
abstemious on their part or just a reflection of the fact that they
were satisfied and happy to go along with it. I presumed it was all
being reported. But when the thing had first been produced in full
and handed to ministers, three of us had to present to ministers and
explain it in detail and answer a lot of questions. The thing we
were holding our breath on, at the end, was what was to be said
about publishing it.

From this account, then, there is no evidence of pressure or interference
from Secretary of State or DES officials, nor of fixed constraints. Given
that some form of national testing was required, the determination of its
form, in the first instance at least, was given over to a group primarily
drawn from the educational establishment. Part of this 'hands off'
approach may have been aimed at achieving some reduction in the fears
being expressed by teachers as to the oppressive and untoward effects of

testing – 'taking the sting out', as one civil servant put it (see below). However, it is clear that later curriculum working groups, on mathematics, science and history in particular, were subject to forceful 'guidance' and pressure from DES officials. These groups certainly did not have an independent status. They operated within political and bureaucratic constraints. But it would seem that the Secretary of State did not discuss the TGAT report in Cabinet before deciding to publish. (Given subsequent events, speedy publication may have been doubtful if he had.) He may have been keen to get the report tabled during the Committee stage of the Education Bill in the House of Commons.

It is also evident from Paul Black's account that the setting up of the committee and the publication of the report represented a political commitment by the Secretary of State to a new form of partnership in the development of the National Curriculum. This was not a commitment that was necessarily shared elsewhere in government or in the Conservative Party. It quickly became clear that the Prime Minister for one was not happy with the TGAT report. On 10 March 1988 a letter (dated 21 January) from Margaret Thatcher's office to Tom Jeffery, a Private Secretary at the DES was leaked to the press.

Dear Tom,

National Curriculum Task Group on assessment and testing report

The Prime Minister has had the opportunity to look in more detail at this Report which your Secretary of State published last week. Although she agreed to your Secretary of State welcoming the Report as the broad framework into which attainment targets could be fitted, there are a number of aspects which she finds disturbing.

First, the Committee seemed to have designed an enormously elaborate and complex system. They suggest it requires setting up *two* new powerful bodies: the Schools Examination Council and the National Curriculum Council, and a major new role for LEAs. Is this necessary? And has the sort of approach advocated in the Report in fact been put into practice with the proposed degree of elaboration in any large group of schools?

Second, the Prime Minister notes that the philosophy underlying the Report is that tests are only a part of assessment, and that the major purpose of assessment is diagnostic and formative rather than summative. As a result the method of assessment places a heavy responsibility on teachers' judgements and general impressions. She is also concerned to note the major role envisaged for the LEAs in implementation of the system.

Third, the Report does not pull together the overall costs of the exercise, but the general impression is that these will be very large.

In view of the recommendation in Section xix, the Prime Minister wonders whether, for example, the group has considered the likely costs of training teachers prior to implementation and the regular annual costs of teachers' time once the system was in operation.

Fourth, the Prime Minister also notes that, presumably as a result of the complexity of the proposals, the new assessment system could not be introduced in less than five years. Although she recognises the importance of careful preparation and introduction of the new arrangements, she is concerned that the process might take so long.

The Prime Minister would be grateful if your Secretary of State could take these concerns into account in his further consideration of the Report and the continuing dialogue with the Task Group.

I am copying this letter to the Private Secretaries to other members of E[EP].

Yours, Paul.

Paul Gray.

The major points in the letter rehearse many of the established political concerns which had underpinned the development of Conservative education policies in the 1970s, particularly the distrust of curriculum agencies, of LEAs and of teachers, and a preference for examination-type testing. On the day of the leak the *Independent* commented: 'The nub of the argument is that she wants formal nationwide tests geared to targets which all children of a particular age will be expected to reach. In effect, they would be pass/fail exams'.

One of the key points about TGAT was the conversion of the Secretary of State from an age-related system – what all 8-year-olds should know – to a criteria-related system. Convincing Mrs Thatcher was a different matter. The *Guardian* noted: 'Mr Baker's close colleagues acknowledge that Mr Baker has a difficult task in persuading Mrs Thatcher that the Black proposals go far enough'.

Update: It is interesting to consider the points made on Mrs Thatcher's letter in the light of subsequent recommendations from SEAC to the Secretary of State on 'National Curriculum Assessment Arrangements' (letter and paper 13 July 1989). The paper notes that:

'the Education Reform Act, the working group reports on individual subjects, the NCC Consultation Reports and attainment targets for mathematics, science and English now specified by Statutory Orders, have contained emphases or specific suggestions at variance with each other or with details of the TGAT Reports,

some of which your Department has called to our attention. This
paper addresses these issues'.

(p.2)

In fact, the paper would seem to indicate at several points significant
moves away from the principles of TGAT. In particular, Teachers'
Assessments are subordinated to Standard Assessment Tasks, both in
recording and reporting student achievement (or, more appropriately
now, student assessment). 'The SAT assessment is "preferred" to TA,
where it is available' (p.4), and, 'Our recommendation, subject to test in
the 1990 pilot exercise, is that the SAT results were available, should be
used for recording and reporting purposes instead of TA, except where
this makes a change to a profile component result which the teacher
wishes to query' (p.5). The diagnostic and formative aspects of assessment would seem to be downgraded by these emphases. The *Observer*
(22 October 1989), commented on the SEAC paper:

> The Prime Minister has won a long-running battle with the
> educational establishment over how Britain's seven million pupils
> should be tested as part of the new national curriculum. Mrs
> Thatcher has overruled the advice of Government-appointed
> experts as well as that of her former Education Secretary, Mr
> Kenneth Baker, by insisting that children are rated according to
> nationally prescribed tests rather than by teachers . . . Mrs
> Thatcher's determination to downgrade teachers' views and force
> schools to rely more on banks of national test now appears to have
> won the day.

(p.4)

The *TES* (20 October 1989) reported: 'Three members of the Task
Group on Assessment and Testing (TGAT) which designed the blue-
print for national testing now say that decisions taken this summer have
destroyed the TGAT structure and will undermine the potential benefits
of the National Curriculum' (p.6).

One critic, Norman Thomas, former Chief Inspector for Primary
Schools, commented:

> If they (teachers) are given the impression that their own
> continuous assessments are not valued, they can hardly be expected
> to give the process the time and thought it requires. They may even
> fall back on commercially-produced tests to do the teacher
> assessment.

Another, Professor Jack Allanson, said in reference to the systems of aggregation suggested in the SEAC report: 'It's pulling away from the TGAT system of criterion referencing. It doesn't matter how well you do on separate bits provided the weighted average comes out right.' It is interesting to consider these 'adaptations' of the TGAT system in relation to the New Right arguments discussed in chapter 3.

However, as Paul Black outlines, while there may have been doubts in No. 10, the reception of the report by other parties in the education policy complex was more positive and supportive. The general feeling about TGAT among educationalists was one of relief. The general view was that things could have been worse, much worse. Not untypically, the *TES* report on the conference of the Primary Education Study Group noted that: 'there was still general support for the sophisticated approach of the Task Group on Assessment and Testing. But there were also fears that, without extra time and staffing, all the assessment would overload and distort the work of teachers' (25 November 1988, p.8). Stuart MacClure, editor of the *TES*, speaking to the conference described the report as 'a brilliant way of fooling both sides, giving politicians their league tables and market pressures, while promising teachers arrangements which protected their view of good practice' (ibid.).

It seems possible, although by no means certain, that in the Cabinet sub-committee where the report was formally discussed, Kenneth Baker was presented by the Prime Minister with a crude choice: 'You can have the TGAT Report or the Higginson Report (which was proposing major reforms of A-levels and sixth-form education), but not both'. He chose TGAT, and Higginson was not accepted (at this time).

I think the other part of that story is that the three supplementary reports which completed our job were submitted at the end of March, and there was no decision, we could not find out what the policy decision was going to be on national assessment. I was away for a month. When I came back I found nothing was settled, and in fact all of April, all of May, nothing happened, except that it became increasingly clear that it would be difficult to adopt a very different assessment framework, because the science and maths working parties had nearly finished their work and they were working to the TGAT framework, as they had been instructed to do. So it was a very strange situation, that a Cabinet committee decision to not adopt the framework would have delayed or led to serious need for very rapid change. Quite why it was delayed so long before being decided is a matter of speculation. There is no hard evidence that the TGAT decision and the decision on Higginson were taken at the same time. But it was when the Secretary of State answered a parliamentary question on June 10th, which date is engraved on my heart, that it became clear that he was accepting the main principles.

(Paul Black, chairman of TGAT)

One of the senior civil servants interviewed (D) certainly rejected the view that the Higginson report was sacrificed for TGAT.

They were there at the same time, and I saw the press reports which attributed it to Mrs Thatcher, saying 'You can have one but not the other.' It's nonsense really; Kenneth Baker made it quite clear in his statement to Higginson that he too was strongly in support of the principle of breadth but that he believed that the system could only take so much turbulence and to his mind you could achieve breadth with five subjects, just like Higginson wanted, with building blocks of the traditional eight period A levels and four period AS levels.

However, senior civil servant (C) appeared to suggest that just such a trade off had occurred.

As you know, we set up a task group on assessment and testing, which came up with a very good report, which successfully reconciled both meeting the government's objectives, or certainly Mr Baker's objectives, and removing a lot of the sting from the point of view of the education profession. And the more thinking people in the education profession said, 'Yes, we can work with this'. And getting that signed up was quite a major thing to happen. And the acute observers will have noticed that the statement on that was made at roughly the same time as the statement on the government's response to Higginson, and they can draw their own conclusions about what kind of trade-offs went on on that.

In a news discussion of the rejection of Higginson a BBC reporter commented 'the government seemed committed to retaining A-levels as the gold-standard of education' (*World at One*, 22 November 1989). In the same programme in an interview, Angela Rumbold, junior Education Minister, commented:

The government is very clear about the importance of maintaining the standards of A-level. We do have to address the needs and requirements of the very able youngster in our society. And I fear that much of what has been suggested will edge away at the very high standards of our A-levels.

Again it is interesting to consider this in terms of the cultural restorationist agenda outlined in Chapter 3.

Such points of political exchange are more interesting than important in themselves. The leaked letter and the initial rejection of Higginson indicate at least the scepticism with which No. 10 viewed the re-entry of educationalists into the policy process. Testing, it would seem, was not going to provide the straightforward means of disciplining schools and reasserting traditional teaching methods that was being urged by the cultural restorationists. In a CPS response to TGAT and other curriculum developments associated with the National Curriculum (prepared by Sheila Lawlor 1988) it is baldly argued that:

> The CPS Core Curriculum sets out curricula for English, Maths and Science. In order to ensure that pupils leave school literate, numerate and with a modicum of scientific knowledge, it should not extend beyond these three core subjects, nor attempt to do more than set minimum standards in basic knowledge and technique.
>
> It is regrettable that these aims appear recently to have been abandoned by those in charge of producing and implementing education policy. As the following pages show, the official committees, the DES and Her Majesty's Inspectorate no longer adhere to the belief that teachers should teach and pupils should learn a simple body of knowledge and a simple set of techniques.
>
> (p.5)

This document both reasserts doubts about the wisdom of having a broad, detailed National Curriculum at all, and is scathing in its rejection of innovations in teaching method and subject organisation (like Cockcroft and like the objectives-based approach thrust upon the HMI by Keith Joseph). Also the CPS paper presents serious misgivings about the reports produced by the National Curriculum subject working parties.

As indicated above, the initial colouring in of the National Curriculum boxes was done by subject committees nominated by the Secretary of State. Committees on science, maths and English were the first three to be set up and to report. A brief discussion of the work of these committees and the reception of their reports will provide some insight into the new processes of curriculum policy making established by the provisions of the ERA. The maths and science groups were set up in June/July 1987. The memberships were based on recommendations made by HMI and DES officials, but it is clear that one or two suggestions were rejected by the Secretary of State on evidence that they had previously displayed 'attitudes not supportive of a National Curriculum and National Testing' (group member). Indeed, according to a report in the *Independent* (7 June 1988, p.2): 'Mrs Thatcher has asked to be informed of all proposed appointments to working groups and committees – she takes a keen interest in education because that is the only department she has run as a Minister'. (A similar veto was evident in making appointments to the NCC – Professor Peter Mortimore and Sir Christopher Ball were excluded.) The memberships of the working groups were important in symbolising the seriousness and the reasonableness of the National Curriculum exercise: the seriousness being a political matter, demonstrating to Party and Prime Minister that the National Curriculum was under control, and the reasonableness being an educational matter, demonstrating to teachers that educational considerations were to the fore and that the groups would not be vehicles for the excesses of the 'loony right'. The cultural restorationists were concerned that the National Curriculum could well be captured by the educational establishment if their representatives were to dominate the working groups, NCC and SEAC.

A DES official (C) explained:

> The NCC and SEAC are both ways of involving people from the
> professions, the educational professions, also of involving other
> people. They are deliberately set up not just as educational bodies,
> and have networks which are not purely educational networks, but,
> if you like, they are a recognition that there is a hell of a lot out
> there to be done and not all of it can be done from the DES. So,
> yes, it's a taking things away from the hands of the nasty HMI and
> DES officials, whom we all know are people to be hated. But it
> seems to be a perfectly sensible, logical way of operating. The
> thing which does reflect some of the view about the education
> establishment that comes from the right wing is that they are
> deliberately set up, not as representative bodies but as bodies
> reflecting different interests. In other words, they are not based on
> nominations by the Teacher Associations, nominations by the
> Local Education Authorities. They are Ministerial appointments.
> Now that's seen as being vastly sinister by some people and vastly
> sensible by others. I happen to fall into the vastly sensible group. It
> seems to me that you have got to have a small body if it's going to
> be effective . . . and I do actually regard it as being a perfectly
> legitimate function for elected ministers to exercise patronage and
> appoint people . . . I do think it's a fairly significant change in the
> kind of body. How the relationship between the DES and these two
> bodies works out, where the balance of power will lie, who does
> what, I just don't know. We are going to have to see how it goes.
> All I do know is that there is one hell of a lot of work and we are
> going to have to work closely together to make it happen.

New Right 'representives' were appointed to the maths and English working parties (and TGAT). Professor Sig Prais of the National Institute for Economic and Social Research was a member of the mathematics group, and Brian Cox, founder of the *Black Papers*, was appointed as Chairman of the English group. This seemed to indicate greater seriousness than reasonableness (see press reports below). The National Association for the Teaching of English was denied official representation on the group. A member of the mathematics working party commented:

> Professor Sig Prais was a member of that group and he was also a member of a number of right-wing pressure groups, including the Centre for Policy Studies. He has been widely reported as pressing for a National Curriculum, because of his studies which reported mathematical attainments as particularly low here in comparison with other countries, and his belief that this was the cause of our national industrial decline. We knew that he had a relationship with the head of the Central Policy Unit at No. 10 Downing Street, and that therefore the reports of what was going on in the group were quick to get back to the Prime Minister. One of his colleagues from the National Institute for Economic and Social Research was also a member of the TGAT group and it was clear that these two were working together.

Each of the working groups offer a microcosm of struggles within the educational state over definition and control of subject knowledge. They indicate both the reworking of the policy process and the potential for dislocation and conflict within that process.

Maths counts!

The working group reports as the main basis for Statutory Orders will become the primary source of curriculum planning for schools over the next ten years. Programmes of study and attainment targets will at least considerably constrain, if not wholly determine, the realisation of subjects in the classroom. In several respects the maths group is the most interesting of the early working parties and I will deal with its work in greatest detail. At the heart of its deliberations, in particular in the clash between Sig Prais and the rest of the membership, was a fundamental disagreement about the nature and purposes of school mathematics. Margaret Brown, a group member, explained the grounds of these disputes.

> Professor Prais, for instance, was continuously arguing his case, that we should have a uniform curriculum for all children and that this should be based on very traditional skills in mathematics and that children which could not pass these at the end of each key stage should be kept down. The rest of the Committee, including the industrialists, were very much opposed to this view, for two

reasons. One was that they felt the curriculum structure should be in terms of a mathematical progression of concepts and skills that were not necessarily age related. Children should progress up the structure as fast as they were reasonably able to go. This would not have the effect of holding back the brighter children nor would it mean that the children at the bottom were either pushed up faster than they could cope with the work or held back in younger classes to repeat the year. The second reason for disagreement was in the nature of the mathematics to be included. The rest of the Committee felt that the routine pencil and paper skills that were favoured by Professor Prais were outdated in the age of the calculator and the computer, although children should have good mental skills and have the ability to understand and interpret the use of the machines that were available. We also favoured a much wider curriculum which included spatial and statistical skills, and particularly the ability to apply these and to solve problems. There were also other issues to be argued out in the Committee.

At the point of the submission of the group's interim report to the Secretary of State two members resigned, each in their different ways frustrated by the process in which they were involved. They were Roger Blin-Stoyle, the Chairman, and Sig Prais; in addition John Dichmont (a primary school head) stopped participating in the work of the group.

Roger Blin-Stoyle saw the problems within the group as fundamental.

What happened was that basically the working group, in its early days really, although it couldn't bring itself to say this, didn't accept its terms of reference, that is to say it did not believe in setting attainment targets at age 7, 11 and 14. And so by the time we had to produce our first interim report, there was still agonising over that and that's why it was that the report didn't meet all the things that Kenneth Baker expected.

According to press reports Professor Prais resigned 'saying that drill and rote-learning, including long division, were the only way to bring English school-leavers to the same standard as the Germans, Japanese and French' (*Observer* 14 August 1988, p.4).

As explained by a group member, the interim report was not received well by Kenneth Baker and was compared unfavourably with the science group's effort.

On reception of the report, the Secretary of State said that he felt it was a pretty poor effort, full of jelly and without much specific content. He contrasted it with the science report which was very much longer, and he said he felt that they had done a great deal more work. It was at this time that he accepted the resignation of the Chairman, perhaps not surprisingly, and also Professor Prais formally announced his resignation from the Committee. This was because he had failed to get any support within the Committee and therefore it was clearly a waste of his time to continue. He managed nevertheless to engineer maximum publicity for his resignation, and to take the opportunity again to state his view that the working group were going in the wrong direction in not going back to traditional pencil and paper skills. He also accused the Committee of being dominated by the HMI, which was perhaps not entirely unjustified. Normally a working group would have had as its Secretary a professional civil servant, and this was in fact the case for the other two groups. Because the DES felt it was short of staff they drafted in a science HMI for us. It's fair to say that she played a fairly active role and liaised to a great extent with the staff HMI for mathematics, who was also an active member of the group (although technically an observer). They both had a considerable advantage in that they were full time on the Committee whereas the rest of us were trying to carry on with our normal jobs. This meant that tasks were often passed to them that might more appropriately have been dealt with by the Committee itself.

At this stage the group was 'near to disbanding'. A new Chairman, a non-mathematician, Duncan Graham was appointed from among the existing members (later to become Chairman of the NCC), and he took a more directive role, 'He was extremely keen not only to deliver the final report on time but to make sure that there was no doubt that this would be accepted by the DES and Secretary of State' (group member). New members were drafted in (to 'stiffen' the group) and civil servants began to sit in on meetings. The group was broken up into sub-committees with specific writing briefs. The task rather than the principles were now to the fore.

During this time the Committee was working under considerable pressure. We were continually up against lack of time to discuss or redraft the work of the subgroups and there is some unevenness about the sections in the final draft. It saddens me in particular that not only was there no opportunity to carry out any research or trialing of the targets we wished to put forward, but that there wasn't really even sufficient time to draw upon existing research or to consult experts in the field.

Furthermore, key points of tension remained. A particular bone of contention arose over the issue of pencil and paper algorithms versus practical problem solving and investigations. The new progressives and the industrial member in the group, in advancing the latter (and advocating the use of calculators in place of the former), found themselves ranged against their chairman, the DES officials and the Secretary of State. As one of the industrial members, already quoted, commented, 'Nobody ever does long division . . . It's ludicrous . . . and all The "declining standards seems to be based on tests of that sort . . . if you can multiply six vulgar fractions, well yes, but who ever does?'(Dr Ray Peacock). This dispute 'nearly drove the group apart'.

> All the professional members of the Committee and the industrial representative were very much against children being drilled in long arithmetical procedures when they had calculators available. But it was very difficult to convince the Department and the Chairman, and it was clear that there would be problems, in turn, in convincing the Secretary of State of this. We wanted the accent to be very much on calculator methods . . . And to be able to use them intelligently and interpret the results . . . It was only a last-minute compromise that enabled us all to agree the wording of the final report.

Opposing definitions of what is to count as school mathematics are in play here. Crucial issues and points of struggle which arose in the work of the working party, or which were taken up in the DES and in Cabinet, or which were addressed in the NCC consultative exercise combine to constitute the subject in a particular way. Thus on the question of algorithms, despite the compromise, and after the publication of the report, 'the Secretary of State has insisted on putting back the algorithims'.

The *Observer* (11 December 1988) reported:

> A fresh dispute between advocates of modern and traditional mathematics will erupt this week with the publication of a Government working party report on what children should learn when the National Curriculum is in place.
>
> Mr Kenneth Baker, the Education Secretary, intends to curb the advance of modern maths by overruling the group's advice that children do not need to learn how to do long division or multiplication without a calculator.
>
> Mr Baker, who has the backing of the Prime Minister and the Cabinet Committee on education which considered the report last month, believes some parts of it need tightening up.
>
> He also wants more emphasis on skills and knowledge and less on practical applications of maths.

(p.4)

Again, while the group put a strong emphasis in their report on the processes of using and applying mathematics, this recommendation was lost in the NCC consultation process. 'In fact over 80 per cent of those consulted agreed with keeping practical applications as an important profile component. This was overruled by the need to please the Secretary of State' (group member). It was explained in interview:

> Most of the professional members of the Committee were very keen to have assessment of how children applied their mathematics. It has been the case in Britain, as in other countries, that children have been well drilled in mathematical procedures, but, given an open ended situation, have been unable to use the mathematics they are supposed to know. We felt, therefore, that it was very important to have all through a child's education the opportunity to use what they knew in solving problems – sometimes real life problems but sometimes mathematical investigations. However, it was clear that mathematical investigations couldn't be very high on the agenda, because this is regarded as rather esoteric stuff . . . Therefore investigations had to be hidden under a rather larger umbrella of practical applications of mathematics, which sounded more entrepreneurial and robust.

The *TES* (9 December 1988, p.9) commented:

> Plans for maths in the National Curriculum have been revised extensively to put more emphasis on basics, despite overwhelming opposition from the 2,286 people and organizations who responded during consultations.
>
> The National Curriculum Council was this week clearly unhappy at having to make the changes to the final report of the maths working group – as it was with the changes Mr Kenneth Baker, the Education Secretary, demanded in the science report.

Commenting on both the maths and science groups, Paul Black explained:

> despite all the general pedagogic insights and philosophy, which is excellent in the science and maths reports, when they came down to it, they knew how to do the detailed job (of producing programmes or study and attainment targets) for knowledge and understanding, or at least make it tight and hard . . . and didn't know how to make it look good in the novel areas (investigations, practical mathematics) . . . Roughly the story is that what came out of the working parties wasn't strong enough to stand up. It didn't convince the DES and others. The NCC had to toughen it or abandon it, and they had a go at toughening that aspect, which was

profile component three in mathematics, and part of a profile
component in science. And they succeeded in toughening it in the
science, to a point where it was viable and sustainable in their
view, and they could put it forward and know that it would win,
and they had to give up the mathematics because they weren't
going to win, they thought. And that is the difference in the amount
of work that had been put into developing the assessment or the
techniques in the two areas, and mathematics hadn't got as far, and
the reason why the science had got further and could fill the gap
was APU science.

The groups differed in their ability to realise particular preferred versions of their subject. The outcome of struggles were not necessarily
foregone or automatic, although the possibilities of intervention
weighted things in the favour of the Secretary of State. Essentialist
views of what is, or is not, real mathematics or science are deployed. On
the whole DES officials and the Secretary of State were sceptical about
the attempts in both groups significantly to move away from a firm
'knowledge and understanding' basis to the subjects. Nonetheless there
was a degree of receptiveness to the new pedagogies being expounded.
Paul Black again:

I don't think the DES ever raised serious worries about the profile
component in science on the open-ended investigation. They did
want it toughening. They did feel some of the stuff that it was
bracketed with, which was about group work, was not sustainable.
Not because of bias against that, intrinsically they just thought it
was a different set of ideas being approached which weren't central
to science, and were either not approriate and certainly hadn't been
dealt with in appropriate detail. But there wasn't any great
difficulty about getting that in, if it could be done properly.

But, in several respects, the Secretary of State and the Cabinet tended to
reiterate the CPS view on mathematics teaching. The CPS document on
The Common Core says of recent developments in mathematics
teaching.

Mathematics, like other subjects, has suffered from the shift of
emphasis away from pupils being taught a clear body of
knowledge. Instead of teaching basic arithmetic in the early stages,
many teachers have, over the last twenty years, set out to introduce
pupils to complicated mathematical concepts without an adequate
foundation.

(CPS 1988 p.30)

Here, in relation to mathematics, new progressivism is under attack.

What is apparent here in small-scale and close focus are the more general ideological interests and definitions outlined in chapter 1. The new progressives and reforming old humanists in the HMI and DES, in this instance supporters of 'modern' maths, are confonted by the cultural restorationists in government and the New Right.

These are struggles over subject knowledge in 'crucial sites' of influence and definition. There are some woolly compromises and some losses and victories for each camp. There is no simple or direct translation into the National Curriculum of either New Right or new progressivist views. In the case of mathematics the relevant HMIs were evidently committed to a Cockcroftian view, and the industrial representative was strongly supportive of the 'progressive line'. The DES, the Secretary of State and the new Chairman seemed to take a middle line, accepting some aspects of the 'new mathematics' but holding also to certain sticking points of traditionalism, like the opposition to the use of calculators. The fate of 'discrete mathematics', which appeared in the interim report, is an interesting example of the limits of both professional and industrial argument.

> The Chairman was very much against including this because he felt it was not commonly understood by either himself or the Secretary of State and refused to be reassured by the Committee that much of this mathematics was extremely important in its industrial applications, including the kind of applied logic that's used in computer programming and in industrial planning. I believe if we had been more politically sensitive about selling this area we could actually have got a higher profile for it in the final report. In the event we tried to slide as many of these ideas as we could into other targets.
>
> (group member)

In this phase of curriculum policy making, the locus of decision making is located firmly inside the educational state, to the extent that significant aspects of school mathematics are being discussed in Cabinet sub-committee. The establishment professionals drafted in to give form and credibility to the National Curriculum are being kept on a tight leash. Education has moved to the very centre of the political stage. Thus, we arrive at something of a paradox. On the one hand the working parties and the setting up of the NCC do allow the educationalist voice back into the policy complex; on the other the degree of control over, intervention in and monitoring of curriculum matters from government and civil service is at an unprecedented level.

English, whose English?

The internal workings of the English working party have been decidedly less dramatic than those of the mathematics one, but the reports of the group have received considerable public attention. English has consistently been in the forefront of public and political dispute between contending interests since its emergence as a separate school subject in the late nineteenth century. English has been regarded as a key subject in the 'political education' of the masses (see Ball, Kenny and Gardiner 1989). In particular, at various points, governments have attempted to intervene in the field of English teaching in order to discipline 'wayward' practitioners and rectify 'unacceptable' deviations from that version of English which best suits the interests of dominant political elites. At stake are views of what literacy involves, of what counts as being literate, and what is seen as the 'real' uses of reading and writing skills. In the context of the National Curriculum it is also important that Kenneth Baker took a personal interest in English teaching and has firm views about priorities. It is particularly interesting to consider the press handling of the English working party reports.

As noted above, Brian Cox, *Black Paper* founder, was appointed to chair the working party for English, which reported in two stages: 5-11 and 11-16. Many commentators expected draconian reports requiring a return to traditional methods and content in English teaching. The *Guardian* (10 May 1988) asked 'Is the future of English safe with Professor Brian Cox?'. But the headline in the *Observer* (20 November 1988) following the publication of the 5-11 report of the working party reads, 'Professor Brian Cox, one-time scourge of the "progressive" teachers as editor of the notorious "Black Papers", now finds himself under attack for rejecting traditional methods of teaching "Standard English" ' (p.15). And the same newspaper (18 June 1989) headed its report of the publication of the 11-16 report of the working group, 'English Report rekindles grammar row' (p.4). The particular focus of the outcry from right-wing commentators concerned the report's apparent rejection of the primacy of Standard English and the need for the teaching of formal grammar. The primary report describes Standard English as, 'one dialect among many' and argues for the need for grammar to be taught not separately but 'in context'. The secondary report does not list grammatical terms which should be learned, and recommends that speaking and listening be given equal weight with reading and writing when children are tested at 11 and 14. Further, there is no list of authors for study, nor a set of attainment targets for literature in the report. 'Group members could not agree between themselves or with Education Secretary Kenneth Baker on which other writers (apart from Shakespeare) were appropriate for study' (*Observer* 18 June 1989). The *Observer* (20 November 1988) comments, again referring to Brian Cox, that 'The maverick extremist of the Sixties appears a moderate in the Eighties'.

Sheila Lawlor, speaking on behalf of the CPS, features repeatedly in the rebuttals of Cox; she is reported as accusing the Cox group of:

> not really believing in Standard English. They speak of a child's entitlement to Standard English, but nowhere do they set out clearly what must be taught.
>
> It's a great disadvantage to children from homes where correct English isn't spoken. You are creating a social divide between children who will learn correct English at home and those who won't.
>
> (*Observer* 20 November 1988)

The shift here from Standard to the use of 'correct' English is significant. As to the 11-16 report she is reported as 'preparing a riposte' and quoted as saying that: 'There may be some sense in giving some children practical training in how to write a letter but it would be wrong to suggest that the essay is not a very good training for most children' (*Observer* 18 June 1989). However, the response from the government was more muted, again according to the *Observer*: 'Professor Griffiths (Head of Mrs Thatcher's policy group in No. 10), Whitehall sources say, returned the report from Downing Street with the message that a little more emphasis on grammar would satisfy the Prime Minister (20 November 1989).

Again it is possible to see the emphasis being tightened in the process between the final report stage and the drafting of statutory orders. A 'little more emphasis' is exactly what the Secretary of State asked for in submitting his version of the 5-11 report to the NCC for consultation. In his letter to Duncan Graham (Chair of the NCC) (15 November 1988) he says:

> The report is printed in full, with our comments. In general it forms a useful basis for the proposals. *We have, however, modified the group's recommendations in some important respects* and are asking the National Curriculum Council to do some further work.

Again the Secretary of State is making curriculum policy, and determining school knowledge in the most direct sense. He goes on:

> Bearing in mind our proposals for the first attainment target for writing, the Council will need to suggest a strengthening of the programmes of study to ensure that grammatical structure and terminology are appropriately reflected.

And such a 'little more emphasis' is exactly what was provided by the NCC consultation report on the 5-11 report. Duncan Graham, in his covering letter to the Secretary of State, notes that the consultation report:

> proposes a curriculum in English which reflects its view [the Council's] that mastery of grammatical structure goes hand in hand with the development of pupils' capacity to use language. This has been ensured by emphasizing the importance of language within the attainment targets which have been strengthened and widened accordingly.

The response in the report is summarised as:

> Council recommends that the increased emphasis on language study, including grammar, set out in the revised programmes of study and statements of attainment, should be incorporated into draft Orders (NCC 1989b, p.21).

This recommendation is made despite the Council's noting that:

> while most respondents rejected the Secretary of State's wish for greater emphasis on mastery of grammatical structure, a number also held the view that there was a need for increased knowledge about language for all pupils. The working group's report, in its chapters on Standard English and linguistic terminology, contributed positively on this issue. Council, too accepts that pupils require an increased knowledge about language
>
> (NCC 1989 p.19).

The non sequiturs here are interesting, particularly in the way they tend to obscure the fact that the Council is siding with the Secretary of State and a minority of those consulted against the views of the working party and the majority of those consulted. However, in at least one other area – the relative weighting to be given to the speaking and listening and reading and writing profile components – the Council does endorse the original report rather than the Secretary of State's amendments. Here the political and educational are clearly set over and against each other. These issues serve to indicate some of the symbolic as opposed to substantive aspects of the role of the working parties and the consultation process. Expert advice and consultation may provide credibility for the National Curriculum but are set over and against political preferences and entrenched old humanism in the curriculum policy process. However, the complexity of this process, particularly in relation to the National Curriculum, should not be underestimated. I am not suggesting that the process is a sham – the struggles are real, those which take place both within and between the groups and agencies involved. The DES and the Secretary of State may differ on particular points of issue from the educational establishment, and particularly those I have called the new progressives, but they also often differ from the Conservative cultural restorationists in No. 10 and in ginger groups like the CPS.

This is evidenced by one senior civil servant (C) who spoke about the way in which the bases of the National Curriculum and National Testing were established within government and within the DES.

> I think it's fair to say that with the original proposition, ten subjects, there was a certain amount of not so much horse trading as just straight outright opposition to begin with, which Kenneth Baker won. Plainly and simply he said, 'We must have this kind of National Curriculum. Look at what our competitor countries are doing, look at what the best schools are doing, the independent schools', and that was that. It started off from April '87 which is when he made his announcement to the Select Committee that he was going to legislate, and that he was going to legislate for this kind of curriculum. He said ten subjects; in the Conservative Party Manifesto for that summer it didn't say ten subjects. But nonetheless, having heard that April statement, we went on working on that basis. There was an attempt at a later stage to cut it down, influenced by CPS thinking, to something more like the core subjects. And certainly there was a large argument about how much time in the curriculum should be taken up by those ten subjects, which wasn't anything we were going to legislate about anyway, contrary to a lot of people's perceptions. So that was a quite hard-won argument. The other thing which I think was a major source of continuing discussion was the nature of assessment and testing.

Roger Blin-Stoyle of the SCDC illuminates another aspect of this political process with regard to the National Curriculum, the particular importance of 'subjects'.

> He seemed very wedded to the subjects, I think unwisely. But I can see the problem that Kenneth Baker had. If you presented things in terms of areas of experience, it can look very wishy-washy to those who are not in the educational establishment and most MPs are not of course and most parents aren't either. The general consumer knows what English and physics and chemistry are. They don't know quite what is meant by 'areas of experience'. But in the SCDC we felt there was too much emphasis on subject presentation

in the National Curriculum document, it was a pity that the HMI approach wasn't used. Personally I am sorry that more wasn't learnt from the Scottish experience. They've done a lot of work, way in advance of England, on curriculum matters, but the DES started from scratch . . . Political complexions may have come into this. I think it is doubtful whether No. 10 would have accepted something formulated in terms of 'areas of experience'. It is clear that they like the old-fashioned subjects – reading, writing, science and maths – that should be the core curriculum and the rest can go to hell.

In all this the New Right are an important point of reference; as an ideological ginger group they can sometimes set the tone for policy making, but may not make policy. A DES civil servant (E) offers a view of this.

The way in which I think I would analyse it, and this may be over-simplistic, is that they created the political climate within the Tory party in which it was acceptable to go for a National Curriculum and indeed to legislate about it. Partly because they were weaving up and down and saying things are so bad at the moment. But their impact on the actual form of the legislation and the actual form of the assessment arrangements has been fairly toned down, muted. In other words, they've got the principle, but not the practice.

In the light of CPS responses to the National Curriculum working groups this seems an appropriate representation. The pursuit of ideological purity and party commitments has to be set in the context of the work of the civil service with ministers in translating ideologies into policies and in relation to the interface between the DES and the educational establishment. The DES's contribution to the policy process is not insignificant and in relation to curriculum issues the officials may operate as policy 'brokers'.

SJB: Given what I was saying just now about a department view on the curriculum, is it sensible to think about a department view or views that are separate from those of the Secretary of State?

(C): Yes, I think that that is true of any departmental policy, or any department that has certain things which stem from the longer-term perspective, that seem a good way of going about things, developing things. And if you like, that's one of the advantages of the British civil service system, that you do have an element of continuity or forward thinking built in. Which is not to say that officials are going to pursue that if they are going to have ministers come in who are going to pursue a different line. Very much the contrary. What it does mean is that when ministers come in with a framework which says, 'We want to legislate about curriculum', they will put up advice. Now ministers may reject that advice, and say, 'No, we want something different', or they may say, 'Yes, that looks like a good idea'. That's a perfectly normal civil service/minister way of working. The manifesto is always, from all sides of the spectrum, a pretty broad brush document, and it is very unusual for any government or minister to come in with a fully worked-up idea of what he wants to do. So that the civil service longer-term view then tends to come in and fill the vacuum, but it may get very much switched around. And it is the usual sort of iterative process and that iterative process also takes in views not just of ministers and politicians and civil servants, but also the kind of response that you get from out there, from a large number of sources, as soon as you start flouting ideas. So the whole formulation of policy is complex.

8

Endnote

Complexity has been one of the major recurring themes of this study. It is also the basis of my brief concluding comments. Education policy is infused with economic, political and ideological contradictions; in the analysis developed here it emerges as a site of struggles 'among status communities for domination, for economic advantage, and for prestige' (Collins 1977 p.3). Not everything can be reduced to the requirements of production, nor to the play of political ideologies. 'Ideological cultural practice' and political necessity *are* significant as well as, and aside from, 'economic practice' (Whitty 1985 p.34). The curriculum, as I have tried to demonstrate, is a particular focus for contradiction and struggle. The economic provides a context and a 'vocabulary of motives' for reform. The overall repositioning and restructuring of education in relation to production is evident. But in curriculum terms the economic, expressed as either vocational or technical initiatives, remains marginal, although settlements and compromises between contending interests do vary from subject to subject.

The DES, while willing to acknowledge and exploit, where useful, arguments relating education to economic need in a specific sense, has maintained a stance towards the curriculum in general which I have called reformist old-humanism. It is a stance which incorporates a commitment to certain educational verities, like the subject, a belief in the efficacy of assessment-led control, and in the need for selection and curriculum differentiation. But it also includes a view of curriculum change as a process of adaptation to economic and technological change. In the arena of policy making this can be set in antagonistic relation to three other positions within the curriculum field: the cultural restorationism of the New Right, the industrial-training lobby of the schools/industry movement and the DTI, and the new progressivism of the education intellectuals. We may discern the representatives of the state at work in this arena of conflict, attempting to construct new compromises for the curriculum which balance out disparate

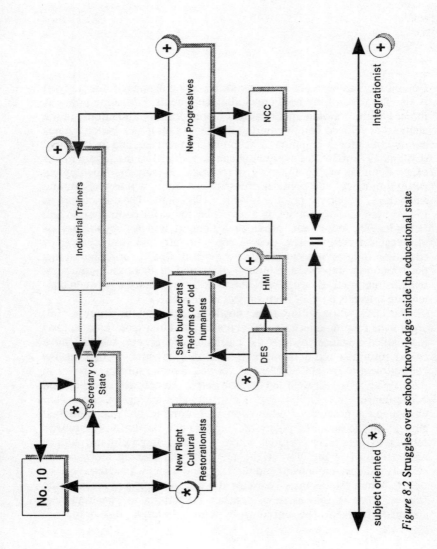

Figure 8.2 Struggles over school knowledge inside the educational state

imperatives and interests. (See figure 8.2 for a heuristic representation of contending influences inside the educational state.)

One aspect of these new compromises is a new view of partnership, wherein individual teachers are now franchise holders of the National Curriculum responsible for its delivery; they are urged to make the new system their own. This is a very different form of partnership from that which operated within education policy in 1976, the point at which we began. The 'policy community' of education is now constituted very differently. Certain groups are maginalised or excluded altogether.

The complexity of curriculum conflict and the changing, sometimes surprising, nature of alignments between factions makes it difficult therefore to sustain a simplistic analysis which reduces these political and ideological conflicts directly or solely to the effects of changes and contradictions in capitalist production. However, as I made clear in chapters 4 and 5, changes in capitalist production do provide one compelling dynamic for educational change, and representatives of capital are influential contributors to the field of curriculum conflict. The arguments of these representatives are privileged in some sections of the state but not in such a way as to influence decisively the outcome of struggles over the definition and purposes of education. Nonetheless, the generalised and cumulative effect of organisational and curricula changes in schools may have gone some way towards establishing a new correspondence between certain factions of capital and certain forms of schooling.

Furthermore, aside from the organic intellectuals of conservatism (the New Right) and the needs of the economy, the practical politics of education must also attend to the pragmatics of control and the limits and possibilities of change in the system. The interests and concerns and progressive impetus of the educational establishment can only be ignored to a certain extent if co-operation is also required from them in making change work. According to Shilling (1988) policy is a dialectical process and outcomes are constrained 'by the potential power schools are able to exercise as "front-line organizations"' (p.11).

Some of the tensions and contradictions in this politics of education are refractions of broader tensions and contradictions embedded in Thatcherism and the ideological constitution of the Conservative Party. Thatcherism attempts to stand both for modernisation and progress and for tradition and stability. The neo-liberal influence emphasises an orientation to the future, constant adaptation to new circumstances and an absence of state controls; the neo-conservative influence stresses an orientation to the past, traditional values and collective loyalties. Education is thus contested in terms of its role in both restoring authority and responding to the contemporary logic of capitalist development. The internal cultural and ideological dynamics of these struggles serve to underline Williams' (1962) point, which was quoted in chapter 1, that: 'An educational curriculum, as we have seen again and again in past periods, expresses a compromise between an inherited selection of interests and the emphasis of new interests' (p.172). The pattern and outcome of these compromises *are* different at different historical moments. The outcomes cannot simply be read off from events or structures elsewhere.

But the ERA is not just about control over the definition of school knowledge. It is also about control over teachers and teachers' work. It rests upon a profound distrust of teachers and seeks to close down many of the areas of discretion previously available to them. In doing this it brings into being a massively over-determined system of education. The National Curriculum and National Testing provide the belt and braces of central controls, and the market offers a further carrot-and-stick mode of constraint. Embedded in all this are confused and contradictory views of the 'new teacher', ranging from the innovative and competitive *petit*-professional to the harrassed, reactive teaching technician. In some respects LMS may encourage headteachers to treat teachers as commodities, interchangeable with books, equipment, paint and new desks.

The 1988 Act can also be read as signalling the break-up of a national state education system. There is massive potential for greater diversity among schools, but beyond this the separation between the state and private sectors is being blurred and new sources of funding (CTCs and local sponsorship) are given formal recognition in current government policy. Alongside this, aspects of the Act reduce significantly the historic role of local government in educational provision and management.

However, it is crucial to recognise that the analysis of the noise and heat of reform and the making of national policy still begs questions about the implementation and realisation of reform in schools and classrooms. The struggles over interpretation and accommodation go on.

Appendix 1

List of acronyms and abbreviations

ACC	Association of County Councils
AMA	Association of Metropolitan Authorities
AMMA	Assistant Masters and Mistresses Association
BTec	Business and Technicans Education Council
CASE	Campaign for State Education
CATE	Council for the Accreditation of Teacher Education
CBI	Confederation of British Industry
CEA	Conservative Education Association
CPS	Centre for Policy Studies
CPVE	Certificate of Pre-Vocational Education
CSE	Certificate of Secondary Education
CTC	City Technology College
DES	Department of Education and Science
DOE	Department of the Environment
DTI	Department of Trade and Industry
ERA	Education Reform Act (1988)
FEU	Further Education Unit
GCE	General Certificate of Education (O and A levels)
GCSE	General Certificate of Secondary Education
HMI	Her Majesty's Inspectorate
IEA	Institute of Economic Affairs
ILEA	Inner London Education Authority
ILTA	Inner London Teachers' Association
IoD	Institute of Directors
LEA	Local Education Authority
LMS	Local Management of Schools
MESP	Mini-Enterprises in Schools Project
MSC	Manpower Services Commission
NAGAM	National Association of school Governors and Managers
NAHT	National Association of Head Teachers

NATFHE	National Association of Teachers in Further and Higher Education
NC	National Currriculum
NCC	National Curriculum Council
NCES	National Council for Educational Standards
NCPTA	National Council of Parent-Teacher Associations
NSG	Non-Statutory Guidance
NT	National Testing
NUT	National Union of Teachers
PSHE	Personal, Social and Health Education
SAT	Standard Assessment Task
SAU	Social Affairs Unit
SCDC	Schools Curriculum Development Committee
SCIP	Schools Curriculum Industry Partnership
SEAC	Schools Examination and Assessment Council
SEC	Schools Examination Committee
TA	Teacher Assessment
TGAT	Task Group on Assessment and Testing
TES	Times Education Supplement
TVEI	Technical and Vocational Education Initiative
YTS	Youth Training Scheme

Appendix 2

List of interviewees and comment on interviews

Alan Ainsworth	Personnel Manager, Imperial Tobacco/CBI Education Committee
Digby Anderson	SAU
Sherrall Andrews	Industrial Society
Derek Betts	NATFHE
Prof. Paul Black	Chairman of TGAT, Deputy Chairman of NCC
Prof. Roger Blin-Stoyle	Chairman of SCDC
Michael Boxhall	Tesco/Chair of CPVE Board
Sir Rhodes Boyson MP	Former Education Minister
Dr Margaret Brown	Mathematics Working Party
Sheila Browne	Former Chief HMI
Sir Wilfred Cockcroft	Chairman of SEC
Dimitri Coryton	Chair of CEA
Baroness Cox	Former Education Minister, CPS, NCES
Lord Donaghue	Former adviser to James Callaghan
Alan Evans	Education Officer, NUT
Charlotte Gibbons	NAGAM
Bryony Griffith	Former Education Desk, Conservative Central Office
Alan Grunow	Secretary of AMA
Philip Halsey	Chairman of SEAC
Keith Hampson MP	Former Education Minister
David Hart	General Secretary, NAHT
Allen Hazelhurst MP	Vice-Chairman of backbench Education Committee
Lord Joseph	Former Education Secretary
Robert Joy	Institute of Directors
Kevin Keohane	Director, Roehampton Institute
Brian Kington	Public Issues Manager, IBM

Keith McWilliams	Former Chief Executive, Schools Council and SCDC
Phillip Merridale	Chair of Hampshire Education Committee, ACC, Burnham Committee
Lord Mulley	Former Education Secretary
Sir Peter Newson	Secretary of ACC
Dr Ray Peacock	Research Co-ordinator, Philips UK
Jack Peffers	SCIP
Pauline Perry	Former HMI
Sir Reg Prentice	Former Education Secretary
Stuart Sexton	IEA, former adviser to Mark Carlisle and Keith Joseph
Rev. Dr George Tolley	Former Head of Quality Division, MSC
George Walden MP	Former Education Minister
Tony Webb	Director of Education, CBI
Damian Welfare	Parliamentary Officer, AMA
Raphael Wilkins	Former Special Adviser to Commons Committee on Science and Education
Prof. John Woolhouse	Former Chairman of MSC

plus six serving and two former DES civil servants

Total = 49

These interviews were conducted over an eighteen-month period in 1988–89. In all but two cases the respondents allowed me to tape-record our discussion and most were conducted on the respondent's 'home ground'. Very few of the people I interviewed requested to see or approve the material from their interviews that I intended to use. Some of the civil servants did require to see the extracts I intended to quote, but nothing of substance was removed as a result. But it was in the process of clearing the interviews that I decided not to name the civil servants I interviewed. In effect, attribution had to be traded-off against the freedom to quote. (I had received only four negative replies to my letters requesting an interview.)

Because of the limitations of space only a very small proportion of the 1200 pages of transcripts is quoted in the text and many of those interviewed are not quoted directly at all.

References

Adam Smith Institute (1984) *Omega Report – Education Policy*, London, Adam Smith Insitute

Alder, M. and Raab, G. (1988) 'Exit, Choice and Loyalty: the impact of parental choice on admission to school in Edinburgh and Dundee', *Journal Of Education Policy*, 3, (2), pp.155–80

Althusser, L. (1969) *For Marx*, London, Allen Lane

Anderson, D. (1982) *Detecting Bad Schools: A Guide for Normal Parents*, London, The Social Affairs Unit

Apple, M. (1986) *Teachers and Texts*, London, Routledge and Kegan Paul

Ashford, D.E. (1981) *Policy and Politics in Britain: The Limit of Consensus*, Oxford, Blackwell

Atkins, M.J. (1982) *Foundation Courses in a Sixth Form College: A Case Study*, Unpb. Ph.D Thesis, University of Nottingham

Atkins, M.J. (1986) 'The Pre-Vocational Curriculum: A Review of the Issues Involved', *Journal of Curriculum Studies*, 19, 1, pp.45–53

Audit Commission, The (1986) *Towards Better Management of Secondary Education*, London, HMSO

Ball, S.J. (1981) *Beachside Comprehensive*, Cambridge, Cambridge University Press

Ball, S.J. (1986) 'English Teaching, the Educational State and Forms of Literacy', paper presented at the Symposium on Research in Mother Tongue Education, University of Antwerp

Ball, S.J. (1987) *The Micro-Politics of the School*, London, Methuen (reprinted by Routledge)

Ball, S.J. (1988) 'Staff Relations during the Teachers' Industrial Action: context, conflict and proletarianisation', *British Journal of Sociology of Education*, 9, 3, pp.289–306

Ball, S.J. (1989) 'Through the Secret Garden and into the Secret Room: political culture and educational policy-making', paper presented at the conference 'Education Policy and Ethnography', St Hilda's College, Oxford

Ball, S.J., Kenny, A. and Gardiner, D. (1989) 'Literacy and Democracy: policies and politics for the teaching of English' in I. Goodson and P. Medway (eds) *Bringing English to Order*, Lewes, Falmer Press

Barcan, A. (1986) 'English: Two Decades of Attrition', in D. O'Keeffe (ed.) *The Wayward Curriculum*, Exeter, The Social Affairs Unit

Politics and policy making in education

Barnett, C. (1972) *The Collapse of British Power*, London, Eyre Methuen

Barraclough, G. (1967) *An Introduction to Contemporary History*, Harmondsworth, Penguin

Bates, I. (1989) 'Versions of Vocationalism: an analysis of some social and political influence on curriculum policy and practice', *British Journal of Sociology of Education*, 10, 2, pp.215–32

Bates, R. (1983) 'Administration of Education: Towards a Critical Practice', *International Encyclopaedia of Education*, Oxford, Pergamon

Baudrillard, J. (1988) *Selected Writings* (ed. M. Poster), Oxford, Polity Press

Becher, A. (1989) 'The National Curriculum and the Implementation Gap', paper prepared for the Open University

Beck, J. (1983) 'Accountability, Industry and Education', in J. Ahier and M. Flude (eds) *Contemporary Education Policy*, Beckenham, Croom Helm

Belsey, A (1986) 'The New Right, Social Order and Civil Liberties', in R. Levitas (ed.) *The Ideology of the New Right*, Oxford, Polity Press

Bennett, N. (1976) *Teaching Styles and Pupil Progess*, London, Open Books

Bernstein, B. (1967) 'Open School Open Society', reprinted in *Class, Codes and Control, Vol. 3*, London, Routledge and Kegan Paul

Bernstein, B. (1971) 'On the Classification and Framing of Educational Knowledge', in M.F.D. Young (ed.) *Knowledge and Control*, London, Collier/Macmillan

Bernstein, B. (1975) 'Visible and Invisible Pedagogies' in *Class, Codes and Control, Vol 3*, London, Routledge and Kegan Paul

Bernstein, B. (1977) 'Aspects of the Relations between Education and Production', in *Class, Codes and Control, Vol.3, 2nd Ed.*, London, Routledge and Kegan Paul

Bernstein, B. (1985) 'On pedagogic discourse' in *Handbook of Theory and Research in the Sociology of Education*, New York, Greenwood Press

Bonefeld, W. (1987) 'Reformulation of state theory', *Capital and Class*, No. 33, pp.96–128

Bosanquet, N. (1983) *After the New Right*, London, Heinemann

Bottomore, T., Harris, L., Kiernan, V.G. and Miliband, R. (1983) *A Dictionary of Marxist Thought*, Oxford, Blackwell

Bowe, R. and Whitty, G. (1984) 'Teachers, Boards and Standards', in P. Broadfoot (ed.) *Selection, Certification and Control*, Lewes, Falmer Press

Bowis, J. (1988) *ILEA – The Closing Chapter*, London, Conservative Political Centre

Bowles, S. and Gintis, H. (1975) *Schooling in Capitalist America*, London, Routledge and Kegan Paul

Boyson, R. (1975) 'The Developing Case for the Educational Voucher', in C.B. Cox and R. Boyson (eds) *Black Papers 1975: The Fight for Education*, London, Dent and Sons

Briault, E. (1976) 'A distributed system of educational administration', *International Review of Education*, 22, 4, pp.429–39

Brown, M. (1989) 'Programmes of study in the National Curriculum for Mathematics: A fit prescription for teaching and learning?', paper

presented at the BERA annual conference, University of
Newcastle-upon-Tyne

Bucher, R. and Strauss, A.L. (1961) 'Professions in process', *American
Journal of Sociology*, 66, 2, pp.325–34

Bullock Report, The (1975) *A Language For Life*, London, HMSO

Burton, F. and Carlen, P. (1977) 'Official Discourse', *Economy and Society*,
6, 4, pp.377–408

Callaghan, J. (1987) *Time and Chance*, London, Collins

Campbell, R.J. (1989) 'HMI and Aspects of Public Policy for the Primary
School Curriculum' in A. Hargreaves and D. Reynolds (eds) *Education
Policies: Controversies and Critiques*, Lewes, Falmer Press

Castells, M. (1977) *The Urban Question*, London, Edward Arnold

CCCS (1981) *Unpopular Education*, London, Hutchinson

Chitty, C. (1988) 'Two Models of a National Curriculum: Origins and
Interpretation', in D. Lawton and C. Chitty (eds) *The National
Curriculum, Bedford Way Papers 33*, Institute of Education, University of
London

Cockcroft, W.M. (1982) *Mathematics Counts!*, London, HMSO

Cohen, P. (1980) *Folk Devils and Moral Panics*, Oxford, Martin Robertson

Cole, P. (1983) 'Work Experience Programs in Schools: some Suggestions for
Program Reorientation', *Discourse*, 3, pp.22–32

Collins, R. (1975) *Conflict Sociology*, New York, Academic Press

Coopers and Lybrand (1988) *Local Management of Schools: a report to the
DES*, London, Coopers and Lybrand

Cousins, M. and Hussain, A. (1984) *Michel Foucault*, London, MacMillan

Cox, C.B. (1981) *Education: The Next Decade*, London, Conservative
Political Centre

Cox, C.B. and Dyson, A.E. (eds) (1969) *Fight For Education: A Black Paper*,
London, The Critical Quarterly Society

CPS (1988) *The Common Core*, London, Centre for Policy Studies

Dale, R. (1979) 'The Politicisation of School Deviance: Reactions to William
Tyndale', in L. Barton and R. Meighan (eds) *Schools, Pupils and
Deviance*, Driffield, Nafferton

Dale, R. (1982) 'Education and the Capitalist State: Contributions and
Contradictions', in M.W. Apple (ed.) *Cultural and Economic
Reproduction in Education*, London, Routledge and Kegan Paul

Dale, R. (1985) 'The Background and Inception of the Technical and
Vocational Education Initiative', in R. Dale (ed.) *Education, Training and
Employment: Towards a New Vocationalism*, Oxford, Pergamon

Dale, R. (1988) 'Implications for Progressivism of Recent Changes in the
Control and Direction of Education Policy', in A. Green and S.J. Ball (eds)
Progress and Inequality in Comprehensive Education, London, Routledge

Dean, J. and Steeds, A. (1981) *17 Plus: The New Sixth Form in Schools and
FE*, Windsor, Nelson–NFER

Demaine, J. (1988) 'Teachers' Work, Curriculum and the New Right', *British
Journal of Sociology of Education*, 9, 3, pp.247–64

Dennison, W.F. (1984) *Educational Finance and Resources*, London, Croom
Helm

DES. (1977a) *Education in Schools: a Consultative Document*, London, HMSO
——(1977b) *Circular 14/77*, London, DES
——(1977c) *The Curriculum 11–16*, London, HMSO
——(1978a) *Mixed-Ability Work in Comprehensive Schools* (Matters for Discussion No.6), London, HMSO
——(1978b) *The Primary Survey*, London, HMSO
——(1980a) *A Framework for the School Curriculum*, London, HMSO
——(1980b) *A View of the Curriculum*, London, HMSO
——(1981a) *The School Curriculum: A Recommended Approach*, London, HMSO
——(1981b) *Curriculum 11-16: A Review of Progress*, London, HMSO
——(1982a) *Education 5–9: An Illustrative Survey*, London, HMSO
——(1982b) *Mathematics Counts (The Cockcroft Report)*, London, HMSO
——(1983a) *Curriculum 11–16: towards a statement of entitlement*, London, HMSO
——(1983b) *The School Curriculum, Circular 8/83*, London, DES
——(1983c) *The New Teacher in the School*, London, HMSO
——(1984a) *Circular 7/84 Work Experience*, London, DES
——(1984b) *Parental Influence at School*, London, DES
——(1984c) *Organization and Content of the 5–16 Curriculum: A Note from the DES*, London, DES
——(1984d) *Teacher Quality*, London, DES
——(1985a) *The Curriculum from 5 to 16*: (Curriculum Matters No.2), London, HMSO
——(1985b) *Better Schools*, London, HMSO
——(1985c) *Education 8–12*, London, HMSO
——(1985d) *Science from 5–16: A Statement of Policy*, London, DES
——(1986a) *Local Authority Policies for the School Curriculum*, London, HMSO
——(1986b) *City Technology Colleges: A New Choice of School*, London, DES
——(1987) *The National Curriculum 5–16: A Consultation Document*, London, DES
——(1988) *National Curriculum: Task Group on Assessment and Testing – A Report*, London, DES and Welsh Office
Donald, J. (1979) 'Green Paper: Noise of Crisis', in R. Dale, G. Esland, R. Fergusson, and M. Macdonald (eds) *Schooling and the National Interest Vol 1*, Lewes, Falmer Press
Dreyfus, H.L. and Rabinow, P. (1982) *Michel Foucault: Beyond Structuralism and Hermeneutics*, Brighton, Harvester Press
Duncan, S. and Goodwin, M. (1985) '*The Local State and Local Economic Policy. Why the Fuss?*', Policy and Politics, 13, (3), pp.227–253
Dunleavy, P. and O'Leary, B. (1987) *The Theories of the State*, London, Macmillan
Ernest, P. (1989) 'Introduction' in P. Ernest (ed.) *Mathematics Teaching: The State of the Art*, Lewes, Falmer Press

Finn, D., Grant, N. and Johnson, R. (1977) 'Democracy, education and the crisis', in CCCS, *On Ideology*, London, Hutchinson

Fitz, J., Edwards, T. and Whitty, G. (1986) 'Beneficaries, Benefits and Costs: an Investigation of the Assisted Places Scheme, *Research Papers in Education*, Vol.1, No.3

Foucault, M. (1971) 'Theories et institutions penales', Annuaire du College de France 1971–72

Foucault, M. (1972) *The Archeology of Knowledge*, London, Tavistock

Foucault, M (1977) *The Archeology of Knowledge*, London, Tavistock

Foucault, M. (1978) *The History of Sexuality Vol.1*, New York, Pantheon

Foucault, M. (1979) *Discipline and Punish*, Harmondsworth, Peregrine

Foucault, M. (1980) *Power/Knowledge: Selected Interviews and other Writings 1972–77*, C. Gordon (ed.), Brighton, Harvester Press

Foucault, M. (1981) 'The Order of Discourse', in R. Young (ed.) *Untying the Text*, London, Routledge and Kegan Paul

Fowler, G., Morris, V. and Ozga, J. (1973) *Decision-Making in British Education*, London, Heinemann/Open University Press

Fowler, W.S. (1988) *Towards the National Curriculum: discussion and control in the English education system*, London, Kogan Page

Francis, M. (1986) *The ILEA Elections 1986: a survey of the political and ideological issues*, MA in Urban Education dissertation, King's College London

Friedman, M. and Friedman, R. (1980) *Free to Choose*, London, Secker and Warburg

Fritzell, C. (1987) 'On the concept of relative autonomy in educational theory', *British Journal of Sociology of Education*, 8, 1, pp.23–36

Gamble, A. (1986) 'The Political Economy of Freedom', in R. Levitas (ed.) *The Ideology of the New Right*, Oxford, Polity Press

Gerwitz, S. and Ozga, J. (1990) 'Partnership, Pluralism and Education Policy: A Reassessment', *Journal of Education Policy*, 5, 1, pp.35–46

Gleeson, D. (1987) 'Introduction', in D. Gleeson (ed.) *TVEI and Secondary Education: a Critical Appraisal*, Milton Keynes, Open University Press

Gleeson, D. (1989) *The Paradox of Training: Making Progress out of Crisis*, Milton Keynes, Open University Press

Goodson, I. (1983) *School Subjects and Curriculum Change*, London, Croom Helm

Grace, G. (1984) *Education and the City*, London, Routledge and Kegan Paul

Grace, G. (1987) 'Teachers and the State in Britain: a Changing Relation', in M. Lawn and G. Grace (eds) *Teachers: the Culture and Politics of Work*, Lewes, Falmer Press

Grant, W. and Nath, S. (1984) *The Politics of Economic Policymaking*, Oxford, Basil Blackwell

Habermas, J. (1976) *Legitimation Crisis*, London, Heinemann

Hall, S. (1980) 'Popular-Democratic vs Authoritarian Populism: Two Ways of "Taking Democracy Seriously" ', in A. Hunt (ed.) *Marxism and Democracy* London, Lawrence and Wishart

Hall, S. (1983) 'The Great Moving Right Show' in S. Hall and M. Jacques (eds) *The Politics of Thatcherism*, London, Lawrence and Wishart

223

Hall, S. Critcher, C., Jefferson, T., Clarke, C. and Roberts, B. (eds) (1978) *Policing the Crisis*, London, Macmillan

Hall, S. and Jacques, M. (eds) (1983) *The Politics of Thatcherism*, London, Lawrence and Wishart

Hargreaves, A. (1983) 'The Politics of Administrative Convenience', in J. Ahier and M. Flude (eds) *Contemporary Education Policy*, Beckenham, Croom Helm

Hargreaves, A. (1987) 'Educational Assessment – A Test For Socialism' in R. Williams and C. Lacey (eds) *Ecology, Development and Education*, London, Kogan Page

Hargeaves, A. (1989) 'The Crisis in Motivation and Assessment', in A. Hargeaves and D. Reynolds (eds) *Education Policies: Controversies and Critiques*, Lewes, Falmer Press

Hargreaves, A. and Reynolds, D. (1989) 'Decomprehensivization', in A. Hargeaves and D. Reynolds (eds) *Education Policies: Controversies and Critiques*, Lewes, Falmer Press

Haviland, J. (ed.) (1988) *Take Care Mr Baker!*, London, Fourth Estate

Hayek, F. (1973) *Law, Legislation and Liberty, Vol.1: Rules and Order*, London, Routledge and Kegan Paul

Hayek, F. (1976) *Law, Legislation and Liberty, Vol.2: The Mirage of Social Justice*, London, Routledge and Kegan Paul

Hayek, F. (1979) *Law, Legislation and Liberty, Vol.3: The Political Order of a Free People*, London, Routledge and Kegan Paul

Hayek, F. (1986) *The Road to Serfdom*, London, Routledge and Kegan Paul

Hennessey, P. (1989) *Whitehall*, London, Secker and Warburg

Hillgate Group, The (1987) *The Reform of British Education*, London, Hillgate Group

Hindess, B. (1981) 'Parliamentary democracy and socialist politics', in M. Prior (ed.) *The Popular and the Political*, London, Routledge and Kegan Paul

Hirsch, J. and Roth, R. (1986) *Das neue Gesicht des Kapitalismus, Vom Fordismus zum PostFordismus*, Hamburg, VSA Verlag

Holloway, J. (1987) 'A Note on Fordism and Neo-Fordism', *Common Sense*, No.1, Edinburgh

Holt, M. (1982) 'The Great Education Robbery', *Times Education Supplement*, 3 December, p.11

Hopper, E. (1971) 'The Classification of Education Systems', in E. Hopper (ed.) *Readings in the Theory of Education Systems*, London, Hutchinson

Horton, T. (ed.) (1987) *GCSE: Examining the New System*, London, Harper & Row

Jamieson, I. (1986) 'Corporate Hegemony or Pedagogic Liberation: the schools/industry movement in England and Wales', in R. Dale (ed.) (1986) *Education, Training and Employment: Towards a New Vocationalism*, Oxford, Pergamon

Jamous, H. and Peloille, B. (1970) 'Professions or self-perpetuating systems? Changes in the French university-hospital system', in J.A. Jackson (ed.)

Professions and Professionalisation, Cambridge, Cambridge University Press

Jessop, B. (1985) *Nicos Poulantzas, Marxist Theory and Political Strategy*, London, Macmillan

Jessop, B., Bonnett, K., Bromley, S. and Ling, T. (1984) 'Authoritarian Popularism, Two Nations and Thatcherism', *New Left Review*, No. 147

Jessop, B., Bonnett, K., Bromley, S. and Ling, T. (1988) *Thatcherism: A Tale of Two Nations*, Oxford, Basil Blackwell

Johnson, R. (1989) 'Thatcherism and English Education: breaking the mould or confirming the pattern?', *History of Education*, 18, 2, pp.91–121

Joseph, K. and Sumption, J. (1979) *Equality*, London, John Murray

Kenway, J. (1987) 'Left Right out: Australian Education and the Politics of Signification', *Journal of Education Policy*, 2, (3), pp.189–204

King, A. (1975) 'Overload: problems of governing in the 1970s', *Political Studies*, 23, pp.284–96

Kogan, M. (1975) *Educational Policy-Making*, London, Allen and Unwin

Kogan, M. (1978) *The Politics of Educational Change*, Manchester, Manchester University Press

Kogan, M. (1979) 'Different Frameworks for Education Policy-Making and Analysis', *Educational Analysis*, 1, 2, pp.5–14

Kogan, M. (1982) 'Changes in Perspective', *Times Education* Supplement, 15 January, p.6

Labour Research (1987) Web of Reaction: right-wing groups and activists, 76, 10, pp.7–12, London, Labour Research Department

Laclau, E. and Mouffe, C. (1985) *Hegemony and Socialist Strategy*, London Verso

Lawton, D. (1986) 'The Department of Education and Science: Policy Making at the Centre' in A. Hartnett and M. Naish (eds) *Education and Society Today*, Lewes, Falmer Press

Lawton, D. and Gordon, P. (1987) *HMI*, London, Routledge and Kegan Paul

Levitas, R. (1986) 'Competition and Compliance: The Utopias of the New Right', in R. Levitas (ed.) *The Ideology of the New Right*, Oxford, Polity Press

Littler, C. and Salaman, G. (1982) 'Bravermania and beyond: recent theories of the Labour Process', *Sociology*, 16, 2, pp.215–69

Lindblom, C.E. (1979) 'Still Muddling, Not Yet Through', *Public Administration Review*, No. 39, pp.517–26

Lipietz, A. (1985) *The Enchanted World, Credit and World Crises*, London, Verso

Lodge, P. and Blackstone, T. (1982) *Educational Policy and Educational Inequality*, Oxford, Robertson

Lonely, M. (1986) *The Politics of Greed: The New Right and the Welfare State*, London, Pluto Press

McClure, S. (1988) *Education Re-formed*, Sevenoaks, Hodder and Stoughton

McCullough, G. (1986) 'Policy, politics and education: the Technical and

Vocational Education Initiative', *Journal of Education Policy*, 1,1, pp.35–52

Macdonell, D. (1986) *Theories of Discourse*, Oxford, Blackwell

Mace, J. (1986) 'Education and Science', in *Public Expenditure Policy 1984/5*, London, Croom Helm

McLennan, G., Held, D. and Hall, S. (1984) 'Editors' Introduction' to G. McLennan, D. Held and S. Hall (eds), *State and Society in Contemporary Britain*, Oxford, Polity Press

McPherson, A. and Raab, C. (1988) *Governing Education: A Sociology of Policy since 1945*, Edinburgh, Edinburgh University Press

Marks, J., Cox, C. and Pomian-Szednicki, M. (1983) *Standards in English Schools*, London, National Council for Educational Standards

Marx, K. (1968) *Capital*, London, Lawrence and Wishart

Maude, A. (1969) 'The Egalitarian Threat', in C.B. Cox and A.E. Dyson (eds) *Fight for Education*, London, The Critical Quarterly Society

Maw, J. (1988) 'National Curriculum Policy: Coherence and Progression', in D. Lawton and C. Chitty (eds) *The National Curriculum, Bedford Way Papers 33*, Institute of Education, University of London

Miliband, R. (1973) *The State in Capitalist Society*, London, Quartet

Moon, J. and Richardson, J.J. (1984) 'Policy-making with a difference, the TVEI', *Public Administration*, Vol.62, (spring), pp.23–33

MSC (1984) *TVEI Review*, London, MSC

Murray, R. (1988) 'Life After Henry (Ford)', *Marxism Today*, October, pp.8–13

NCC (1989a) *An Introduction to the National Curriculum*, NCC/12, York, NCC

NCC (1989b) *National Curriculum Council Consultation Report: English*, York, NCC

No Turning Back Group of MPs (1986) *Save Our Schools*, London, Conservative Party Centre

North, J. (ed.) (1987) *The GCSE: An Examination*, London, Claridge Press

Nozick, R. (1974) *Anarchy, State and Utopia*, Oxford, Blackwell

OECD (1975) *Education Development Strategy in England and Wales*, Paris, OECD

Offe, C. (1976) *Industry and Inequality*, London, Edward Arnold

Offe, C. (1984) *Contradictions of the Welfare State*, London, Hutchinson

O'Keeffe, D. (ed.) (1986) *The Wayward Curriculum*, Exeter, Social Affairs Unit

Ozga, J. (1987) 'Studying Educational Policy through the Lives of Policy Makers: An attempt to close the macro-micro gap', in S. Walker and L. Barton (eds) *Changing Policies, Changing Teachers*, Milton Keynes, Open University Press

Palmer, F. (ed.) (1986) *Anti-Racism: An Assault on Education and Value*, London, The Sherwood Press

Palmer, F. (1986) 'English: Reducing Learning to Short Cut 'Skills' ', in D. O'Keefe (ed) *The Wayward Curriculum*, London, Social Affairs Unit

Pecheux, M. (1982) *Language, Semantics and Ideology: Stating the Obvious*, London, Macmillan

Pietrasik, R. (1987) 'The Teachers' Action 1984–86', in M. Lawn and
G. Grace (eds) *Teachers: The Culture and Politics of Work*, Lewes, Falmer
Press

Pile, W. (1979) *The Department of Education and Science*, London, Allen and
Unwin

Plaskow, M. (ed.) (1985) *The Life and Death of the Schools Council*, Lewes,
Falmer Press

Policy Research Associates (1986) *The House of Lords Debate: Educational
Indoctrination*, London, Policy Research Associates

Pollard, A., Purvis, J. and Walford, G. (eds) (1988) *Education Training and
the New Vocationalism*, Milton Keynes, Open University Press

Prais, S.J. (1987) 'Educating for Productivity: comparisons of Japanese and
English schooling and vocational preparation', *National Institute
Economic Review*, February, London, National Institute of Economic and
Social Research

Prais, S.J. and Wagner, K. (1985) 'Schooling standards in England and
Germany: some summary comparisons bearing on economic performance'
National Institute Economic Review, May, London, National Institute of
Economic and Social Research

Pring, R. (1986) 'Privatization of Education', in R. Rogers (ed) *Education and
Social Class*, Lewes, Falmer Press

Prunty, J. (1985) 'Signposts for a Critical Educational Policy Analysis',
Australian Journal of Education, 29, 2, pp.133–40

Quicke, J. (1988) 'The "New Right" and Education', *British Journal of
Educational Studies*, 36, 1, pp.5–20

Ranson, S. (1985) 'Contradictions in the Government of Educational Change',
Political Studies, No.33, pp.56–72

Ranson, S. and Travers, T. (1986) 'The Government of New Education', in
S. Ranson, B. Taylor and T. Brighouse (eds) *The Revolution in Education
and Training*, London, Longman

Reeder, D. (1979) 'A Recurring Debate: education and industry', in
G. Bernbaum (ed) *Schooling in Decline*, London, Macmillan

Rees, T. (1988) 'Education for Enterprise: the state and alternative
employment for young people', *Journal of Education Policy*, 3, (1),
pp.9–22

Rees, G., Williamson, H. and Winckler, V. (1989) 'The "New
Vocationalism": Further Education and Local Labour Markets', *Journal of
Education Policy*, 4, 3, pp.227–41

Reynolds, D. and Sullivan, M. (1987) *The Comprehensive Experience*, Lewes,
Falmer Press

Rhodes, R.A.W. (1985) 'Power-Dependence, Policy Communities and
Inter-governmental Networks', *Essex papers in Politics and Government*,
University of Essex

Richardson, J.J. and Jordan, G. (1979) *Governing Under Pressure*, Oxford,
Martin Robertson

Riseborough, G. (1981) 'Teachers' careers and comprehensive schooling: an
empirical study', *Sociology*, 15, 3, pp.352–81

Robson, M.H. and Walford, G. (1989) 'Independent Schools and Tax Policy under Mrs Thatcher', *Journal of Education Policy*, 4, 2, pp.149–62

Rustin, M. (1989) 'The Politics of Post-Fordism: Or the Trouble with "New Times"', *New Left Review*, No. 175, pp.54–78

Salter, B. and Tapper, T. (1981) *Education, Politics and the State*, London, Grant McIntyre

Salter, B. and Tapper, T. (1985) *Power and Policy in Education*, Lewes, Falmer Press

Saran, R. (1988) 'Education Policy under the Thatcher Government', *Australian Educational Researcher*, 15, 2, pp.55–65

Saunders, P. (1979) *Urban Politics*, London, Hutchinson

Saunders, P. (1981) *Social Theory and the Urban Question*, London, Hutchinson

Saunders, P. (1986) *Social Theory and the Urban Question, 2nd Ed.*, London, Hutchinson

Schools Council (1980) *The Practical Curriculum*, London, Schools Council

SCDC (1987) *National Curriculum 5-16: Response from the SCDC*, London, SCDC

Schumpeter, J. (1979) *Capitalism, Socialism and Democracy*, London, Allen and Unwin

Schwarz, B. (1987) 'The Thatcher Years' in R. Miliband, L. Pantich and J. Saville (eds) *Socialist Register 1987*, London, Merlin Press

Scruton, R. (1980) *The Meaning of Conservatism*, Harmondsworth, Penguin

Scruton, R. (1986) *World Studies: Education or Indoctrination*, London, Institute for European Defence and Strategic Studies

Scruton, R., Ellis-Jones, A. and O'Keeffe, D. (1985) *Education and Indoctrination*, Harrow, Education Research Centre

Seidel, G. (1986) 'Culture, Nation and "Race" in the British and French New Right', in R. Levitas (ed.) *The Ideology of the New Right*, Oxford, Polity Press

Senker, P. (1986) 'The Technical and Vocational Educational Initiative: an interim assessment', *Journal of Education Policy*, 1, 4, pp.293–306

Sexton, S. (1987) *Our Schools: A Radical Policy*, Warlingham, IEA, Education Unit

Sharp, R. and Green, A. (1975) *Education and Social Control*, London, Routledge and Kegan Paul

Sharp, R. (1980) *Knowledge, Ideology and the Politics of Schooling*, London, Routledge and Kegan Paul

Shilling, C. (1987) 'Work Experience as a Contradictory Experience', *British Journal of Sociology of Education*, 8, 4, pp.407–24

Shilling, C. (1988) 'Work Experience and Schools: Factors Influencing the Participation of Industry', *Journal of Education Policy*, 2, 2, pp.131–48

Shilling, C. (1989) 'The Mini-Enterprise in Schools Project: a new stage in education-industry relations', *Journal of Education Policy*, 4, 2, pp.115–24

Smith, A. (1976) *The Wealth of Nations*, Oxford, Clarendon Press

Stronach, I. (1988) 'Vocationalism and Economic Recovery: The Case Against Witchcraft', in S. Brown and R. Wake (eds) *Education in Transition*, Edinburgh, Scottish Council for Research in Education

Svi Shapiro, H. (1980) 'Education and the State in Capitalist Society: Aspects of the Sociology of Nicos Poulantzas', *Harvard Education Review*, 50, 3, pp.321–31

Taylor Report, the, (1977) *A New Partnership for our Schools*, London, HMSO

Taylor, I. (1987) 'Law and Order, Moral Order: The Changing Rhetorics of the Thatcher Government' in R. Miliband, L. Pantich and J. Saville (eds) *Socialist Register 1987: Conservatism in Britain and America: Rhetoric and Reality*, London, Merlin Press

Taylor-Gooby, P. (1985) *Public Opinion, Ideology and State Welfare*, London, Routledge and Kegan Paul

Thornbury, R. (1978) *The Changing Urban School*, London, Methuen

Turner, R. (1960) 'Sponsored and Contest Mobility and the School System', *American Sociological Review*, 25, 5

Walker, A. (1981) 'Social Policy, Social Administration and the Social Construction of Welfare', *Sociology*, 15, 2, pp.255–71

Wallace, G., Meyann, R. and Ginsberg, M. 'Teachers' Response to the Cuts' in J. Ahier and M. Flude (eds) *Contemporary Education Policy*, Beckenham, Croom Helm

Weinstock, A. (1976) 'I Blame the Teachers', *Times Education Supplement*, 23 January

Wexler. P. and Grabiner, G. (1986) 'America during the Crisis', in R. Sharp (ed) *Capitalism, Crisis and Schooling*, South Melbourne, Macmillan

Whitty, G. (1985) *Sociology and School Knowledge*, London, Methuen

Wiener, M. (1981) *English Culture and the Decline of Industrial Spirit*, Cambridge, Cambridge University Press

Williams, R. (1962) *The Long Revolution*, Harmondsworth, Penguin

Williams, R. (1973) 'Base and Superstructure in Marxist Cultural Theory', *New Left Review*, 82, pp.3–16

Williams, R. (1978) *Marxism and Literature*, Oxford University Press, Oxford

Worthen, J. (1987) 'GCSE English: A Cause for Concern', The Salisbury Review, 5, 1, and in J. North (ed.) (1987) *The GCSE: an Examination*, London, Claridge Press

Worsthorne, P. (1978) 'Too much Freedom', in M. Cowling, (ed) *Conservative Essays*, London, Cassell

Wright, M. (1981) 'Big Government in Hard Times: The Restraint of Public Expenditure', in C. Hood and M.A. Wright (eds) *Big Government in Hard Times*, Oxford, Martin Robertson

Wright, E. O. (1979) *Class, Crisis and the State*, London, New Left Books

Wright, N. (1977) *Progress in Education*, London, Croom Helm

Young, P. (1985) 'Do schools make a difference?' in D. Reynolds (ed.) *Studying School Effectiveness*, Lewes, Falmer Press

Index

accountability 138
Adam Smith Institute 34, 50
Advisory Committee on the Pay and
    Conditions of Teachers 50, 85, 97
agency 9, 14
Ainsworth, Alan 112, 114, 116
A-levels 195
Alder, M. and Raab, G. 67, 91–2, 219
Allanson, Jack 193
Althusser, L. 9, 219
AMA 168–9, 170, 184
AMMA 184
Anderson, D. 32, 55, 219
Andrews, D. 32, 55, 219
Andrews, Sherrall 106, 118, 121–2
anti-racism 46, 47, 48
appraisal, of teachers 97, 120,
    121–2, 171
APS 62, 84, 88, 91
APU 135, 166, 203
Ashford, O.E. 7, 12, 219
assessment (*see also* National
    Testing and GCSE) 52–5, 75, 95,
    105, 106–8, 111, 125, 127, 133,
    135, 157, 158, 164, 174, 182–4,
    187–98, 199–202
Atkins, M.J. 93, 208, 211
Audit Commission 87, 219
'authoritarian populism' 28, 41

Baker, K. 8, 50, 54, 92, 114, 115,
    116, 117, 119, 121, 144, 148, 157,
    159–60, 167, 169, 172, 173–82,
    190, 193, 194, 195, 199, 201, 202,
    205, 208

Ball, Sir Christopher 196
Ball, S.J. 2, 30, 170, 219
Ball, S.J., Kenny, A., Gardner, D.
    205, 209
Barcan, A. 47, 219
Barnett, C. 71, 219
Barraclough, G. 1, 220
Bates, I. 133, 220
Bates, R. 124, 127, 220
Baudrillard, J. 25, 220
BBC, 195
Beck, J. 77, 220
Belsey, A. 8, 220
Bennett, N. 27, 220
Bernstein, B. 28, 56, 79–80, 124–8,
    220
Better Schools 144, 147–8, 152, 157,
    158, 175, 176, 178, 181, 182, 188
Black Papers, the 23, 24–30, 45, 50,
    51, 58, 71, 73, 88, 89, 113, 143,
    205
Black, Paul 135, 161–2, 187,
    189–90, 191, 194–5, 202–3
Blin-Stoyle, Roger 164–5, 199, 208
Bonefeld, W. 15, 16, 130, 220
Bosanquet, N. 34, 35, 220
Bottomore, T. *et al.* 86, 220
Bowis, J. 55–6, 220
Bowles, S. and Gintis, H. 125, 220
Boyson, Sir Rhodes 51, 52, 88, 143,
    144
Branson, Richard 118
Briault, E. 7, 220
Brown, Margaret 188, 198–9, 200
Browne, Sheila 154–5, 162, 166, 176

Btec 83
Bucher, R. and Strauss, A. 152, 221
Bullock, Report, the 25, 221
Burke, Edmund 35
Burnham Committee 50, 169

Callaghan, J. 23–4, 31–2, 70–1, 77,
    138, 140, 143, 221
Campbell, R.J. 146, 150, 221
Carlisle, Mark 42, 43, 180
Castells, M. 77, 221
CASE 184
CATE 166
CBI 107, 110–11, 112, 114, 116,
    117, 122
CCCS 12, 13, 19, 29–30, 34–5, 144,
    221
CEA 8, 41
centralisation 58, 139, 156
Chitty, C. 156–7, 221
Circular 14/77 147, 151
City and Guilds 83
Cockcroft, Report, the 6, 106, 152,
    156, 176, 187, 196, 204
Cockcroft, Sir Wilfred 168, 174–5
Cohen, S. 26–7, 221
Collins, R. 211, 221
commodity form, the 81–3, 86–7,
    89, 90, 97
competition 35, 39, 60–9, 85, 93, 98,
    120, 169
comprehensive schools (including
    comprehensivism) 11, 24, 25, 26,
    27, 28, 29–31, 45, 50, 55, 62, 73,
    89, 91, 117
Conservative Party 15, 19, 26, 41,
    42, 49, 64, 90, 113, 119, 143, 175,
    178, 181, 191, 208, 209, 213
Coopers and Lybrand 68, 221
Coryton, Dimitri 41
Cousins, M. and Hussain, A. 48–9,
    90
Cox, B. 197, 205, 221
Cox, B. and Dyson, A. 23, 24, 26,
    221
Cox, Baroness Caroline 44, 48, 50,
    184
CPS 34, 44, 139, 175, 181, 182, 183,
    196, 198, 203, 205, 207, 208, 209,
    221
CPVE 83, 93, 94, 95, 96, 106, 109,
    118, 126
Crick, B. 8
crisis in education 24, 27, 31, 128,
    142
crisis management 19, 108, 129
cross-curriculum work 110–13
CTCs 62, 68, 85, 92, 101, 113–19,
    129, 179, 214
cultural restorationists 6, 24, 27, 28,
    48, 54, 58, 84, 93, 100, 102, 113,
    129, 135, 185, 195–6, 197, 204,
    207, 211
curriculum 4–6, 25, 45, 46–9, 69, 70,
    76, 101, 102, 110–11, 118, 130,
    133–72, 196, 199, 208
cuts in education spending 79–81

Daily Mail, the 27
Dale, R. 11, 14, 27, 71, 76, 100, 102,
    221
Dean, J. and Steads, A. 93, 221
Demaine, J. 49, 221
Dennison, W. 12, 221
DES 4, 6, 8, 12, 15, 19, 20, 21, 30,
    33, 51, 62, 63, 70, 74, 76, 91, 93,
    96, 97, 101, 111, 112, 113, 119,
    123, 130, 136, 137–72, 173,
    181–3, 185, 189, 190–210, 211,
    221–2
Dichmont, John 199
differentiation 90–4
discourse 17–18, 21, 27–42, 46, 48,
    50, 52, 56, 58, 70, 73, 75, 77, 87,
    90, 91, 100, 108, 110, 113, 118,
    124, 129, 136, 145–6, 150–2, 153,
    155, 157, 166, 185
DOE 20, 74, 76, 112, 130
Donaghue, Lord Bernard 138–41,
    142, 144
Donald, J. 17, 71, 222
DTI 5, 6, 8, 19, 20, 76, 112, 113,
    130, 211
Duncan, S. and Goodwin, M. 56, 222
Dunleavy, P. and O'Leary, B. 2, 13,
    222

Dunn, B. 85

economic policy 77–9
Education Act (**1980**) 61, 166 ✔
Education Act (**1986**) 158 ✔
Education in Schools **1977**, 71, 142,
    153–4, 155
education market place 59–69, 86
    see also 'the market') 87, 90, 93,
    98
Education Reform Act (**1988**) 43,
    51, 54, 59, 60–9, 85, 87, 97, 98,
    101, 117, 121, 123, 124, 129,
    133–72, 175–7, 181, 182, 184,
    188, 192, 196, 214 ✔
'educational bureaucrats' 5, 133
'educational establishment' 18, 45,
    49, 53, 58, 100, 130, 190, 193,
    197, 207, 209, 213
educational policy making 9–11 (*see
    also* policy)
educational state (*see* the state)
effective schools movement 89–90
egalitarianism 25, 28, 55, 58
English National Curriculum
    Working Party 204–7
entrepreneurship 36, 72, 121
ERC 47
Ernest, P. 6, 222
Evans, Alan 163, 166, 178–9

family 40, 41, 45
FEU 4, 20 ,96, 111, 112
Finn, D., Grant, N. and Johnson, R.
    17, 222
flexibility 103, 104–6, 125–6, 127,
    130
Foucault, M. 17, 18, 22, 23, 31, 34,
    59, 90, 150, 223
Fowler, G. *et al.* 7, 223
Fowler, W. 153, 154, 156, 158, 223
*Framework for the School
    Curriculum, A* (DES **1986**) 155–6,
    161, 163
freedom 37–8, 39, 44, 64
free-market (*see* 'the market)
Friedman, M. and Friedman, R. 36,
    223 ✔

Fritzell, C. 81–3, 87, 94, 125, 223

Gamble, A. 36, 223
GCSE 45, 53–4, 83, 93, 101, 107–8,
    111, 135, 156, 164, 173–4, 177
Gerwitz, S. and Ozga, J. 12, 161, 223
Gleeson, D. 76, 100, 102, 128, 223
GMS 46, 62, 63, 68, 85, 91, 169,
    177, 183
Goodson, I. 152, 223
Grace, G. 20, 79, 223
Graham, Duncan 133, 134, 200, 206
grammar schools 29, 30, 45, 48, 62,
    92, 116, 129, 130
Grant, W. and Nath, S. 79, 223
Great Debate, the 23, 31–2, 71, 73,
    75, 77, 89, 137, 140, 143, 147, 168
Green Paper, the (**1977**) (*see
    Education in Schools*)
Grunow, Alan 168–9, 170
Guardian, the 192, 205

Habermas, J. 26, 223
Hall, S. 33, 41, 223
Hall, S. *et al.* 26, 223
Hall, S. and Jaques, M. 28, 224
Halsey, Philip 176
Hampson, Keith 143, 146, 159
Hargreaves, A. 13, 14, 15, 68, 95,
    108, 224
Hargreaves, A. and Reynold, D. 11,
    224
Hart, David 63, 64, 67–8
Hayek, F. 35–9, 51, 56, 58, 61, 62,
    63, 66
Hazelhust, Alan 42
headteachers 67–8, 88, 97, 98, 120,
    122–3, 158, 179, 214
Hennessey, P. 160, 224
Higginson Report, the 108, 194
Hillgate Group, the 43–59, 113, 224
Hirsh, J. 15, 224
Hirsh, J. and Roth, R. 15, 224
HMI 7, 20, 21, 70, 86, 133, 136,
    138, 139, 140–72, 173–4, 182,
    185, 190, 198, 200, 203, 208
Holloway, J. 16, 224
Holt, M. 101, 223

Holt, Sheila 109
Hopper, E. 128, 224

IEA 34, 43, 104
IEDSS 47
ILEA 45, 54–6, 135, 147
Independent, The 93, 119–20, 191, 196
indoctrination 47
Industrial Society, the 121
'industrial trainers' 4–6, 74, 76, 83, 100, 101, 113, 118, 129, 130, 211
Industry Year 72
in-service education 49–50, 97
I.O.D. 120

Jamieson, I. 72, 75, 100, 102, 104, 126, 224
Jamous, H. and Peloille, B. 170, 224
Jessop, B. 15, 224
Jessop, B. *et al.* 41, 124, 125, 225
Johnson, R. 6, 225
Joseph, Sir Keith 8, 28–9, 43, 53, 62, 63, 64, 83, 88, 116, 117, 119, 139, 143, 144, 157–9, 162–4, 166, 169, 171–2, 173–81, 188, 196
Joseph, K. and Sumption, J. 37, 225
Joy, Robert 106, 108, 120–1, 123

Kenway, J. 32–3, 225
Keynsianism 35–6, 225
King, A. 36, 225
Kington, Brian 106, 114–115
Kogan, M. 1, 3, 16, 161, 225

Labour Party 29, 30, 31
Laclau, E. and Mouffe, C. 23, 225
Lawlor, Sheila 196, 205–6
Lawton, D. 6, 225
Lawton, D. and Gordon, P. 149, 161, 225
LEAs 7, 8, 12, 30, 33, 45, 46, 62, 68–9, 76, 84, 85, 86, 91, 97, 133, 138, 140, 150–1, 153, 162, 165–6, 167–72, 179, 185, 191, 197
Levitas, R. 24, 42, 225
'liberal humanists' 4–6, 58, 102, 144, 150–7

liberty (*see* freedom)
licensed teachers 50, 97
Lipietz, A. 124, 225
Littler, C. and Salaman, G. 123, 225
LMS 51, 59, 65, 67–8, 69, 87, 97, 98, 121, 123–4, 134, 183, 214
Lodge, P. and Blackstone, T. 137, 161, 225
London Evening Standard 56

McClure, S. 149, 153, 194, 225
McCullough, G. 76, 225
Mace, J. 80, 225
Macdonell, D. 18, 29, 56, 225
MacGregor, J. 148, 181
McLennan, G., Held, D. and Hall, S. 20, 226
McPherson, A. and Raab, C. 11, 226
McWilliams, Keith 159, 163–5, 178
magnet schools 92
management 97, 120–4, 127–32, 171
marketisation 86–90
'market, the' 35, 36, 38, 50, 52, 53, 56–7, 58, 60–9, 84, 88, 94, 105, 120, 124, 167, 178, 214
Marks, J. *et al.* 55, 226
Marx, K. 87, 226
Mathematics National Curriculum Working Party 102, 198–204
Maud, A. 25, 226
Maw, J. 151, 226
Merridale, Phillip 169–71
MESP 94, 109
Mortimore, Peter 196
Mowat, C.L. 24
MSC 20, 76, 77, 83, 85, 93, 96, 101, 104, 113, 137, 226
multiculturalism 40–1, 45, 46
Murray, R. 124, 126, 226

NAGAM 184
NAHT 62, 67–8, 184
NATE 198
NATFE 184
nation 39–40, 41, 48, 61
National Curriculum 42, 54, 56–9, 65, 68, 87, 92, 93, 98, 101, 109, 110, 111–13, 114, 141–6, 148,

150, 153–6, 158, 169, 173–210,
211, 214
national testing (*see also* assessment)
51, 68, 98, 101, 111
NCC 37, 112, 133, 134, 135, 149,
166–7, 178, 185–7, 191, 197, 200,
201, 202, 204, 206–7, 226
NCES 34, 36, 44
NCPTA 184
neo-conservatism 8, 34, 39–42, 43,
46, 52, 54, 56, 129, 213
neo-liberalism 8, 34–40, 43, 46, 52,
54, 56, 72, 74, 88, 129, 139, 173,
213
neo-Marxism 12, 13
New Partnership for Our Schools, A
144
'new progressives'/new
progressivism 6–7, 100, 101, 102,
135–7, 172, 176, 185, 200, 203,
207, 211
New Right, the 4, 6, 8, 11, 18, 21,
22, 23–69, 70, 74, 87, 100, 129,
133, 149, 150, 160, 172, 176, 185,
189, 194, 197, 204, 209, 211, 213
new vocationalism 71, 74, 75–80,
83, 84
NIESR 197–8
North, J. 53, 101, 226
No. 10 Policy Unit 183, 188, 198,
206
No Turning Back Group of MPs 50,
226
Nozick, R. 35, 226
NUT 71, 163, 184

Observer, the 92, 119, 193, 199,
201, 205, 206
OECD Report, the (**1975**) 160, 226
Offe, C. 19, 81, 82, 226
'old humanism' 4–6, 24, 100, 118,
129, 207
open enrolment 60–9, 86, 183
'opting out' (*see* GMS)
Ozga, J. 1, 226

Palmer, F. 47
parental choice 33–4, 43, 46, 52,

57–7, 58, 60–9, 70, 88, 91
parents 8, 33–4, 43–4, 70, 84, 87,
120, 138
partnership 145–6, 148, 154, 161,
169–72, 177–9, 191, 213
Peacock, Ray 102, 107, 201
Pecheux, M. 18, 226
Peffers, Jack 110
Perry, Pauline 139–42, 150, 151,
171–2, 176, 177
Peston, Maurice 175
Pietrasik, R. 170, 226
Pile, W. 12, 149, 226
Plaskow, M. 163, 227
pluralism 12, 13, 19
policy (including policy making,
policy formation, policy struggle)
3, 7–8, 10–13, 22, 32, 33, 42, 44,
58, 59, 76–7, 79, 101–2, 118, 126,
129, 130, 141, 142, 145, 150, 160,
162, 165, 171, 176, 183, 185, 189,
196, 198, 204, 207, 209–10,
211–14
policy analysis 3, 9
policy communities 19, 71, 134, 213
policy sociology 1
politicised subjects 25–8, 47–8, 53,
54, 55
Pollard, A. *et al.* 83, 227
post-Fordism 124–32, 136
Practical Curriculum, the (Schools
Council **1980**) 155
Prais, S. 180, 188, 197, 198–9, 227
Prais, S. and Wagner, K. 183, 188,
227
Pring, R. 84, 227
privatisation 78, 84–5
profiles 95
proletarianisation 97–9
PSHE 83
Prunty, J. 2, 3, 130, 227
'public educators' 4–6, 136

Quicke, J. 48, 227
Quinton, Peter 35

racism 40
Ranson, S. *et al.* 137, 227

records of achievement 83
Reeder, D. 76, 227
Rees, G. *et al*. 96, 227
Rees, T. 95, 227
'reformist old humanism' 6, 100, 203, 211
relative autonomy 9, 13, 20, 80–4
Reynolds, D. and Sullivan, M. 30, 227
Richardson, J. and Jordan, G. 19, 227
Riseborough, G. 30, 227
Robson, M. and Walford, G. 84, 227
Rumbold, Angela 54, 195
Rustin, M. 126, 227

Salter, B. and Tapper, T. 5, 7, 11, 12, 48, 137, 149, 161, 227, 228
SATs 193
Saunders, P. 9, 13, 16, 19, 130, 131, 228
SCDC 20, 110, 149, 159, 160–5, 208, 228
Schools Council 20, 76, 138, 149, 150–1, 155, 160–5, 176, 177, 228
School Curriculum, the (DES **1981**) 155, 156, 163, 166
school governors 67–8, 69, 88, 98, 123, 158
schools/industry movement 72–3, 75–80, 94, 101, 116, 124, 138, 211
Schumpeter, J. 63, 228
Schwarz, B. 39, 41, 228
Scruton, Roger 35, 39, 47, 228
SEAC 54, 133, 134, 166, 176, 185, 191, 192, 197
SEC 163, 164
Secondary School Science Review 186
Secretary of State for Education and Science, the 62, 67, 85, 114, 115, 139, 142, 145, 152, 153, 156, 160, 166, 171, 173–81, 185, 187, 189, 191–2, 200, 201, 203, 204, 206
Seidel, G. 40, 228
Seldon, A. 63, 228
Select Committee on Education and Science 8
Senker, P. 96, 228

Sexton, S. 23, 43–59, 98, 228
SHA 148
Sharp, R. 100, 228
Sharp, R. and Green, A. 102, 228
Shilling, C. 94, 96, 213, 228
'sink schools' 91–2
Smith, Adam 35, 74, 228
Smith, Sir Alex 162
Social Affairs Unit 32, 34, 47, 49–50
social policy 11, 77, 79
'star schools' 91–2
state, the 12–14, 15, 16, 19–21, 34–9, 46, 77–8, 95, 113, 118, 130, 211, 213, 214; educational state 198, 204, 212–3; local state 20
St John Stevas, N. 23, 43, 60, 143
Stronach, I. 74, 132, 228
Svi Shapiro, H. 3, 228

TAs 193
Taylor, Cyril 119
Teacher Quality (White Paper **1984**) 171
teachers 25–8, 49–52, 55, 70, 73, 88, 89–90, 97–8, 128, 129, 138, 157, 170–2, 191, 213, 214
teacher training 49–50, 192
teacher unions 7, 12, 30, 33, 76, 93, 150, 160, 162–3, 166, 179, 197
TES 112, 115, 153, 166–7, 193, 194, 202
testing (*see* national testing)
TGAT 53, 135, 187–98
Thatcher, M. 36, 37, 41–2, 63, 79, 157, 178, 181, 191–2, 193, 194, 195, 196, 201
Thatcherism (including Thatcherist, Thatcherite) 3, 15, 16, 28, 37, 39, 43, 59, 72, 73, 77, 79, 84, 87, 93, 118, 124, 213
THES 16, 61
Thomas, Norman 193
Thornbury, R. 25–6, 229
Thornycroft, Lord 184
Times, The 28–9
Tolley, Revd Dr George 104–5, 109, 116
Treasury, the 19, 93

Turner, R. 130, 229
TVEI 76–80, 83, 93, 94, 95, 96, 101,
    102, 106, 109, 110, 111, 112, 116,
    118, 126
Ulrich, Walter 147, 164
'ungovernability' 36, 38

View of the Curriculum, A 155, 156,
    161, 162, 166
vocationalism 94–7, 100
'vocational progressivism' 101–19,
    136
vouchers 45, 63–4, 68, 87–8, 177

Walker, A. 1, 229
Webb, Tony 107, 117
Welfare, Damian 184
Wexler, P. and Grabiner, G. 56, 58,
    229

Whitty, G. 185, 211, 229
Wiener, M. 71, 229
Wienstock, A. 73, 229
Wilkins, Raphael 179
William Tyndale 27, 34
Williams, R. 4, 7, 11, 13, 24, 100,
    118, 136, 214, 229
Williams, Shirley 23, 140, 143, 151,
    152, 153, 162
work experience 96, 113, 115
Worsthorne, P. 40, 229
Worthen, J. 53, 229
Wright, E.O. 3, 229
Wright, N. 25, 229

Yellow Book, The 146, 153, 162
Young, Lord 113
Young, P. 89, 229
YTS 85, 93